Robert Pierpoint

ALSO BY TONY SILVIA
AND FROM MCFARLAND

*Fathers and Sons in Baseball Broadcasting:
The Carays, Brennamans, Bucks and Kalases* (2009)

*Baseball Over the Air: The National Pastime
on the Radio and in the Imagination* (2007)

Robert Pierpoint

A Life at CBS News

TONY SILVIA

Foreword by Bob Schieffer

McFarland & Company, Inc., Publishers
Jefferson, North Carolina

All photographs are from the Robert Pierpoint Collection, University Archives, University of Redlands.

Library of Congress Cataloguing-in-Publication Data

Silvia, Tony.
 Robert Pierpoint : a life at CBS news / Tony Silvia ; foreword by Bob Schieffer.
  p.   cm.
 Includes bibliographical references and index.

 ISBN 978-0-7864-7414-1 (softcover : acid free paper) ∞
 ISBN 978-1-4766-1575-2 (ebook)

 1. Pierpoint, Robert.   2. Television journalists—United States—Biography.   I. Title.
 PN4874.P49S55 2014
 070.92—dc23   2014018789
 [B]

British Library cataloguing data are available

© 2014 Tony Silvia. All rights reserved

No part of this book may be reproduced or transmitted in any form or by any means, electronic or mechanical, including photocopying or recording, or by any information storage and retrieval system, without permission in writing from the publisher.

On the cover: Robert Pierpoint outside the Correspondents Club in Hong Kong (Robert Pierpoint Collection, University Archives, University of Redlands)

Printed in the United States of America

McFarland & Company, Inc., Publishers
 Box 611, Jefferson, North Carolina 28640
  www.mcfarlandpub.com

For Belmira Miranda Silvia,
from whom I learned the value
of stories to peoples' lives and
gained the will to tell them

Table of Contents

Acknowledgments — ix
Foreword by Bob Schieffer — 1
Introduction — 5

1. Beginnings: From Redlands to Stockholm — 9
2. New Blood: Meeting Murrow and Covering Korea — 23
3. Bureau Chief: The Far East — 38
4. Back Home: Marriage, Family and the White House — 51
5. Back Row: Tennis, Television and Politics — 111
6. After the White House: Casting a Critical Eye — 126
7. Last of Murrow's Boys: A Journalist's Professional and Personal Legacy — 151

Notes — 159
Bibliography — 167
Index — 169

Acknowledgments

There are so many people to whom I'm indebted, first for their belief in this project, and second for their help. To begin, the Robert Pierpoint family: his sons, Eric and Stan (Alan), his daughters, Kim and Marta, their wonderful mother and the love of Bob's life, Patricia, and his devoted sister, Ruth. It can't be easy to give someone you don't know complete access to your loved one's life. It's a leap of faith. Thanks to you each for taking it. Your trust, confidence, and acceptance inspired me to write this book.

To Bob's former colleagues, both at CBS and the other networks, your input has been invaluable and appreciated. Bob Schieffer, who wrote the foreword, was the very first to sign on to the project and, in turn, led me to so many others who were interviewed for this book—Eric Engberg, Phil Jones, Bill Plant, Susan Zirinsky, Lesley Stahl, Roger Mudd, and Dan Rather among them. As word spread that I was writing a biography of Robert Pierpoint, so many more came forward to help. It taught me how important it is not to be liked but to be respected. Robert Pierpoint was both, but, if asked, I'd like to believe he would prefer the latter.

Marta and Kim Pierpoint pushed me to talk with their father's lifelong friends, not simply his professional peers. Doing so helped complete a portrait of Robert Pierpoint, the person whose life was spent in, but not solely consumed by, journalism. There was so much more to their dad's life and they insisted I include it. For that, too, I'm thankful.

David Fite, Vice President of Academic Affairs at Robert Pierpoint's treasured alma mater, the University of Redlands, immediately saw the value of this project and didn't hesitate to invite me to campus in 2012, to lecture and teach about Pierpoint and journalism. He provided the support needed to conduct my research in the university's archives.

The archivist of the Robert Pierpoint Collection, Nathan Gonzales, helped my research a year before I arrived on campus, always pointing me in the right direction and providing anything needed. A friend of Bob, he also had some great stories, a few of which are included here.

Stan Marvin, program manager of KRCB-TV, went well above and beyond to locate, on film no less, two interview programs conducted with Bob for the Santa Barbara PBS affiliate in 1998. Not only did he find the film, but he had it transferred to video for me. I'm appreciative.

In Wisconsin, Harry Miller, now retired from the University of Wisconsin Historical Society, was always there answering questions from a distance and helping once I arrived in Madison on a chilly November morning. Having access to Bob's reporter notebooks, early film reels, audio tapes, and other memorabilia was invaluable. I felt I'd found gold. It hit me one afternoon that probably only two people ever handled, let alone read, some of these materials—Robert Pierpoint and me.

Foreword

by Bob Schieffer,
CBS News Chief Washington Correspondent

I first met Bob Pierpoint the night before John Kennedy died. Kennedy spent that night in my hometown, Fort Worth, Texas, and in those days I was the night police reporter at the *Fort Worth Star-Telegram*.

It was a night like Fort Worth had never seen. Ten thousand people had shown up at 10 p.m. at Carswell Air Force Base to see *Air Force One* arrive and they gave Kennedy an overwhelmingly friendly welcome.

They were there because the next morning he and Vice President Johnson and their wives would be attending a bipartisan breakfast at the Hotel Texas before the short trip to Dallas.

We kept the Fort Worth Press Club open late to welcome the traveling White House press corps, and when the last edition of the *Star-Telegram* was put to bed, well after midnight, I went to the Press Club to meet all the famous reporters that I knew only from their by-lines and the images we had seen on TV.

One of the first faces I recognized was that of Bob Pierpoint. In those days, I was something of a "print snob," had no ambition to be on TV, and generally looked down on TV reporters—especially local ones—as being sort of second-class journalists. Truth is, some were just that—old dance band announcers who wouldn't have known a story if it had bitten them.

Newspapers had their share of drunks and other phoniness too, but we newspaper guys somehow overlooked them. But for all my misplaced bias, I had always admired Walter Cronkite and his CBS News crew so when I saw Pierpoint at the Press Club I headed straight for him (after getting a drink, of course).

He could not have been nicer, and two minutes into the conversation I knew I was talking to a real pro. This was not some golden voice; in fact, Pierpoint had kind of a squeaky tenor. No, this was someone who was completely immersed in his job, politics and the fun and fascination of being a reporter.

A half-century later, after working with him and knowing him through several decades, I find myself saying the same thing: he couldn't have been nicer and he was a real pro.

In every newsroom I ever worked in there was always someone like Pierpoint—the person you could turn to for help when you didn't know where to go on a story. The guy who knew the history, knew where things were, often didn't get the credit, was usually underrated but absolutely essential. Someone whose love of the profession and what it does or is supposed to do overrides the pettiness, the office politics, the nonstop gossip and the bickering that is part of every newsroom. That was Pierpoint.

All our lives changed the day after I met him. The next morning in Dallas, John Kennedy was gunned down. It would be the first in a series of violent events to shock the nation, change our culture and change journalism.

From that weekend on, a nation in which most people depended on print for their news, and really didn't believe anything until they saw it written down in black and white, became a nation in which most people turned to television for their news.

From his seat on the press bus at the rear of the motorcade that brought Kennedy to downtown Dallas that day, Pierpoint heard the three shots ring out.

But that was all he knew, and because he knew nothing more, he refused to go on the air until he reached Parkland Hospital where Kennedy had been taken and where he found more information. Today's bloggers might find that hard to believe, but there was a time when pros didn't go with a story until they had a story, and Pierpoint was a pro with a passion for accuracy.

It was Pierpoint's bad luck that when Vice President Johnson took the oath in Dallas to replace Kennedy, he decided to return immediately to Washington, which meant Pierpoint and the rest of the White House press corps would return with him.

With Pierpoint gone, it was left to CBS's dashing young southern bureau chief Dan Rather to cover the dramatic and still-unfolding story in

Dallas—the first but not the last time Pierpoint would find himself in Rather's shadow. Because of his work in Dallas, Rather would become chief White House correspondent and Pierpoint, who had covered the White House since Eisenhower, would be his number two.

The assignment was not without friction, and the rivalry that existed between them was legendary at CBS News. It is also one of the fascinating parts of this book, but it is to the credit of both men that neither allowed White House officials to play them one against the other. It was not for the lack of trying, especially during the Nixon administration.

When Rather arrived, Pierpoint managed to make the best of a bad situation, as he did so many times during his career. When it became clear that Pierpoint was not going to be the reporter delivering the spot news from the White House each night, he stepped back and began concentrating on longer investigative pieces, efforts that would earn him two Emmys.

This book is more than Bob Pierpoint's story. As good biographies should, it tells us the story of the subject's world as seen through his experiences, in this case the very small but enormously influential world of the White House press corps—a clubby, mostly male world in Pierpoint's day that is glaringly different from today's Washington.

Tony Silvia peeks behind the White House curtain to tell us how it was during the administration of Eisenhower, the war hero who was beloved by the public but so impersonal that reporters were never quite sure he knew their names.

Silvia tells how Pierpoint once tried to get a comment from John Kennedy and used a beautiful White House visitor as "bait" in hope of attracting Kennedy's attention. Kennedy took the bait, stopped to chat with the lady but moved on before Pierpont could ask a question.

Pierpoint was never one to back away from a fight and managed a few with every president he covered. Lyndon Johnson tried to revoke his press pass, and it was to a Pierpoint question that Richard Nixon issued his withering denunciation of the press, "You can't be angry with those you don't respect."

I will leave it to Tony to tell the tale, but he also recounts my favorite Pierpoint story, the day Bob found himself in a White House bedroom, interviewing a totally naked Lyndon Johnson. "I was not sure how that day was going to end," Pierpoint said to me years ago when he told me the story.

When I came over from the Pentagon beat to replace Rather at the White House in 1974, I wasn't sure how I would be received by Pierpoint. But he treated me the same way he had when I met him that long-ago night before the Kennedy assassination in 1963. He couldn't have been nicer and he was a real pro. "I'll help you all I can," he said. "We both work for the same outfit, CBS News."

Every newsroom needs a guy like that, and Bob Pierpoint was ours for a long time.

Introduction

It was a Sunday morning like any other. On Sundays, my routine doesn't vary. It begins with a leisurely hour and a half of the best journalism on television, *CBS Sunday Morning*, a weekend buffet of tasteful, appetizing stories that are well written, well told, and somehow appeal both to the brain and the heart at the same time. It was October 23, 2011, and this Sunday morning was about to become both a profoundly sad and remarkably transformative day in my life.

Charles Osgood, the broadcast's host, informed us that Robert Pierpoint, a legendary CBS News correspondent of some 40 years, who covered six presidents in his time as White House correspondent, had passed away. I knew the name, but little else. As I had grown up in the age of Cronkite on CBS, I had some vague familiarity with his work. If I remembered anything at all, it was the impression of a man who roamed the radio and television landscape of his day with luminaries like Cronkite himself and, before him, Edward R. Murrow. That was about it.

Over the next two years, I would come to know the man "Bob," as his close friends and family called him, nearly as well as I would come to know "Robert," the more formal name by which the public knew him. I would come to respect him, his work, and his unflinching standards for the field he loved: journalism. I would come to know him as a man who achieved what most of us try to achieve: that elusive balance between what we do for a living and how we live.

As you read this man's remarkable biography, from a boyhood which he spent mostly in isolation, to a great adventure in the world's capitals, to a place at the highest table of our own nation's capital, it's important to keep in mind a number of factors.

First, Robert Pierpoint was one among a special group of people named "Murrow's Boys," after the man generally referred to as "the father of broadcast journalism," Edward R. Murrow, the patron saint of CBS News at a time when radio was the dominant news medium and carrying through to the time when an upstart medium named television was in its infancy. He was there when no one had a blueprint, when the rules weren't fully formed, when audience research and focus groups hadn't been implemented, and when it was a very special thing to be a network correspondent, let alone a network White House correspondent.

As a CBS colleague told me, the White House correspondent in Pierpoint's day had a unique role. There were no satellites. There was no Internet. Social media was socializing with others while watching an evening newscast in real time on one of three networks. Not only all the domestic news we received, but virtually all the foreign news we knew, was dependent upon the networks' White House correspondents. As Bob's former colleague Eric Engberg put it, "They were important. Today, they don't have the heft or public understanding that those guys in Bob's era had." In an era when technology rules and rapidity of transmission often outpace judgment and expertise, today's White House correspondent has a diminished role in the public eye.

Then again, so do "journalists," in the broader sense. Lightweight, consumer model mini-cameras, many a personal cell phone, make it possible for anyone to be a journalist. Or do they? Just because we have more to look at doesn't mean we see more or know more. Without context, we simply have images. Without expertise, we merely have noise. That's one of the lessons I learned from studying the life and times of this remarkable man, and I hope you do, too.

In Pierpoint's day, journalism was still seen by the networks as a public service, not a profit center. The goal was to shed light on important issues, not simply to light up screens. Ultimately, Robert Pierpoint went from a man of his time to beyond his time. His message: Keep fighting even after your time on the job is done. Work is not what you do; it's what you believe. Robert Pierpoint's message, *in* his time and *since* his time, resonated with me as being relevant to *our* time.

There were a lot of things I didn't know about this man on that October morning in 2011. For one, I didn't know he had written his own book, *At the White House*, in 1981. I initially feared that would make this book redundant. I was wrong. It was a guide, but not a complete picture. The complete picture is what you now hold in your hands.

I also didn't know how many of the people we now look to as luminaries in broadcast journalism, several of them in his former role as CBS News White House correspondent, looked to him for inspiration. I do now. Many came forward wanting to contribute to his biography. That, too, is remarkable.

Bob's daughter Marta sent me a message during a stage in the writing of this book. It read: "A few family members just read this and we think you must have met our father/husband/grandpa Bob. He would have felt exactly as you described!" I never did meet Bob Pierpoint. But I wish I had. And I hope what you are about to read makes you feel like you *have*.

1

Beginnings: From Redlands to Stockholm

Beating the Odds

The coughing and wheezing were familiar to the frail, diminutive boy who spent nearly every day since his birth in 1925 among adults in various stages of tuberculosis. Sanatoriums were places where, for much of the 20th century, asthma patients were treated like those with what came to be known as "TB." The prescribed treatment plan, too, was the same: bed rest and isolation in places far from social contact, away from friends and family. Like tuberculosis, asthma was then a fully debilitating disease. It became a constant companion for Bob, who would grow into *Robert* Pierpoint. He would never outgrow the ailment.

The days were long, the nights longer. His parents, Charles and Emma, did all they could, but there were so many setbacks. Their son wanted *so* badly to run and play like the other kids in their California town. But he wasn't like other kids. "Apparently, I was practically born with asthma," the boy would recall as a man, many years later. "Asthma influenced my life for many years afterward, and may have been the best thing that ever happened to me."[1]

He never forgot two things. The first was what was at the time considered to be a "semi-cure"—the burning of a kind of Chinese incense which did help his breathing, but also stunk up the house. The other was the first time he had to leave that house for one in a series of sanatorium stays. Mother and son each felt the pain. For the mother, saying good-bye was the worst, leaving young Bob in the hallway, in the care of others. For the son, there was the feigned bravery, turning around so his mother wouldn't see him cry. He put his hands behind his back and waved with his fingers.

It was an image no parent could ever forget, and this one—Emma Pierpoint—never did.[2]

It wasn't always time spent in the medical facilities of the day. There were respites, even if they resembled treatment facilities. One was a camp for kids like him, in the hills near Monrovia, California, far enough from constant fog and dampness that defined Redondo Beach—and aggravated the boy's breathing. There were only twice-a-month visits by his parents, but the tradeoff was an escape from the winter cold—and the opportunity, for the first time in his young life, to wear shorts and tee-shirts and a light jacket. The food wasn't great, but he breathed easier. After a year, he returned to Redondo, but a pattern was established: back home, back to treatment, even living with a family whose home was further inland, away from the irritants that blocked his breathing. It broadened him, though he couldn't have known it at the time, by serving as his first contact to people from different cultures, a strong foundation for his future work.

The duration of trips back home varied, depending upon his progress. Half days at school, back in bed every afternoon was the unforgiving rule. It didn't leave much time for play. It did allow a lot of time for dreams. No one knows for sure, but those years between infancy and high school must have forged the kind of determination you need to survive in a career where many gasp, either for air (as in air *time*) or in awe: the rarefied world of Washington, D.C., far from the family home in Redondo Beach, and home to the elite group of journalists known as White House correspondents.

There were signs along the way that the family couldn't help but notice. Once, when he was 13, the young Bob Pierpoint learned of an airplane's crash in the mountains nearby his home. He and his father headed in the direction of the crash, young Bob gathering facts on the scene and pretending to be a radio reporter, "doing his Robert Pierpoint thing at an early age," observes his son Eric, who remembers hearing a recording of his father's earliest broadcasting effort decades later at his grandmother's house.[3]

That was a good day. Many others, however, were routine, a "very difficult period," recalls his sister, Ruth. As the younger sibling, and the healthy one, she was assigned to help Bob occupy his time, playing cards and generally keeping up his spirits. "I was about 10," she remembers. Among her duties: making her brother what she calls "liver cocktails," a concoction of chopped up liver and onions on which he existed. At the time, it was thought of as, if not a cure, at least a helpful tonic. "His diet was limited, but his attitude wasn't," says Ruth.[4]

Of course, the family felt lucky to have him home, even if for a short time. A regimen of living in hospitals and sanitoriums became the young boy's "normal." He spent two years in one sanitorium in Pasadena. His parents were allowed to see their son only once a month, his sister even less. The home visits, sometimes for a night, sometimes over a weekend, could also be painful, giving his parents a reason for both hope and disappointment. It wouldn't be long before the heavy breathing resumed. His wheezing could be heard throughout the house. "It was obvious he wasn't getting rid of it," recalls his sister. Despite that, she adds, "When I was growing up I couldn't believe how well he handled it."

The young boy had a lot of thinking time, everyone agrees. Inwardly, he might have felt deprived, but outwardly Robert Pierpoint was developing his personality. During this time, his sister says, he wrote a paper about himself. "I know I can't do everything everybody else does," he wrote, "so I decided to develop my personality and sense of humor." He impressed Ruth, then 10. "The fact that he figured out that he wanted to be liked for himself and that he figured out how to do it, I think was amazing."

He was shorter than most boys his age and the asthma limited his ability to play sports. He made up for both by figuring that he had to make friends fast—and did so. It was another life skill that would serve him well. One thing that made him popular was the fact he studied hard, got good grades, and became useful to the other kids his age who might need "coaching," what today we'd call tutoring. It all became, he would say decades later, a wonderful learning process that shaped and defined his adult personality.

Those in the household at the time thought it amazing that young Bob Pierpoint eventually outgrew some of the effects of his childhood asthma; however, there were also times where he wouldn't admit to an attack. All this took both an emotional and a financial burden on the Pierpoint family. Several moves would come before Bob's teenage years, always due to a turn in his health, sometimes a climate change—as in too much fog—that could exacerbate his condition. That was on top of the money spent on hospitals and sanitariums.

Finally, the Pierpoints decided against sending their son away every other year and, instead, moved the whole family inland. Charles Pierpoint got a new job with a Bank of America branch and they moved to Whittier, California, to what the younger Pierpoint, now a teen, would write was a "lovely new home, overlooking orange groves in East Whittier." There was a bonus: living next door was a boy his own age. Both were seventeen and became immediate friends. His name was Dick Hogsett and they would soon take on new adventures together.

During his senior year, 1942, at Whittier High School, he was elected class president. His outgoing personality became a shield against the disease that for so long separated him from his peers. The family moved, but he didn't want to go. He had begun to create the persona that would grow into, not a politician, but an observer of politicians. Those around him at the time began to recognize his leadership qualities and intelligence. He also, amazingly, began a lifelong connection to sports, one that would eventually lead to tennis, but in high school centered on running.

Given the odds against him, the frail young boy, had a stature and voice—affected as it was by shortness of breath—that were anything but the stuff of athletes or globe-trotting journalists, "It's remarkable that a little guy with asthma and a squeaky voice ran track," says son Eric. "He also was surprisingly popular." He learned to hide his affliction so well that, to this day, some of his closest friends—in and outside journalism—profess they had no idea that he was asthmatic.

Always there was prayer. A strict Baptist household meant that the kids—Robert and Ruth—went to church every Sunday and not once, but twice. Whether influenced by concern for her son's health or her own upbringing, Emma Pierpoint was "the strong one when it came to religion," Ruth recalls. It made things difficult for the Pierpoint children, whose friends all went to the local Congregational church. The last place the Pierpoint siblings wanted to go was to the Baptist church. Having had so little contact with young people his own age, the young Robert Pierpoint resented the intrusion of religion, even at this early age, a factor that, ironically, may have contributed to his adolescent search for independence. Much later in life, this strict religious upbringing was influential in many decisions he would make—about travel, career, and politics. The time would come when, to the young asthma sufferer, religion of the kind he was forced to practice became to him the essence of "brainwashing," says his sister.

Brainwashing or not, the Pierpoints took solace, finally, in what seemed to be an answer to their prayers or, at least, an important turning point in their son's health. The Pottenger Sanitorium in Monrovia, California, was considered by many at the time to be revolutionary in its care for both asthmatics and tuberculosis patients.[5] The family, though cautious, began to feel that their son was, if not cured, at least recovering. It had been over a decade and a half, but confidence began to build in young Robert's capacity to survive. More importantly, at age 17, Bob himself began to believe it was time to move away from the home in which he had barely lived to see a world he had hardly seen.

Moving Away

The yearning to spread his wings came soon after the young Bob Pierpoint's exposure to Dr. Pottenger's asthma therapy. The years of bed rest brought him newfound strength and a craving for adventure. So, too, did the desire to get away from his strict religious upbringing. It became a major motivating factor throughout much of his life. In reflecting back on this part of his childhood, Pierpoint himself described it as a process of going "from hardshell Baptist to secular liberal," a journey which, he wrote, "took almost half a century, but was well worth the trip." It was intricately linked to his parents' own journey through a complex maze of religious beliefs that both inspired thought and instilled doubt in their son.

    His father, Charles Pierpoint, when the young Robert was born in 1925, was the cashier of a small bank called the Farmers and Merchants National Bank of Redondo Beach (it later became Bank of America). His mother, Emma Adkins Pierpoint, was a housewife who once worked for the Edison Company in Pasadena before marrying. She delighted in playing the piano in her brother's jazz band. Both were born in 1900; each had very different religious roots. Emma was raised as a strict Baptist, Charles as a Quaker; however, he later left the Quaker church, along with his family, and became a Methodist. Charles Pierpoint, however, retained his Quaker pacifist beliefs and during World War I did not enlist for the military, but instead worked on a farm where crops were raised to support the troops.[6]

    Emma Adkins, at this same time, lived on a farm overlooking the Sacramento River in Red Bluff, California. When the farm fell fallow, due in part to her father not being especially adept at making a living from the land, the Adkins family ended up in Pasadena. As Emma's musical prowess expanded—she had been schooled in classical piano, but soon learned jazz—she played in her brother Herb's orchestra. Meanwhile, Charles Pierpoint, the sober banker by day, had learned to play the drums and became a musician by night. Emma's brother, Herb, hired him to play in his orchestra and that's where the two met. They eventually married and, recalled Robert Pierpoint looking back, "that's when the Baptist religion, which mom had apparently inherited from her southern-oriented parents, persuaded my Dad to abandon the more liberal Methodists and become a Baptist." They soon moved to Redondo Beach, where Charles was hired at a small local bank and where they joined the First Baptist Church. "When I came along, that's where I was deeply and constantly instructed in Baptist beliefs and the Bible," wrote Robert, reminiscent of his younger sister Ruth's story of attending church not once, but twice, on Sundays. Even asthma didn't serve as an excuse for missing services. It's one reason the family now remembers him having a much better relationship with his father than his mother. The religious undertone was present, but not pronounced, in Charles Pierpoint, but omnipresent in Emma Pierpoint's dealing with both her children.

None of this "took" for the young Robert. "My earliest recollection about the Redondo Baptist Church began at around the age of ten," he wrote, "when I saw and heard my parents and their friends taking 'communion' in the church. This consisted of grape juice (wine was not allowed for Baptists) and wafers. What bothered me was that the preacher explained these were the 'blood' and 'body' of Jesus Christ. Even symbolically, this sounded to me like a pagan rite, something like cannibalism."

He was "mystified," as he put it, by other beliefs and traditions of the Redondo Baptist Church. He once asked his mother why they were so opposed to wine or any form of alcohol, pointing out that the Bible states Jesus had changed water into wine. Her answer, along the lines of "The Bible didn't say he drank it," didn't satisfy his youthful skepticism. He also found it hard to accept the idea that both his parents thought dancing and card playing were sinful, especially on Sunday (although they played in a dance band and would play bridge, but never on Sunday).

Call it youthful rebellion or an early adherence and respect for facts. Robert Pierpoint had begun to develop a reporter's sense for questioning the status quo, scrutinizing the seemingly inscrutable. "What bothered me most of all about the Christian faith," he would write toward the end of his life, "was that one had to accept all that heavy baggage or could not be 'saved' and go to heaven. That truly sounded like a catch 22." He had fought too long, too hard to breathe to become suffocated by what he saw as an oppressive form of control.

Religion was a contributing factor to the young man's development, but not in the sense his parents—his mother especially—had intended. It pushed him away from acceptance and toward argument. As son Eric put it, throughout his life, for Robert Pierpoint, "it was very important for him to get at the argument of what was going on." He may not have accepted formal religion, but he did see value in the opportunity it presented to analyze, assess, and argue. Its influence would reassert itself constantly throughout his professional life in ways that neither he nor his parents could have predicted. It presaged his passion for social justice and even-handedness in politics and in society.

The push back against religion also moved him forward toward education, which he came to see as one of the major antidotes to blindly accepting the ideas or statements of others, especially those in power. Like many young people of his day and since, the son rejected the parents' beliefs, but saw a reason why they acted in strict adherence to those beliefs:

> I cannot blame my parents too much for all of this. Mom had not even finished high school, while Dad had graduated from high school and done some study of the law in adult education classes. After all, they only believed

what most of their fellow Baptists, and many other Christians believed, and what their minister told them.

So, when, in 1943, he decided to enlist in the navy, it was both an escape and an acknowledgment. He escaped that which he could not accept. It was the beginning of a life based on finding fact, rather than following faith. Entering the service would the first step and, as he reflected back on his life, "education had a great deal to do with my journey." It would lead him away from home and back again, to countries around the globe and to the largest stage in all of journalism.

Service Calls

It was an odd pairing—Robert Pierpoint and the U.S. Navy. His asthma alone was reason to question how well he would do in the service of his country. He had by now become extremely adept at hiding his respiratory problems from others, so getting past the screening tests and physicals must have come easily. World War II was well underway when Pierpoint enlisted in 1943, motivated in part by a desire to travel, but mostly to learn. Those who knew him best say learning was paramount, something that motivated him throughout his life. That being the case, the Navy promised, but didn't deliver; it did, however, feed the desire for education while hardly satiating the appetite.

He and his next door neighbor in Whittier, Dick Hogsett, joined the navy together at 17, when the war was entering its second year. They were promised that if they signed up each would receive at least two years of college and then a commission. Almost immediately upon his enlistment, the navy sent Pierpoint to the California Institute of Technology, where the plan was to turn the curious young seaman into a scientist or engineer. What initially seemed like a good move almost instantly turned bad. He alone was sent to Caltech, while Hogsett and his other buddies who signed up out of high school were dispatched to the University of Redlands. It was where he wanted to go for more than one reason: he also had a sweetheart there.

Pierpoint became part of what was then called the V-12 Navy College Training Program, a newly minted training initiative aimed at supplementing the number of commissioned officers in the U.S. Navy during World War II. It lasted from July 1, 1943, until June 30, 1946. Joining as he did right after graduation from Whittier High School in May 1943, Robert Pierpoint was among the first enrollees in the new program and one of 125,000 overall during its years in operation. He was not alone, either, in terms of those who would become notable graduates of the program, including future U.S. Secretary of State Warren Christopher (who Pierpoint would later in life count among his closest friends) and entertainment luminaries like Johnny Carson.[7]

The V-12 program was a cooperative one, involving 131 American colleges and universities, the goal being to grant bachelor's degrees to future officers, both in the navy and the Marine Corps. Pierpoint's goal was, as stated, to gain the education that came with the training. Caltech, however, was not a good match. For one, it was heavy on training and light on what he really loved: the liberal arts, principally history and sociology. Neither was taught in the V-12 program. Therefore, "it was not something he would be interested in," says his sister, Ruth. "It was the wrong choice at the right time."

Given his restless desire to make up for a lost childhood due to asthma, she says her older brother saw it as "a waste of his time and energy." One day Robert himself would say that "the war and my years at Cal Tech had cheated me of most of the liberal arts courses I would have enjoyed in peace time." Even worse, he wrote, "I spent four miserable semesters at Cal Tech, taking almost every weekend to travel to Redlands." His misery did not go unnoticed. "As it became clear to the officers running the program at Caltech, I was no budding engineer or scientist." He got a "D" in a physics course, but straight A's in the few liberal arts classes Caltech offered. His poor showing left his commanding officers with two choices: send him to a different school or flunk him out and ship him off to boot camp and then out to sea.

Fortunately, as unfortunate as it may seem, asthma again became a determining factor in his life's course. "After four semesters at

A young Robert Pierpoint soon after enlising in the U.S. Navy in 1943, during World War II. Pierpoint did not see action; instead he was sent to California Technical Institute as part of an officer training project. The navy, in many ways, disappointed him, as he wanted to study liberal arts at Caltech, but the navy had other ideas, channeling him toward engineering.

Caltech," he recalled, "the navy discovered that my records showed I had a history of asthma, therefore could not become an officer." The navy brass decided midshipman's school might be a better fit, both from an academic and a health perspective. He eventually completed the program and received his commission as an ensign, but never saw a tour of duty, instead being granted a medical discharge.

It proved to be a fortuitous as well as a formative time in Robert Pierpoint's development, since it allowed him, under the GI Bill, to attend the University of Redlands in California.[8] It was an institution for which there was a great deal of affinity within the Pierpoint family. His grandmother taught there. His father was the university's business manager. In time, both the Pierpoint children would attend, as would their own children. Immediately upon his admission, Robert, now barely in his second decade of life, took on a challenging course of study, top-heavy with history, sociology, and politics. "There I studied more history and sociology and became even more skeptical about religion," he wrote.

Specifically, he would remember how "one history professor in particular was important in my ongoing journey, as he emphasized in several ways that the liberal developments throughout history always marked progress for civilization." Pierpoint began to concentrate his studies on such "liberal developments": the Declaration of Independence, the freeing of slaves by Lincoln, and women's right to vote, each of which he termed "liberal-backed changes." The unnamed history professor had a profound influence. "This professor's constant lesson was that liberal causes may suffer setbacks, but eventually will prevail if civilization is to survive." Pierpoint was serious of mind and purpose; most who met him during this time probably saw a young man who seemed much older and more driven than his peers.

All was not stoic studying for Robert Pierpoint, however, which is to say he did retain an adolescent fascination with the opposite sex. Early in his time at the University of Redlands, he met two women who would become central figures in his life, one for a shorter period of time than the other, but both intertwined with his journey—both personal and journalistic. Even during his Caltech time while in the navy, Pierpoint and a friend named Bryns Fagerburg—also in the officer training program—began dating girls enrolled at the University of Redlands. When he eventually enrolled there himself, Robert met Donna Knight, a young woman with whom he became captivated, developed a relationship, and married. Donna was a close friend of his sister, Ruth, also a Redlands student. Around the same time, he met another young woman, for whom he felt a great deal of respect. Patricia Adams was her name; they met in class and talked a great deal about anything and everything.

They were in the same sociology course, ironically titled "Marriage and the Family." He recalled their first meeting: "In the class was a bright and attractive co-ed named Pat Adams. We did some studying together, and became good friends."[9] They were not romantically involved—by the time of their meeting in the sociology class he had already married Donna—but there was something about her that Robert admired, the easy way she handled herself and the ease with which he conducted himself in her presence. They would meet again, but not until many years passed and Pat Adams had also married a young medical student, becoming Pat Adams Porter and giving birth to three children.

Before then, the young man who had already done a lot of living, more perhaps than many who knew him in the days of his chronically ill youth could have imagined, took the next major step. The years at Redlands had become an incubator for his burgeoning sense of social justice. The result became a belief that knowledge was essential to our country, indeed to any society. That belief would one day grow into one of the basic tenets of how he would practice journalism. It brought him next to Stockholm, Sweden, where Pierpoint would have his first encounter with news reporting.

"After graduating from the U. of R., I realized that I needed more education," he wrote. Plan A had been to enter law school. He received an assurance from the dean at Stanford Law School, after much persistent lobbying, that he would be admitted as a law student; the recommendation, however, was that he take a year of study abroad first. In the summer of 1947, Pierpoint applied and was accepted to the University of Stockholm, for studies in history and economics. He sailed aboard a ship called the *Gripsholm* in what would become a grand adventure. His wife, Donna, traveled with him. Eventually, his sister, Ruth, would also join him, urged by her brother to exercise her independence from what he saw as their mother's tyrannical religious fervor. She would provide company for Donna when Robert worked, while also establishing herself in a secretarial job.

For about a year, they lived with a Swedish family and Pierpoint learned the language. He once laughed about its usefulness, remarking to an interviewer, "What good is it?" It was good enough, Pierpoint found, to land him a translator job with the Swedish Broadcasting Corporation. Soon, through a series of circumstances, he would parlay that into becoming a reporter, more for fun than money. "It was a fateful and fulfilling decision," he would one day write, looking back on his days spent in Scandinavia.

Indeed, it was.

A Lucky Break

There was little to recommend him as a radio broadcaster to the Swedish Broadcasting Corporation in 1948. Without his facility for the Swedish language (which he sometimes would "affect" even when speaking English), the young American's somewhat squeaky voice would not have garnered him a second listen. Neither would his resume for RADIO-JIANST (Swedish Radio), on which he listed his experience as "usual part-time jobs such as service-station work and clerking during high school and college days."[10]

Between his studies and his radio work, Pierpoint found time to travel, and during one of his trips, to Helsinki, Finland, he was among the first group of American war veterans to visit that city. He called it a "rocky" time in Finland, with a quarter of its population preparing to vote for communist rule. Pierpoint knew that Czechoslovakia had recently become a Soviet satellite state and he met a number of Finnish war veterans who told him the same thing was about to happen in Finland.

Ears open, Pierpoint sensed he was onto an important story. He wrote a letter to CBS News back in the U.S. in which he offered his services reporting for the network from Helsinki. His letter went unanswered. Next, he got a tip from some of the same sources that there would be an upcoming strike organized by the communists and a coup would be attempted against the Finnish government. Showing his perseverance in the face of rejection, Pierpoint wrote CBS again. This time his letter received attention. He was hired as a "stringer"—a part-time reporter by CBS. "It was 1949. I did one radio broadcast a week, and got paid $25," he recalled nearly sixty years later.

Among the stories he filed for CBS from Scandinavia over the next two years were accounts of conflict, bloodshed, and destruction. A sampling of these stories shows just what kind of reporter Robert Pierpoint, at a tender age, was developing into. First, there's this broadcast from January 15, 1949. In succinct, yet descriptive, prose, it paints the scene for listeners.[11]

> Finland seems almost strangely quiet this morning for the day preceding an important presidential election. The calm is particularly noticeable because of the storms which have risen to plague this country's prime minister ... during the past two weeks. First came the note from Soviet Russia demanding to know why the Finnish government has not surrendered some 300 so-called war criminals, in violation of the Russ-Finnish armistice of 1944. This was obviously nothing but a move to intimidate the Finns in view of the hot Presidential battle between the communists and the other political parties.

In another, from August 12, 1949, he makes the listener feel as if he or she is there, standing beside the reporter: "All of Scandanavia is turning anxious eyes eastward today, as trouble brews in Finland. Last night Swedes were told over their national radio, in a direct broadcast from Helsinki, that their eastern neighbor is once again in serious danger from communist-dominated labor unions."

The series of reports culminates on August 19, 1949:

> Finland witnessed its first bloodshed yesterday as illegal communist-led strikes increased in number and intensity. In the northern industrial town of Kemi one worker was killed and 18 persons were injured as a crowd of 1500 tried to storm across a dam heavily guarded by police.... In a speech over the Finnish National Radio last night Minister of the Interior Simonen stated: "You can be fully assured that the government can and will maintain order throughout the country." So far the minister seems to be correct.

Throughout all of these reports, a strong sense of "scene" prevails, in which the youthful Pierpoint is developing his style as a radio reporter. In addition to his radio work, during this period he dabbled in film, narrating and appearing in a little-known and seldom seen, promotional film for the Swedish State Railways titled *Sunlight Cruise*. In one of his earliest forays into the visual medium, he uses film to paint pictures, a departure from the formative reports in which words were his paintbrush.[12]

It begins with an eight-day trip on a "luxurious rolling hotel," clear to Swedish Lapland and back. He introduces himself on camera at the start of the short film: "It's me, Bob. You'll be seeing lots of me in the next two thousand miles or so. I don't know what I'll remember best about this trip. Perhaps it will be the day these girls from a Swedish farm gave us such a warm welcome ... or the time we drank mead out of old Viking drinking horns. Lumbering on along the river made it a big impression on us and apparently we made a big impression on the Swedes. Lapland is lovely in the summer."

The trip begins in Stockholm. "Many say the bridges in this city make it one of the most beautiful in the world," he tells us. We then see a monkey with its owner, many local people, travelers and a crew. We see a library with the oldest non–Latin Bible in existence, burial grounds of royals, cows and goats in the mountains, local food and customs, and so on. We see the Arctic Circle and the circle crossing ceremony. He warns the viewer about those "Lapland mosquitoes."

"This is spectacular country and gives our photographers an opportunity for many splendid pictures." He says he didn't know what to expect, but it has "lovely scenes, great hotels, and a mild climate, at least in the summer." He throws in the fact that the sun is visible for 50 days straight at this latitude.

Best of all is the point where we see the 25-year-old Robert Pierpoint on camera: "This is station LAPP, the voice of the midnight sun, with your star reporter Bob Pierpoint, bringing you the regular edition of the news compiled from all corners of the world. And, as an added feature, your daily gossip column of events and personalities aboard the midnight sun land cruiser." Here we see the burgeoning journalist, with shots of Bob lying back on the train, hovering over, no doubt, a prop microphone and pretending to do an actual radio news broadcast.

It's likely that the Swedish Railways film was an experiment, a lark, the kind of work that a young man feeling his way in a new field would produce, if only to learn new skills (not to mention generate some modest income). While not at all a work of journalism, it foreshadows the use of the same visual techniques later adopted by television news, a medium Robert Pierpoint would one day help shape. It also provides a light-hearted, eminently human counterpoint to the more serious journalistic side he was developing, even at such an early age.

For someone who came to Sweden more for social and political reasons, Pierpoint had caught the journalism "bug." Originally, his attraction to the country had been mainly based in its social policies, not its news organizations. He had come there to extend his learning, making up in some ways for what he perceived he'd missed by not attending college. The Swedish government, at that time, was known for having developed a successful middle ground between capitalism and communism; to the graduate student devoted to ideals of social justice, the country itself was its own attraction. Broadcasting brought him closer to the culture.

He spent barely two years in Sweden, yet its impact upon him during a formative time in the young Pierpoint's development cannot be overstated. It was where he first cut his teeth on radio, flirted with what would become the new visual medium of television, and embraced the first of many cultures which would fascinate him. "Bob was as Swedish as he was American," says a close family friend, Mary Silverman. Silverman, later in the correspondent's life, heard from Pierpoint how very much he believed in the system Sweden had for its people—especially in terms of its education and health care. "Especially in his later years," she says, "he kept in touch with his Swedish friends and people in the Swedish embassy. The things he learned in Sweden were things that stayed with him for the rest of his life."[13]

Sweden was only the beginning. So, too, was his stringer work for CBS. Soon, the young Californian commanded the attention of a man across the world—a tall, chain-smoking, deep-voiced, brooding figure who was fast becoming the radio voice of a generation. It was a voice the young reporter had heard many times before, every night, in his parents' living room back in Redondo Beach. It was a long way from home and, for Robert Pierpoint, home would soon become even further away.

2

New Blood: Meeting Murrow and Covering Korea

A Chance Encounter

Robert Pierpoint was feeling pretty good about himself, and why not? He was 25 years old, working in a foreign country, having a great adventure, and stringing for CBS (then called the Columbia Broadcasting System). It was 1950 and that $25 weekly paycheck wasn't small change. He also had broken a big story that led to the contact with CBS and, even though it hadn't turned into a full-time job, he had hope. Not bad for someone who not only hadn't studied journalism but who came to Stockholm with no intention of working in journalism. His whole purpose had been to study the nation's economic system, to look at the possibility that a large government could coexist with democracy and with social justice—a concept he would study throughout his life.

Still, throughout his life, Pierpoint would often joke about being in the right place at the right time. In this instance, the right time was a chance meeting with the daughter of the owner of a large Swedish munitions company. That meeting led to a dating relationship, and on one particular night he accompanied the young woman to the Nobel Peace Prize awards ceremony in Stockholm. The American author William Faulkner was being presented with the Nobel Prize for Literature and his acceptance speech that evening was highly lauded and instantly publicized around the world. Not surprisingly, the event also attracted the attention of CBS News back in the U.S. The network was in search of a recording of Faulkner's acceptance speech.

A cable arrived in Stockholm. It was for "Mr. R. Pierpoint" and it was from CBS Radio. He'd received cables from CBS before; after all, he had been a stringer for over a year now. But this one was different. Pierpoint's eyes were immediately drawn to the name of the sender: Edward R. Murrow. *The* Edward R. Murrow. It was a personal message from Murrow to him asking for a favor. Pierpoint's mind spun. What could the great Edward R. Murrow of CBS want from him, a 25-year-old who had barely scratched the surface of broadcasting—especially compared to Murrow, the voice of World War II, the man who reported from the rooftops of London during the blitzkrieg and came into the homes of every American with a radio throughout the war years? Even in the strict Baptist Pierpoint household, 8 to 8:15 every night was reserved for listening to Murrow on CBS radio. The Pierpoints even had a world map in their breakfast room, showing the places Murrow talked about around the world and, after his broadcasts, Charles Pierpoint would quiz his children on what they had just heard.

Could he get his hands on a recording of Faulkner's speech for use on *Hear It Now*, asked Murrow? Murrow's popular radio program was one Pierpoint had heard hundreds of times from thousands of miles away. Like any good journalist, Pierpoint worked his sources. In this instance, he found a colleague at the Swedish Broadcasting Corporation who could secure a recording of the Faulkner speech. That act alone solidified a friendship between Murrow and Pierpoint. Murrow never forgot the favor. Pierpoint never forgot the cable. He kept it to the end of his life.

Pierpoint was in awe of Murrow's style; some even say he was "smitten" by the legendary broadcaster's attention. Murrow had been the voice of the World War II generation, a man whose credibility came from time spent on the front lines and in the realm of danger. His star, which always shone brightly, would only shine brighter at CBS, through the aegis of programs like *Hear It Now* on radio and its eventual television equivalent *See It Now*. He was a hardnosed, hard-edged reporter's reporter and a man's man. The ever-present cigarette (sometimes two, one pursed between his lips, another burning in a nearby ashtray) was among his trademarks. He fought with the powerful, tangled with the miscreant, and tangoed with celebrities. In the complex world of broadcast news, Murrow was a demigod. He surrounded himself, as time went on, with an inner circle that came to be known as "Murrow's Boys," hand-picked correspondents whom Murrow anointed with prestige and power at CBS. To be among them was to be one of the chosen; to be an outsider meant you were ignored.

Robert Pierpoint had no aspirations toward journalism, at least at that time. He had planned to return to the United States and pursue a degree in economics at the University of California, Berkeley. The night he attended the Nobel banquet changed all that. He found it hard to get the idea of Murrow contacting *him* out of his mind. Maybe, he began to think, this broadcasting field was for him after all. If Edward R. Murrow thought so, maybe he should think about it. Another world event made him think even more seriously. The Korean War broke out in 1950.

Already employed as a stringer, Pierpoint took the next step. With Murrow in his corner, he had his superiors at the Swedish Broadcasting Company write a reference to CBS in New York. In one letter, addressed "To Whom it may Concern," the writer, Sven-Bertil Norberg, manager of the network's shortwave division, extols the young Pierpoint's qualifications. He writes:

> Since the fall of 1948, Mr. Robert Charles Pierpoint has been employed as a program producer and broadcaster, under my supervision here at the Swedish Broadcasting Corporation. During that time he has shown himself to have a very good knowledge of Swedish and Scandinavian conditions in general, and economic and political conditions in particular. Without previous radio experience, and in a relatively short time, he has made an outstanding success of our daily feature in English—Sweden Today. Mr. Pierpoint has an alert and intelligent approach to current issues, plus an interesting manner of presenting them to the public. He has always managed well the many and varied tasks assigned him—news analysis, sports programs, travelogues, musical shows, and administrative tasks. I would particularly like to recommend his ambition, interest, and responsibility in whatever job he takes on. He has also shown imagination and ability in organizational work such as the planning of new types of programs. His humor, spirit, and ability make him a valuable and enjoyable person to work with.[1]

The letter was dated February 21, 1951. The application Pierpoint completed for permanent employment with CBS asked, "Where would you agree to be assigned?"

Pierpoint wrote: "Anywhere is OK." By May of that year, CBS would take him at his word. Robert Pierpoint was going to Korea.

"Send in some new blood"

Among all the things that Edward R. Murrow was, there was one thing he wasn't: afraid. Murrow had made his name reporting on war. He was based in London even before the outbreak of World War II in 1940 (he had gone to London in 1937, sent by CBS to head its European operations) and, once war broke out, his daily accounts and descriptions became, for millions of Americans, defining moments. His nightly broadcast from the scene of the blitzkrieg always began with three words: *This is London.*

From late 1939 to early 1940, Murrow risked his life reporting on the bombing of London. He daringly transmitted his reports from a rooftop, ignoring offers to broadcast from an underground shelter. He used the sounds of the war in telling the stories of the war, making them come alive and become real for listeners at home in the U.S. As poet Archibald MacLeish said, according to *The New Yorker*, Murrow "burned the city of London in our houses and we felt the flames that burned it." He would go where the story was, tireless and relentless in its pursuit. When Germany invaded Austria in 1938, Murrow chartered a plane to Vienna to cover the invasion.

He was there in 1945, at the war's end, reporting on the Buchenwald extermination camp, where he described the horrible condition of the concentration camp victims and the "rows of bodies stacked up like cordwood." His was a straight-ahead style, uncompromising and unapologetic. "I pray you to believe what I have said about Buchenwald," went his broadcast. "I have reported what I saw and heard, but only part of it. For most of it I have no words. If I've offended you by this rather mild account of Buchenwald, I'm not in the least sorry."

Although the public perceived Murrow as a solitary figure, he assembled a team of reporters, who came to be known as the aforementioned "Murrow's Boys," a network of skilled journalists, most young and untested, some veterans of the news wire services. One of his biggest strengths was in recognizing potential, and among those he brought to his inner circle were Eric Sevareid, William L. Shirer, and Richard C. Hottelet. His impact on the established medium of radio and the fledgling one of television cannot be overestimated. As one of his biographers has written, "The history of broadcast journalism can fairly be divided into before Murrow and after Murrow."

For Robert Pierpoint, whose only contact with the great Edward R. Murrow at this point had been a cable asking for the recording of a Nobel acceptance speech, the same might be said. His career would soon, similarly, be divided into before and after Murrow. The dividing line was the Korean War. Murrow, always on alert for new talent, had kept his eye on Pierpoint and now the time had come to offer him a job that Murrow, in all candor, did not want. He'd had his fill of war. When the Korean War broke out in 1950, Murrow and his colleagues were supposed to cover it, but Murrow declined. He told CBS, "We've had our war [World War II]. Send in some new blood." Robert Pierpoint didn't know it at the time, but years later learned the truth of how he got to Korea in 1951. "I was part of the fresh new blood," he said.[2]

Robert Pierpoint (center) with his photographer and crew (names unknown) in Korea, 1951. Pierpoint had just been hired by the legendary Edward R. Murrow to cover the war. Murrow felt coverage of the Korean War required "new blood," and Pierpoint was among the first assigned there by CBS. That same year he appeared on the first episode of Murrow's seminal TV news program *See It Now*.

On-the-Job Training

With his formal hire by CBS News as a full-time correspondent covering the Korean War, Robert Pierpoint must have had some doubts about his readiness. Years later he would reflect upon his lack of formal training as a journalist. "Everything was learned on the job," he once told an interviewer. Besides, he trusted, as did the brass at CBS News, Murrow's judgment. There's no question that the untested Pierpoint looked to the iconic Murrow as his guide to becoming a war correspondent.

For one, Murrow had concentrated his reporting on the "human" side of war—its impact on everyday people living everyday lives, both on the battlefield and back home: the soldiers, yes, but also those left behind, the families of those soldiers fighting their own battles. Murrow's rooftop reporting as London was being bombed served as an example to Pierpoint of the precision of language and the power of sound. Throughout his report, Murrow would put the microphone close to the ground or up into the air in order to capture the noise around him: the air raid sirens, bombs, and destruction. He would talk about how the war affected those he referred to as the "little people," in stark contrast to those in power who start wars but seldom see their impact up close. The shopkeepers, haberdashers, apothecaries, and factory workers were front and center in Murrow's reports.

Pierpoint's learning came from what he recalled of hearing Murrow back home in California; from those memories of Murrow's nightly broadcasts, he schooled himself in telling stories that spoke to people, not power. Once he reached Korea, he had two goals: to tell a story as Murrow might and to stay alive. By the second week of 1950, at the very start of the war, twelve correspondents, then of them American, had been reported killed, wounded, or missing. It was one reason that correspondents weren't lining up to cover the war.

During this period, Pierpoint had experienced a personal setback. His short marriage to Donna Knight-Pierpoint was over. His soon-to-be ex-wife had long since returned to the U.S. and filed for divorce in Reno, Nevada. While Pierpoint was "in a state of shock," because he "never saw it coming," says his sister, Ruth, the timing was fortuitous on many levels. First, if he had not been free to date the munitions factory owner's daughter in Stockholm, he might not have had either the means or the opportunity to be of service to Murrow. Second, he was now single and CBS was prioritizing single men to send overseas to cover the Korean War. "They were looking for young, unmarried men," Pierpoint said in an interview, "and I qualified."[3]

Before leaving for Korea, Pierpoint stopped in New York to sign a contract with CBS for more money than he had ever dreamed of making. "CBS dangled a juicy, all-expenses paid contract in front of me," he would later recall. When he showed his father the contract, the reply from Charles Pierpoint was, "You're in show business now." Whether Pierpoint believed it at the time or came to believe so later in life, he made a note to himself that read: "And he was right."

Tested in Battle

Pierpoint would also make a note to himself during this period in his life that he "didn't know what he was getting into." Aware of how untested in battle he was, he sought the advice of his mentor, Murrow. Looking for confidence, he asked whether Murrow really thought he had the mettle both to survive and to hold his own with the well-established reporters in the war zone. Murrow told him not to worry. There were some veteran correspondents in Korea, he said, "but don't worry. They aren't better, they're just older."[4]

The war's expected duration was a few months, not three years. He met with the veteran CBS bureau chief George Herman in Toyko and was given a huge, heavy, awkward tape recorder and directed to a jeep that was awaiting him. "If anything happens to that jeep, you better not come back," Herman told him. Pierpoint made it his business to ensure the jeep survived battle, even if he didn't. It wouldn't be long before both would be tested.[5]

In his very first week, he found himself sitting in a trench on the front line, using that massive tape recorder to tape an interview with an army officer. Suddenly, artillery went off. The officer he was in the middle of interviewing yelled, "Short one," referring to an incoming round of fire. Everyone, Pierpoint included, ducked for cover. A shell almost hit him and the others. Pierpoint would later laugh it off. "That was a close one," he said. While under attack, he'd forgotten that the tape recorder had been rolling the whole time. Realizing he had a story worthy of the best of Murrow's realistic war reporting, Pierpoint needed to get the tape back to the US, but not before machine gun fire erupted. "All I could think of was getting the jeep out of there before something happened to it." The jeep was safe. He was relieved.

The tape also survived and he managed to get it shipped to New York, where Murrow's producer Fred Friendly was working on a CBS radio show called *Hear It Now*. The show focused on historic events and often used sound effects and recreations to dramatize its stories. It was greatly popular with the audience, thanks in large part to Friendly, who had an ear for great writing and drama, and Murrow's authoritative narration. Friendly intercepted the tape and brought it to Murrow, who was impressed and gave the go-ahead to use it as the basis for a *Hear It Now* installment.

In his first week on the battlefield, Pierpoint's fears, both of success and survival, were calmed. He had faced fire and lived. He had possessed the instinct to know what he had on tape and how it could be used to bring American listeners to the battlefield. His report was a great success; Murrow was so pleased with the story that he even phoned Pierpoint's parents to tell them to listen to the broadcast.

Success had another side, the young Pierpoint learned. Soon after the *Hear It Now* segment, he received a cable from CBS, specifically Fred Friendly, who wanted him to go back and do the same story for television. "I cabled them back explaining that it was impossible," said Pierpoint. "I couldn't take lights and cameras to the front. I explained it was night and all they would see would be flashes of light anyway. "Friendly said, do it. Essentially, I made a movie," recalled Pierpoint. "It wasn't my proudest moment as a journalist. But it made them happy. Fred was a tough guy to work for."[6] This would not be as tough as it would get in Korea.

"It is almost impossible to imagine the working conditions when television was in its infancy," wrote Myra MacPherson, a Pierpoint colleague. Their professional paths would cross many times, particularly in Washington decades later. "Film shot in Korea sent from Tokyo took a minimum of three days to get on the air in New York." She documents how a friend of Pierpoint's, a wire service correspondent, once tried using a carrier pigeon as a faster means of transport, but "gave up on that when the first bird took 11 days to get from Korea to Tokyo."[7] There had to be a better way, but it would be many years before its invention. Even then, there are those who today suggest the actual work of Pierpoint, Herman, and their ilk during the Korean War neither suffered from the slower transmission, nor would be improved by the speed of today's technology.

The Face of War

While his personal leanings were against war in general, the young Pierpoint saw the Korean War, specifically, as a somewhat noble cause on behalf of the United States—a position he returned to many times over the course of his life. In his reporting one finds a predilection toward focusing on the good that would come from American involvement in Korea. Part of this possibly came from Murrow's own support of the U.S. position in Korea and Asia in general. Even before the war had begun in earnest, in his nightly broadcast, Murrow had spoken to his audience about the importance of U.S. involvement in the region. According to broadcast historian Dr. J. Fred McDonald:

> Murrow also saw the Korean conflict as a struggle between the Soviet Union and the United States for leverage in world politics. The American nation, he remarked on December 5, 1950, was committed "to the proposition that our foreign policy must be based on strength, ours and that of our allies." The United States, he said, "concluded that the Russians would not negotiate realistically until we had created sufficient 'situations of strength.'"[8]

Not only would Murrow's views help shape Pierpoint's, but the younger man would, before long, play a major role in shaping both Murrow's and Americans' view of that war. The more he became immersed in the conflict, the more Pierpoint searched for those moments when humanity superseded conflict. In so doing, he was moved by much of what he saw. Not all of it was reported—a good deal of what reporters note to themselves ultimately does not make it into their stories—but the experience of studying, analyzing, and making sense of another culture, learned so well in Stockholm, made Pierpoint a keen observer of life at the tender age of 26.

He spent a good deal of his time when not with the troops in the Plaza Hotel, a domicile that sounds a great deal better than it was. The Plaza, not to be confused with its namesake in New York, offered guests little more than a sink, a toilet, and a bed, though Pierpoint recalled that it was possible to get a "pretty good" drink there. Mainly, it was a respite for him from the field of battle, a place to gather and organize his thoughts about what he had seen and heard that day. He assembled them in a series of reporter notebooks, a practice he continued throughout his professional career. Individually and collectively, they present a portrait of the reporter as a young man. Often containing incomplete sentences, they contain quick sketches of his impressions of a place, time, or event. They also provide a glimpse into the raw material of his reports during this period, principally for CBS radio, but also, eventually, for CBS television.⁹

As stated, he was moved by many things he experienced during the Korean War. He made an entry in one notebook regarding an orphanage he saw "which was destroyed—mostly boys—some from GIs. Both cried when left. 1 little kid, who always wants to see American uncle. GI come back at first—sometimes bring food and candy." In one province, he noted an "estimated over ¼ million still left refugees from Han River North.... People falling dead as they get off trucks. Starvation. Homes destroyed and damaged in province."

This reporter "shorthand" displays what Pierpoint was reaching for when creating vivid descriptions of a scene. The goal in radio reporting at the time was to capture the reality of war through short bursts of descriptive prose. The concept was to bring the listener a sense of how ordinary people were being affected by battle. In the above instance, Pierpoint focused on the children, one in particular, who yearned for the American soldier whom he (whether correctly or not) thought to be his "uncle." The missing GI came to the orphanage bringing food and candy, but one day didn't come. The waiting of this child and others for those who may or may not return, noticed by Pierpoint, suggests the kind of reporter he was striving to be: one, like Murrow, whose focus was on average people caught in the middle of war and the heavy price they paid.

In another notebook entry, Pierpoint recorded his observations regarding the people, doctors, and police officers he met in his daily travels.

He wrote how "Korean government people are the better. They cooperate." Medical care," he noted, was substandard, with those in need of care facing a shortage of resources. "Doctors are very poor here—sanitation worse. 6 hospitals full scale for Korean people plus many dispensaries." Then, he includes this curious comment: "I don't think there is an honest Korean. All crooks." The Seoul police force, however, he labels the "best in Orient. Trustworthy, relatively honest—good chief."

Ironically, while in the navy, Pierpoint had never seen action, but as a correspondent he did, at least of a sort. In addition to the close call with enemy fire during his first week in Korea, months later, for a story, he suited up and took part in a U.S. bomber training mission. For this story, he not only wrote a radio report, but experimented with television, using a film crew to record the experience from inception to flight to landing. Along the way, he introduced viewers to the young pilots who risked their lives on foreign soil. To get the "feel" for the job they did and to convey that "feeling" to a rapt audience back home in the United States, Pierpoint became one among them.

With a journalist's sense, he recognized that his subjects would open up more to him if he joined their ranks, if only for a day. Always, however, Pierpoint recognized there was a fundamental difference between him and the military men he covered. "They were real heroes," he wrote. "We correspondents could always get out. They were there for the duration."

The fact that he was himself a young man covering young men must have given Robert Pierpoint an instant advantage over the older correspondents at the time. As his son Eric observed, the war was being fought by young people and the medium of television, in its infancy at the time, was essentially a young medium; "it was young people talking to young people." Radio was his parents' generation, but television was coming of age during the Korean War and Robert Pierpoint was coming of age along with it.

See It Now

The Korean War was, in many ways, a seminal time in the development of television's potential to cover news from a distance. It was a test of the medium's ability to provide stirring pictures to accompany needed information. On the domestic front, TV news had a difficult enough time providing same-day visual coverage. Covering a war a half a world away was a challenge television had not yet faced. World War II had been a radio war. Murrow and Friendly were working to make Korea the first television war.

Robert Pierpoint's primary responsibility, as with all network correspondents, was to file his stories for radio. The networks (principally CBS and NBC at the time) were not geared up to cover a war using camera crews. It had only been five years since World War II filled Americans' homes via radio, and television was an afterthought in terms of war coverage. Television required pictures to synchronize with the words that described a battle. The networks, CBS included, turned to newsreel photographers, as they had no staff. They would buy the film from these photographers, whose first job was to produce the newsreels that appeared in theaters before or between feature attractions. It was cheaper than either hiring or training their own staff (though often both networks would "poach" the newsreel photographers to work for them full-time, believing their experience was worth the expense).

Enter *See It Now*, a program that Murrow and Friendly envisioned as a weekly television offering that would be somewhat like a documentary, but more akin to what we would today call a "magazine" approach to news. The first *See It Now* aired on CBS television on November 18, 1951. Pierpoint's contribution was a filmed report following soldiers from Fox Company, Second Platoon of the 19th Infantry, through a day in their lives. It accounted for roughly half the program's total length and "drew viewers into the actions and feelings of a combat unit about to assault enemy installations on higher ground." The balance of the inaugural *See It Now* followed the pace Pierpoint had set with his 15-minute opening segment, developing the theme of how a donated pint of blood found its way to saving soldiers' lives, wounded soldiers returning stateside, and the first story on the release of American POWs from Korean prison camps.

Pierspoint's work was praised by Murrow and solidified the 26-year-old's place in journalism history by being "among the very first on television to focus on the soldier in a more personal style, as opposed to the newsreel film style that featured battles and material over the story of the individual trooper." His report was so well received that it wasn't long before he was again called upon to report on Korea for *See It Now*. On February 24, 1952, he reported on three wounded GIs, following them from their evacuation in Korea to the base hospitals near their homes back in the United States. Many had interviewed these same GIs, but the young correspondent's work in this program was lauded for its sensitivity, compassion, insight, and even good humor. Always, there was the human touch in his stories.

Never was that more evident than in what has been termed the "culmination of Murrow and Friendly's search for a proper TV news documentary form," the famous "Christmas in Korea" broadcast that aired on December 29, 1953. In it, Pierpoint again interviewed U.S. troops and covered the story of Ethiopian soldiers involved in the war. The "Christmas in Korea" broadcast became a classic for its time and, with it, Pierpoint received perhaps the highest recognition in his young career. As one broadcast journalism historian put it, "See It Now's distinctive format and voice crystallized in its Korea programming, beginning with Robert Pierpoint's 15 minute report ... the full-length 'Christmas in Korea' in 1953 was the crowning achievement."[10]

With all of this praise coming his way, it would have been easy for someone so young to get a big head. Around this time he made a notation in his reporter's notebook as a reminder not to take himself too seriously. "Recently friend warned me against just such today. He is AP war corres [sic]. That he was big hero, asked to speak many times, got to feel pretty BIG then one day spoke for AP before big crowd. Really great job—much emotion—afterward little old lady [told him] I always shop at A&P. So I shall try to keep my emotions AND my illusions to a minimum. I am a reporter—shall do my best to report facts as I see them."

The comment is so telling. It became the very benchmark of his reporting for the next three decades, from the battlefields of Korea to the steps of the White House and all the stops in between. Korea, specifically, was an experience which defined the young reporter early in his life and one of which he never lost sight. Well after his retirement from CBS News, in 1993, he attended a reunion of a hundred or so Korean War correspondents in Washington, D.C., to commemorate the 40th anniversary of the war's end.

In a piece about the reunion he wrote for the *San Francisco Chronicle*, Piepoint recalled events during the Korean War from June 1950 until July 1953. "More than 33,000 Americans died," he wrote, "but they and their comrades who survived saved South Korea from the Communists who started it and who still rule in the north." He maintained that "the millions of Koreans who live today in a democratic and prosperous nation south of the 38th parallel have not forgotten," nor have "100 or so correspondents who covered that war." For him "it was a bittersweet reunion." The losses were personal. Eighteen of his colleagues died covering the war. "Many more are no longer around," he continued, "or were unable to attend because of various infirmities. But there was no regretting the war." He pointed out that President Harry Truman didn't take a public opinion poll before he ordered the troops in. "Few reporters, at least in the first years, ever dubbed it 'Truman's war.' Fewer still expended any ink debating whether the U.S. should be waging a war in Korea at all."

He called it a different time, stating, "there was admittedly debate over whether General Douglas MacArthur should have been allowed to continue the fighting until North Korea surrendered. But Truman settled that one, along with the insolence of a popular general who forgot that in this country the military takes its orders from the civilians at the top." Truman sacked MacArthur. The communists were "chased back north and Moscow learned that its client states could not invade with impunity. The American people learned that every so often we have to fight for a principle. The U.S. military establishment was reminded who is boss." His conclusion: "And the world gained more respect for a nation willing to sacrifice for the freedom of others. Maybe there is a lesson there."[11]

In Korean War coverage there was also a lesson for journalists, particularly those in the profession of television news. In a *New York Times* editorial titled "Not an Anchorman in Sight," James Greenfield, who attended the 1993 reunion, noted that "amid all the quiet talk, it was clear that most of the American correspondents who had covered the war were the last of a breed and that American journalism itself was at the end of an era." As Greenfield points out, "for the most part, the correspondents in Korea were still awash in the patriotic fervor of World War II. For the press in general it was a less questioning, less cynical time." Censorship existed, as the writer states, but there were "few complaints, as long as the censor's touch was light. No one tried to keep you away from the action if you were hell bent on getting yourself killed." The interesting thing that Greenfield points out is that there is virtually no television footage of the Korean war and "there were no anchormen at the reunion."

Ed Murrow "dropped in on the war occasionally," but "those were the days of his *Hear It Now* radio program; *See It Now* came later." Pierpoint is cited as among the CBS radio reporters "who were about the closest anyone came to glamour." The still photo, "not TV, defined the war for many Americans." As a result, "war coverage changed drastically after Korea. TV's wallop was just faster and more powerful than either words or still pictures."[12]

Whether Robert Pierpoint ever came close to "glamour," as Greenfield suggests, is highly debatable, but that was never his goal, beginning as a young journeyman reporter and throughout his career. Despite that, Korea put him in the spotlight long after the war ended. On February 28, 1983, the television program (coincidentally, on CBS) *M*A*S*H* aired its final episode, after twelve seasons (the show ran seven years longer than the actual war itself). The episode chronicled the final days of the Korean War. Pierpoint had broadcast the announcement of the war's end on CBS radio and the show's producers wanted to include it in the plot. Unfortunately, the original recording was deemed too scratchy and was of such low quality that he was asked to reprise his famous broadcast. He rerecorded it, word for word, to improve the sound:

On board a Pan Am flight leaving Korea in 1953, and en route to his next assignment covering Asia as CBS Far Eastern Bureau Chief. His voice announcing the end of the Korean War that year was later used, in 1983, in the final episode of the television series *M*A*S*H*, and heard by an estimated 125 million people.

> *This is Robert Pierpoint speaking to you from Panmunjon. It's one minute before 10 p.m. We can still hear the sound of nearby artillery. At some point during the next few seconds, the guns should go silent as the cease fire officially goes into effect. (the sounds of mortar fire are heard, followed by silence). There it is, that's the sound of peace.*[13]

He was paid SAG (Screen Actors Guild) wages for the work (an earnings statement shows that he made just over $29). Over 120 million people worldwide heard his voice on what remains the highest rated series finale in television history—far more than ever heard the original broadcast. On the importance of his most famous broadcast, Pierpoint once wrote that "for many in combat that last broadcast finally let them think they might live after all. They could begin thinking of the future again."

Korea and his experiences there would remain with Robert Pierpoint for the rest of his life. Significantly, the very last story he did for CBS News, on June 24, 1990, was a *Sunday Morning on CBS* piece looking back at the Korean War and updating the audience on what had happened to some of those soldiers he first met while reporting for *See It Now*, including those from the air force and the bomber training mission he flew). Some of them were "evacuees," those wounded in battle and transported back to the United States, who were part of the original story nearly four decades earlier.

When the Korean War ended on July 27, 1953, Robert Pierpoint was still a very young man at age 28. His knowledge of Asian culture, gleaned from covering the war, would make him a prime candidate for his next assignment, one for which he was once more handpicked by Edward R. Murrow. Despite the number of times he had worked on Murrow's programs, principally the *Hear It Now* broadcast that forged their initial relationship and the pioneering *See It Now* programs on American troops in Korea, up to this point Pierpoint had barely met or spent much time with the great man. That was about to change.

3

Bureau Chief: The Far East

By 1953, Robert Pierpoint had been overseas for three years, working successfully as a foreign correspondent for radio and television's premier network, CBS. His ascension through the network ranks had been due, in large part, to his own hard work, but also to the guiding hand of the man he had barely met: Edward R. Murrow. One thing everyone at CBS knew: you didn't pick Murrow; Murrow picked *you*. In terms of his next assignment, his sister, Ruth, remembers him telling her: "I've had a summons from CBS telling me that if I want to come to the Orient, I have to be there Monday morning." It was fast turnaround. "This was Friday night," says his sister. "That was the very beginning of his meeting Murrow." She recalls being "shocked" that he wanted to do it—that is, spend more time in Asia.

He made a fast trip back to the States where he and Murrow met and talked. The exact content of their conversation isn't known, but one thing is. It was in Murrow's power, by this point, to call all the shots when it came to correspondents' assignments. It was as if he were dividing up the world and giving pieces of it to those he viewed as deserving. Pierpoint, as the second "wave" of "Murrow's boys," was about to be given one of the spoils of the war he had helped cover so well for CBS. As if passing the younger man a drink, Murrow told him, "I'm giving you Japan." The title would be "Far Eastern Bureau Chief."

For the next four years, until 1957, Pierpoint would file reports, for both CBS radio and television, from Japan and the Middle East. It was a reward for doing good work, but also financially rewarding. In 1952, the year before attaining the bureau chief title, Pierpoint made $13,500, ranging from as little as $50 for a short news item to as much as $100 for a *See It Now* segment. In general, his weekly pay was in the vicinity of $275.[1] For comparison's sake, his salary was roughly that of a star major league baseball player—Stan Musial of the St. Louis Cardinals, for example, who made just over $13,000 that year. It was a sizable amount of money, nearly the equivalent of $95,000 in today's currency at a time when a dollar's buying power certainly was far greater than it is now.

That, of course, was only one measure of success and, for Pierpoint, it wasn't the primary one. Foremost for Pierpoint was the adventure, the opportunity to "make 'em itch," a phrase he had heard Murrow use to describe the reporter's responsibility to report, analyze, and criticize in such a way that the audience was made uncomfortable, stirred up, forced to think. It was what Pierpoint, from Korea, had internalized about Murrow through reporting for *See It Now*. It was what fascinated him about the older man, and what made him want to be a part of his inner circle. Most of all, those close to him say, "he was impressed that Murrow wasn't impressed with himself."

In so many ways, the job of a foreign bureau chief agreed with Pierpoint's temperament. In the introduction to *At the White House*, he recalled how "the overseas assignment put me in a privileged position." He liked the fact that "foreign correspondents are their own bosses, thousands of miles from the home office, instant experts on anything they choose to report." Of course, "nitpicking editorial complaints arrive by cable or telephone, but can easily be ignored or evaded with the subtle suggestion that superiors are simply wrong." The best rejoinder, he learned, was "I am here and you are there, is an unanswerable argument."[2]

Acting with this level of independence, he began the job of Far Eastern Bureau Chief with the support of Murrow, the confidence that three years in a war zone brings, and the desire to explain the importance of events in a part of the world he considered central to Americans' understanding. It took him from Tokyo to Vietnam to the Middle East, principally Syria and Lebanon—all areas that were developing hot spots on the globe. His first assignment: Japan, where he lived in the Imperial Hotel, filing his stories for a variety of CBS radio newscasts, most often *World News Roundup*, but occasionally longer pieces for what was called *CBS World Assignment*, a single-topic radio broadcast centering on a specific part of the world. He emphasized the culture of the place where he lived and worked, seeking out, as he had in Korea, those opportunities to bring listeners closer to the everyday experience of a country's citizenry.

He saw and experienced many problems festering within the region and tried to use his own observations and expertise to identify them for his audience. With an openness and youthful sense of exploration, Pierpoint took on the Far East as he had the Korean War. He saw evidence everyday of a growing resentment and resistance of the United States and its policies, something he found disturbing on several levels. Its implication for U.S. foreign policy was a lesson in progress for the young correspondent, who would use what he learned three years later when assuming one of the most coveted positions at CBS News. He made a study of the Asian people and their culture and focused his reporting on, not facts alone, but also context.

While not many of his scripts or recordings of his broadcasts during this period survive, several do and they are telling of how he viewed a country and a region in turmoil. The first is from July 24, 1952, soon after his arrival in Tokyo: "This is a report from Asia. It is a report of the problems and issues and struggles of the Asian peoples. It is report on the successes and failures of American policy in the Far East." In a foreboding tone, he warns: "Unhappily, it is a report on the advance of communism. It is a fact that we are losing the support of the Asian people. Unless the trend is reversed—and soon—we are liable to find ourselves faced with a completely hostile Asia. This would be a disaster from which the free world would never recover. It is not too late—not yet."[3]

The concerns voiced by Pierpoint in his role as CBS Far Eastern Bureau Chief were ones held by the U.S. government at the time, as noted in "Milestones: 1945–1952" of the website of the Office of the Historian, U.S. Department of State:

> The U.S. perception of international threats had changed so profoundly in the years between 1945 and 1950 that the idea of a re-armed and militant Japan no longer alarmed U.S. officials; instead, the real threat appeared to be the creep of communism, particularly in Asia. The final agreement allowed the United States to maintain its bases in Okinawa and elsewhere in Japan, and the U.S. Government promised Japan a bilateral security pact.

That October, general elections were held in Japan. The results allayed the fears of the U.S., for the short term. With a voter turnout of nearly 77 percent, the Liberal Party prevailed, but that didn't mean communism was dead. The struggles would continue throughout the region and Pierpoint would be there to cover them all, mostly from Tokyo, but often traveling outward to bring Americans the bigger picture.

Sensing he was present in a nation—Japan—that was at the crossroads of cultural change, Pierpoint saw himself not as an outsider, in the conventional sense of being the detached reporter covering a story, but as someone who was *living* the story. In this report from May 9, 1954, for CBS radio, he described what it was like to be in the midst of a country's transition: "My assignment is Tokyo Japan. I live here and work here—in this fabulous, teeming, brutal city of seven million people. Tokyo is indefinable—it's neither East nor West—it almost seems like a place suspended in space and time—between Orient and Occident—between the tranquil feudalism of five hundred years ago—and the tense materialism of today." He says he had lived there three years and may live there three more, but "even after that I don't think I will completely understand Tokyo. But I will nevertheless enjoy it."

If the adage that passion for a subject leads to success at work or in life is true, Robert Pierpoint, at this stage in his career, was destined for even greater success than he had already realized. He was a quick study, intuitive in reading the signs of change all around him that might elude other correspondents, and skilled at drawing connections between the past and present. One such example came from a story titled "Report on Japan," filed for *CBS World Assignment* on August 7, 1954. "Nine years ago this week the first atomic bomb mushroomed over the city of Hiroshima. August 6th, 1945 marked the end of Japan's hope for world domination," he wrote. "To the people of Hiroshima—those still surviving in the mass of burning rubble—there was no more question about fighting on for Emperor and honor. Japan was crushed as flat their once-flourishing city. Within a few days the rest of the country would realize this fact almost as acutely as did the people of Hiroshima."

The ability of Japan to survive, he said, was based upon its willingness to adapt: "There was no other course open but to submit to the inevitable— to accept the fact that Japan was licked—to bow to the conquerors—and to start all over again. That is what Hiroshima—and Japan—have done." He goes on to say that "contrary to other cities in Japan, the city of Hiroshima today is well planned and well laid out. At least one beneficial result of the A-Bomb was the complete destruction of a disorganized hodgepodge of buildings and shacks, which were rebuilt along more orderly lines. Of the seventy thousand homes wiped out by the blast of the A-Bomb, over half have been rebuilt. Many of the new buildings are stronger and more attractive than those destroyed."

There weren't many at the time reporting the potential gain for a nation that had been leveled from top to bottom. In fact, Pierpoint, perhaps because of time spent, maybe because of innate curiosity, and possibly out of respect for the country he watched grow out of the ashes of war, was drawn back to Japan many times during his career. During his days at the White House some 25 years later, he returned there during a presidential visit by Jimmy Carter. In a story of July 17, 1979, which he titled "Japan Revisited ... the Born Again Japanese," Pierpoint said, "It came as no surprise to see the physical changes of Japan over the years since I left at the end of 1957. Nowadays it has become a cliché to remark, on returning to

Tokyo, on the astounding modernity of the city, its skyscrapers, its streets clogged with cars and trucks, the lifestyle of its people so much like New York or Paris." He had been there reporting during the rebuilding of the nation and marveled at those advancements made since. "Anyone who has ever bought a Japanese-built television set or car knows that Japan is a leading industrial society. No, it was not that, as impressive as it is, but the changed people, the attitudes of the Japanese themselves as compared with a generation ago, that slowly seeped into my consciousness during the ten days I was there before and during President Carter's recent visit."

Japan wasn't the only nation on which and from which he reported during this period as Far Eastern Bureau Chief. He also reported from the Middle East, gaining both a taste for its culture, an understanding of the deep divides between its occupants, and, as will become apparent in later chapters, a strong opinion of the relationship between the United States and Israel. In a story from November 30, 1956, Pierpoint recorded his observations as a new arrival in Syria:

> To the newly arrived observer, Syria today gives the impression of a country at war. As far as I know at the moment there is no war, but a warlike atmosphere is certainly the feeling here. Driving over in a car from peaceful Lebanon, one begins to notice soldiers scattered here and there almost as soon as the border is past. There are freshly dug trenches zig-zagging across the dry Syrian hillsides, with an occasional output tent visible from the road. ... This city itself gives one that clutch in the stomach that hints of gunfire and destruction.... Our hotel is well-barricaded with sandbags along the its wide-windowed front. There are 125 rooms in this hotel ... normally a top tourist stopover for visitors to the holy lands ... but at present the place is almost deserted except for a few American correspondents.

The tone and cadence of the descriptions contained in this story, as much if not more so than the others during this time in his reporting life, echo those of his mentor, Edward R. Murrow. Using a sharp eye for detail, his report gives the listener a strong sense of "being there," experiencing the scene for the first time along with Pierpoint. In many ways, it's reminiscent of the rooftop reporting of Murrow during World War II, the style of a man Pierpoint once referred to as, among reporters, "one of the greatest I've known." However, there's something that sets Pierpoint apart from Murrow in this respect: he actually lived in the places from which he reported. Often Murrow would spend short periods of time in a location, but return back to New York. Pierpoint, other than occasional trips back to the United States, stayed the course.

There's one thing anyone who knew Robert Pierpoint during this time would notice. He was, starting in Sweden and continuing throughout

Leaning against the concrete balustrade at the Correspondents Club in Hong Kong. Pierpoint spent a good deal of time at the club, drinking and socializing, and garnering a large number of stories, many humorous, about his fellow correspondents. During his four years as Far East Bureau Chief, Pierpoint developed a great appreciation for Asian culture, becoming something of an art collector.

his Far East duties, a student of whatever nation he was covering as a journalist. He spoke some Japanese and had a special affinity for Asian art. A family friend, Peggy Moore, with her husband, met him during this period after being introduced by Pierpoint's father. The Moores were on a freighter that stopped in Japan and, at Charles Pierpoint's suggestion, the correspondent met them. As with so many people he met during this period in his life, they became close friends and connected each time they returned to Hong Kong between 1955 and 1956. "He certainly knew and enjoyed the culture around Tokyo," Peggy Moore says. "The Japanese aesthetic was absolutely amazing to him," she adds. "I think he also appreciated the fact that here is a country with many people per square mile and yet they learn to farm it ... the economy of life there, the way they lived very simply in small quarters with mats that rolled up at night, their graciousness—that all appealed to Bob."

According to another friend from that time, Mary Silverman, "he was fascinated by Southeast Asia, in the same way he had been by Sweden and the Scandanavian countries." Silverman says he had a lot of interaction with Japanese in Malaysia, where "they were really hated," and sympathized with their plight. He also was fascinated by the large buses that would pull into Tokyo at times, with tourists who would "swarm into a store and buy all the merchandise."[4] In time, he became somewhat of a collector of Japanese artifacts himself.

Many of the U.S. correspondents working in Asia at that time brought their wives with them; some lived in private homes, where others, like Pierpoint, lived in a converted hotel. Some of those wives "had become quite expert on Japanese art and culture," Pierpoint once recalled. One day one of them asked Pierpoint "if I wanted her to purchase some fine Japanese artifacts, which were selling at a very low price in those days. I did not know much about Japanese artifacts, but wanted a few souvenirs, so I said please do so." The wife returned with what Pierpoint labeled "a lovely black and gold lacquer kimono tray, several small jade carvings, a gorgeous Buddhist priest's robe with gold and silver thread, and some old and interesting block prints." The objects became valued reminders of his time in Asia, the block prints especially. They would eventually make their way into his home back in Santa Barbara.[5]

He had found, in some ways, another home, one where he had wide acceptance, where his gentle spirit, friends say, was appreciated and reciprocated. Pierpoint became a stalwart of what he would one day label "a great institution"—the Foreign Correspondents Club of Japan. He first experienced it as an old building in downtown Tokyo in the spring of 1951, when assigned to cover the Korean War. It was, as he described it, a five-story building with a large bar (naturally!), a dining area, an open telephone switchboard, a kitchen, and office, plus an elevator to the upper floors. There was a unique feature: the elevator door had a bullet mark from a pistol fired by "a drunk and angry reporter." (As an aside, Pierpoint wrote that the reporter in question worked for the *New York Times* and was irritated by the elevator's slow movement, incompatible with his urgent need to visit the upstairs bathroom.)

The club had a privileged status. It was run by an elected board among the foreign correspondents and was allowed to purchase food and supplies from military stores. They had a cleaning staff of Japanese women and good, mostly American cuisine (cheeseburgers were a favorite). The "real marvel of the Press Club," Pierpoint would remember years later, was the telephone switchboard. It was depended upon, through the help of English-speaking Japanese-American youth whose parents sent them back to their country once they reached high school age, to receive messages from the correspondents' news desks. "One time I forgot to tell the switchboard that I was going to a Japanese movie," recalled Pierpoint much later in life. "Shortly after I left the Press Club, the operator received a cable from New York asking me for an immediate broadcast on a report on the wires that two Japanese fishermen had been covered with ash fallout from the Bikini hydrogen bomb test, and were dying."

The women at the press club switchboard looked everywhere for Pierpoint, combing all his usual haunts around Tokyo, to no avail. When he returned later that night, CBS had been beaten on the story by all the other news outlets. "I, in turn, was beaten by one of the nastiest cables from my boss that I ever received," recalled Pierpoint, "and was almost fired." It was the first, but not the last time. His experience as Far East Bureau Chief for CBS brought him into contact with people and issues which laid a foundation of controversy surrounding his future work. While it was 5,000 miles from his base in Tokyo, the Middle East, through a matter of happenstance, would play into a scenario that two decades later caused a stir between CBS, its listeners, and its sponsors. It all began with a simple trip to cover a sporting event and ended with hundreds of letters urging his removal. The span in between is important in terms of understanding the basis of Robert Pierpoint's beliefs—and why he wouldn't back down.

Pierpoint would often file his reports from Korea via Tokyo, where he would later be based as the network's Far East Bureau Chief. In this instance, he is seen filing a radio report in 1956 to a CBS producer in San Francisco.

Trouble in the Middle East

That level of immersion in the region made Pierpoint highly opinionated on the problems—and the potential solutions—in what he saw as "that troubled part of the world." As part of his Far East Bureau Chief duties, he traveled outside of Japan and the other Asian countries during this time to report on other cultures. Of particular interest to him was the growing Arab-Israeli conflict, which he first experienced during a three-month tour of duty in the Middle East in 1956. "I was still based in Tokyo and on my way to cover the Olympics in Austria when war broke out over the Suez Canal," he wrote in an undated letter to a family member years later. He was ordered to head to Lebanon to cover the Suez War. The British, French, and Israelis had declared war on Egypt, trying to take back the Suez Canal. "The Muslim Arabs were then and are today, very angry over our support of Israel," Pierpoint wrote in his letter. "I cannot say I blame them. Our policy toward the Middle East has been far too heavily influenced by AIPAC and the Jewish community in the USA."[6]

His experience covering the region led him to this conclusion: "I support neither Israel nor the Palestinians, each of which is violently fanatic. I favor a pro–American policy in that area, but have never seen one. I do support the state of Israel, but not the religious fanatics who continue to build illegal settlements on a Palestinian territory. I also support the Palestinians' right to a homeland, but deplore their violence and their efforts to refuse the existence of Israel."

The several tours of duty in the Middle East created a near obsession in Pierpoint to address what he saw as a basic inequity in the way U.S. policy favored Israel. His opinion on the matter continued to grow long after his time as Far Eastern Bureau Chief had elapsed and he was well into his tenure as the network's White House correspondent. It genesis began from the first-hand experience he gained of the region, as well as two events that occurred decades later: the murder of Israeli athletes by Palestinians during the 1972 Munich Olympics and the subsequent retaliation by Israeli interests in shooting down a Libyan aircraft.

He read extensively on the Arab/Israeli conflict throughout his life, but the genesis of his thought process on the Middle East began during his time as Far East Bureau Chief. He was influenced by "The Real Issues in the Arab/Israel/Zionist Conflict," published in 1971 by Elmer Berger; "Abating the Middle East Crisis through the United Nations (and Vice Versa)," by John Lawrence Hargrove, in the *Kansas Law Review*, for a few. His own experiences years earlier, combined with his reading on the subject, led to a controversial radio broadcast on March 7, 1973, that first aired on

CBS's flagship radio station in New York, WCBS. The platform itself, in one of the nation's largest broadcast markets and one with a large Jewish population nearly guaranteed the response it received. The fact that it was repeated six times on March 16 and twice on March 17 expanded Pierpoint's audience, as did a reprint of the editorial later that year in the *Christian Science Monitor*.

Pierpoint, in a well reasoned, impassioned argument, took on the White House for following what he termed a "double standard" when responding to acts of violence and terror by both Israelis and Palestinians. His exact words: "The Israelis have and utilize a formidable political and propaganda force in this country in the form of six million Jews." He urged Americans to "apply more study, balance and fair play to the difficult problem of the Middle East."[7]

The firestorm that followed might have been predictable; its size was not. Over 300 letters poured into CBS's executive offices, many applauding what their writers saw as Pierpoint's courage and honesty. Many more, however, vilified his views, some even charging that Pierpoint's comments were anti–Semitic. The letters ran approximately 3–1 against Pierpoint. Some even called for his firing from CBS. A sampling of audience feedback reveals just how successful Pierpoint had been in his oft-stated goal to "make 'em itch"—that desire "to report and analyze and criticize in such a way that the audience was made uncomfortable, stirred up, forced to think." He certainly succeeded.

A writer named Greta Meier wrote the following, on behalf of B'nai B'rith Women's Chapter in Baltimore: "I want to voice my protest against Robert Pierpoint's 'First Line Report' on Wednesday, March 7th. Your White House Correspondent's commentary on the Middle East situation was anything but objective and unbiased and such reporting only adds more fuel to the fire consuming this troubled area. At the end of his report, Mr. Pierpoint suggested that 'more studied balance and fair play be applied to the difficult problems of the Middle East.' He should only practice what he preaches."[8]

Another listener, from Wooster, Ohio, wrote in support of Pierpoint: "I wish to recommend for a special award in courage and good reporting, the statement made by Robert Pierpoint on March 7, 1973, 'Double Standard in the Middle East.' From the perspective of someone who lived for 35 years in the Middle East, the writer, Edwin Wright, wrote to then CBS News president Richard Salant, "When I read Mr. Pierpoint's statement, I realized freedom of expression is not dead, that we still have a partially open society and that there are individuals honest and courageous enough to tell it as they see it—in this case it was the truth. Many others who read the article agreed with me—but will not write. Long live Mr. Pierpoint and Freedom of Honest Reporting."

Another wrote: "Judging you from your speech, you are an honest, decent fine and just person, and high value as a human, a rare quality."

Still another wrote to CBS: "While it is certainly yours and his prerogative to report the news and to analyze it, it is also incumbent upon the media to, as Mr. Pierpoint mentions, not use the double standard, which he has so eloquently used in trying to compare the Olympic tragedy to the recent Israeli pre-announced commando raids deep into Lebanon, or to compare the admittedly tragic shooting down of a Libyan airliner to the Khartoum massacre is just not playing games in the same ballpark."

Charles Swartz of Providence, Rhode Island, wrote of his "amazement and indignation at your recent news broadcast on the Libyan plane incident. How can you, an experienced and knowledgeable newsman after 'study, balance and fair play' equate the carefully planned atrocities by the Arabs with the sudden defensive reaction in a war situation by the Jews. You are certainly using a double standard and it is weighted heavily against the Jews. I no longer consider you a reliable and truthful reporter of the news."

"I think that all American Jews are entitled to a public apology from Mr. Pierpoint," wrote another from Maryland. "And unless something is done concerning a public apology, I am going to try to discourage my friends from supporting your advertisers."

B.J. Small of Baltimore wrote that "people are influenced by the written word and maybe even more by what they hear and see on radio and television. And therefore a person in your position loses the 'luxury' of being able to give vent to his personal opinions—unless he just doesn't give a DAMN."

Support came from a letter writer in Worcester, Massachusetts: "I wish to take this opportunity to commend CBS for fulfilling its responsibility to the public by broadcasting timely, controversial, and important subjects in an objective and unbiased manner ... the best safeguard of our country and its interest is an informed public who is aware of both sides of an issue ... congratulations to CBS News on its recent objective analysis and reporting on the Middle East."

Another, from Boston, wrote on April 7, "I was very inspired by your commentary on the Mideast, which I heard this morning while getting ready for work. It was one of the rare pieces of journalism that reminded me that honest, accurate, and fair journalism is still alive in the U.S."

Still another from Worcester, Massachusetts, sent "congratulations for your courage and objectivity."

And this from a writer in Sausalito, California: "I want to thank you for your comments of March 10 in the CS Monitor.... Yours is one of the very rare voices of objectivity and so, by default of the others who are not objective, 'fair' to the Arab side of the endless argument about who is right, who wrong, who suffered the most?"

An attorney in San Francisco wrote: "It makes one feel proud to be an American when courageous and honest people like you defy the Israeli pressure and expose American double standards on justice and fair play on the Middle East."

"I do admire the courage and even handedness of your White House Correspondent, Robert Pierpoint ... at last someone has had the courage to draw attention to the fact that U.S.-Mideast Policy has 'lost its sense of fair play and justice.... Congratulations to Mr. Pierpoint," said another letter writer from Arlington, Virginia.

Lawrence Mosher, a writer for the *National Observer*, sent CBS News president Salant a letter expressing "admiration of that editorial and to urge you to resist any pressures being brought against CBS by Mr. Pierpoint's critics."

The largest measure of support Pierpoint received for his broadcast came from a group called the Holy Land State Committee, who, on March 23, 1973, wrote him a letter requesting permission to translate his article (from the *Christian Science Monitor*) into Arabic to send it to "all Arabic papers all over the world." They also urged their members to send letters to network brass to "protest CBS' oppression of speech."

In response to the outcry, the network did a follow-up editorial, in which CBS radio division vice president David Nelson stated, "If we Americans react differently to Arab terrorism than we do to Israeli actions that result in civilian deaths, it is because the two are fundamentally different. It is not, as has been suggested, because there are more well-organized Jews in America than there are Arabs." The network itself seemed to support Pierpoint, but also tried to appease those opposed to his views. CBS vice president William Small defended the use of the network's facilities for Pierpoint's broadcast. Small said "it was perfectly proper" for Pierpoint "to do what he did" because "reporters have the freedom to interpret the news." However, he added that he deplored Pierpoint's remark that implied six million American Jews acted as a bloc in support of Israel.

Recalling that Pierpoint had been interested in social justice from an early age—which, after all, had led him to Sweden where the roots of such interest grew—it's hardly surprising that he took on the topic he did. In many ways, it exemplified his disappointment that religion—any religion—didn't lead to significant social justice. That, as much as his experience in the Middle East, entered into the "Double Standard" commentary. Pierpoint paid a personal price for his views. He lost friends over the controversy. As a family member put it, "there were close friends, some Jewish, that disagreed with him. He felt a jolt, but never regretted it." Still, it was an episode in his life that bothered him long after the editorial receded into broadcast history. "I think it bothered him so because so many people came out on the opposite side and that so many lobbies got them to write," said another family member.

To the end of his life in 2011, Pierpoint was bothered by the reaction of listeners. It was the very antithesis of what became his personal and professional mantra: to present information on important issues in a manner that would make Americans think. Nathan Gonzales was more than likely the very last person to speak with Pierpoint about the issue. It was while visiting him at the family home in Montana in the summer of 2010. "He really did see that foreign policy as a double-standard and I think he was very surprised at how strong that pro–Israel sentiment was," said Gonzales, who is the archivist for Pierpoint's papers at the University of Redlands. "It came up in the last conversation I had with him. He wrote exactly what he had felt. I do get the sense that it hurt him. Because he was doing his best as a journalist to present both sides of what was going on at the time and that there was one side that was so absolutely partial and venomously partial that it surprised him."[9]

Many of these reflections, because they occurred late in his life, had no bearing on what he had achieved across four decades at CBS. They all occurred in direct response to his time spent in the Middle East, which is their value in being discussed at this point in his life, rather than later. They affected his thought process at the time, although he was well ensconced as a CBS news correspondent. The road there often led through and back to his earlier experiences in Stockholm, Korea, Asia, and the Middle East. All of these assignments provided the foundation for his next—and biggest—assignment at CBS, beginning in 1957. He left his position as Far Eastern Bureau Chief, returning stateside to Washington, D.C. So much had changed since his time away that the next several years would require an adaptation to domestic issues on several fronts—both professional and personal. It all began with a trip back to where it all began in Redlands and brought about a major life change he could not have foreseen.

4

Back Home: Marriage, Family and the White House

It wasn't as if Robert Pierpoint, 32 at the time of his appointment by CBS to cover the White House, was looking for a reason to settle down. After all, one bad marriage lasting four years had left him pretty much resigned to the single life. The pressures of travel, deadlines, and the constant need to be near a phone or on a plane were hardly conducive to a family life. It was, as he would say after many years on the job, "one of the most demanding assignments a reporter can have." But then a funny thing happened on the way to Washington.

Throughout his career, he would periodically travel back to Redlands to visit his parents. Barely a year into his new assignment for CBS News at the White House, during one of those trips, a name from his past resurfaced. Patricia Porter, who had been engaged to someone else when she and Bob had first met in college, was still in town, living near his parents. Pat Porter was now living with her own parents, in the midst of a divorce. When she and her husband separated, she had moved back to California from Salt Lake City. Bob heard she was teaching school and had three kids.

Having learned of her return to Redlands from his parents, Bob, who had also been divorced from his first wife in the interim, welcomed the opportunity to reunite with the woman he remembered as "bright and attractive." The two were very much in the same place, each reeling from the effects of a broken marriage, Bob especially. Two years before going to Sweden he had married for the first time, to Donna Knight. It was clearly a bad match, those who knew them both agree. "She couldn't handle his independence, but she didn't tell him that," says his sister, Ruth. The divorce caught him totally off-guard, leaving him "devastated."

Pat, for her part, saw things fall apart with her then-husband, Alan, "because I didn't know where he was a lot at night." She later learned that he spent much of his time at the local pool hall. There were a lot of moves before the return to Redlands. "I had three kids and I was working at home and we had a little house and we moved to a larger house and then back to Redlands," she recalls. It was good preparation for becoming the wife of a network news correspondent, "strong preparation for the travelling life to come," she says.[1]

Bob, sensing he didn't want to miss the same opportunity twice, sought his sister Ruth's advice. By now, he and Pat had visited several times and she had written him a letter. He called Ruth and wanted to come over to talk with her about something. He brought with him the letter. It read: "Don't expect me to be anything but what I am." His question: "Do you think it's genuine?" Her reply: "I thought it was. She didn't want to misrepresent herself." Bob wasn't the only one using his sister as a sounding board on the relationship. Pat, who had always been a good friend to his sister (as had Bob's first wife), asked Ruth "did she know of any reason why Donna would want to divorce him," searching, she said, for anything below the surface she needed to know. Ruth said she knew of none; it was simply a youthful marriage that didn't work and the distance hadn't helped.

Both parties now feeling confident, Bob visited Pat Porter again. She would sometimes visit her stepsister in Baltimore and meet with Bob for dinner. "We met quickly," he recalled in a personal note made years later, "and this time it was love at many sights." He could be persuasive and this time he was especially so. "I persuaded Pat and her three children to move to Washington, D.C., so we could test whether this was TRUE love." It was 1959 and it was not a common occurrence for a woman and her children to move clear across the country with a man to whom she was not married—but then, there were many untraditional aspects to this pairing.

Pat spent that summer with the children in a rental house in Bethesda, near Washington, D.C., while Bob "became better acquainted with [the] children." They were Stan, 10, Eric, 9, and Kim, 8, a trio whom he termed "a handful for this long time bachelor, but we seemed to get along." It had to work with the kids before it was going to work," recalled Stan. Eric, the younger son, wasn't convinced. He locked himself in the bathroom, but then they each received bicycles, which seemed to be a turning point. "It became a new adventure, that's for sure," says Eric.

Matrimony was in the cards. "Dad just came through the door one day and said, 'Fellers, your mom and I are going to get married,'" Eric recalled. In the autumn of 1959, the wedding took place at Bob's sister's home in Weston, Connecticut, but not before an incident that involved the betrothed, their three children, and a police officer. "We loaded up Pat's station wagon with three kids, their baggage, and enough luggage for our honeymoon," Bob recalled. "On the drive up we had specific instructions on how to cross the George Washington Bridge ... and from the maze of roads there I had specific instructions on how to get to Connecticut." While he was worrying about where to turn, he missed a stop sign and "sure enough a cop was there to catch me." He was asked for his driver's license, then the insurance and ownership papers on the car. "The kids stared in fascination," he would one day write. "Following a search of the glove compartment, Pat said they were somewhere in the luggage packed on the wagon's roof. "By this time, the officer was getting a bit restive," writes Bob, "so, looking at the kids, he said 'I assume you are married.'" Bob replied, "No, officer. We are on our way to get married." The cop "threw up his hands in utter frustration, declaring 'I'm sorry I ever stopped you. Get out of here!'"[2]

It was another situation handled nimbly by a man well versed in dealing delicately with sensitive information. They were married the following day in Weston and, as the now father of three remembered it, "We HAVE lived happily ever after as a family, including our daughter, Marta, who was born a few years later." As Pat Pierpoint remembers it, "he figured he should hang on to me."

Kim Pierpoint was seven at the time and remembers being confused by it all. "I had the feeling this was someone important in my mother's life," she recalled. As in any untraditional family, there was quite a period of adjustment, especially for the youngest child. "I remember very clearly being in the courthouse when the adoption papers were signed," she says. "I knew a major shift had occurred. My last name wasn't Porter anymore. I really didn't understand why." She remembers having her second grade teacher call out her name as "Kim Pierpoint" and not recognizing that it was her being called on.[3]

All the kids remember a carryover from their new dad's own upbringing by Charles and Emma Pierpoint. On the nights when Bob wasn't traveling or didn't have a White House–related event to cover, the family would have dinner at the formal dining room table and the children would be quizzed about current events. "If we didn't know the answer, we had to look it up and write a two-page composition," says the second oldest, Eric. "It was very important to him to get at the argument of what was going on."

It was a daunting proposition on many levels for all the newly adopted children. "I thought 'oh, my gosh,' I had a new dad and he's on TV and I have to know what's going on and I'm in the second grade," recalls Kim

Pierpoint, who also recalls that Stan, the oldest, and Bob were intellectual equals. Eric and Bob bonded around tennis, which increasingly became their father's respite from the pressures of reporting at the White House.

It took what Kim calls "gutting it out" and "grit" to work things out. She adds, "we didn't become this instant family." There were two things her new dad would do to assimilate himself into the family structure, she says. First, "at no time did he force us to call him dad. He said if you need to call me Bob, that's fine." Second, he wasn't "about the biological father thing ... he didn't have a clue about how to be a parent, but he took on a lot of the heavy lifting. I thought it was very brave for someone who had no parenting experience."

Three years after the marriage, in 1962, Pat gave birth to a daughter, Marta. By then, Bob Pierpoint had some parenting experience under his belt. Kim Pierpoint says, "The birth of Marta made us whole as a family." Marta Pierpoint agrees. "Because my mother and father got married fairly quickly, I think that when I was born it helped the family blend together as one. They started to think of themselves as a whole family with a baby sister." None of the children, now Pierpoints, ever referred to their father as a "stepdad." The consensus was, and is, that he treated all four equally, having "the same level of expectations for all of us."[4]

Having joined the family as the youngest child, Marta became the latest addition to the dinner table discussions of current events. "I learned more about the world at that dinner table than I ever got in a public school education," she maintains, while recognizing, as her sister did, how much time, energy, and care it required of her father. "He just embraced that," she says. "Later in my life, as an adult, he did say to me there were sacrifices he made. He made them happily and willingly in his career because he wanted his family to be central."

The demanding life of a father with four young children might indeed have competed with the grueling life of a network correspondent, but, according to Kim Pierpoint, "he and my mother had an understanding ... very explicit discussions about how, if they were going to be married, how they were going to make it work with the children. He had his job at CBS and her role would be as mom and she would be home taking care of the kids—not like people are today, where they both work."

Every night he was on the air, usually during the *CBS Evening News, with Walter Cronkite*, Pat Pierpoint would watch closely, preparing for the time when he came home and would ask her "What did I do right and what did I do wrong?" According to Kim Pierpoint, "He needed her."

The new father was determined to make family life and work coexist, despite the fact that he took some heat for getting married—most of all from his role model, Murrow, who, according to Kim Pierpoint, "viewed him as less serious when he married my mother and adopted three kids. He sacrificed for that. The company [CBS] did not endorse that. He got criticism and that hurt him. He didn't flinch. He did what he wanted to do and drew from his experiences as a reporter to try to toughen us up, teaching how to think on our feet."

Soon, the personal life of Bob Pierpoint, father, began to blend with that of Robert Pierpoint, CBS News White House correspondent. One informed the other; they became inseparable, even to the point where Pat and the kids would travel on the press plane with him once or twice a year. "When he would allow us to go on the press plane with him ... he would disappear and you would hear the sound of the typewriter with dad tapping away on the keys," recalls Eric Pierpoint. "And there would be this fog of blue smoke from all the reporters back then who were all heavy smokers and drinkers."

For the Pierpoint kids, it was "a really, really special era." For a man whose childhood had been spent mainly in isolation, it must also have been nothing short of pure joy.

Path to the White House

The decision to return to America after four years (1953–1957) as Far Eastern Bureau Chief appears to have been solely Robert Pierpoint's choice. He relished the idea of calling his own shots, but the time had come to return stateside. "Those were great years," Pierpoint recalled in an interview years later. "I was 10,000 miles away from my boss. Nobody was able to contradict what I wrote. A dream job." "But by 1957, I'd begun feeling as though if I stayed on much longer, I might 'go Asia'. I wanted to avoid that."[5] What exactly he meant by "go Asia" is hard to tell, but, in an ironic twist, his years spent in Korea came back to him in a most unlikely place.

His first story upon returning to the United States in 1957 wasn't at the White House. Like most of his career, Robert Pierpoint's path was anything but linear. He was assigned to cover the integration of the Little Rock, Arkansas, public schools. A group of nine African American students were prevented from entering a racially segregated school by the state's governor. President Eisenhower sent in federal troops to assist in the enforcement of court-ordered integration.

For Pierpoint, it was an especially sad occasion, given his experiences with U.S. troops in Korea, specifically the 101st Airborne battalion, several of whom he had interviewed and profiled for *See It Now* years earlier. He met some of those same soldiers in Little Rock, assisting in the school desegregation efforts. "I got there a little late.... I got there, I think, on the third day," Pierpoint said. "It was a very strange experience for me to see these troops I had seen fighting battles in Korea trying to just help these little black kids get into school. Very shocking to me."[6]

Elaborating on his feelings, he said in a speech years later that "I was quite shocked to see it took American troops in battle gear to ensure that the children of one race could go to school with the children of another race. I, as an American, was ashamed and greatly disturbed."

It would not be the last time Robert Pierpoint would be "shocked." The people he was about to meet, the things he would soon see, and the events he would consistently cover over the next 23 years from the place he called "the news center of the universe" would rival anything he had yet done. As he put it, "Every important occurrence anywhere in the world eventually generates activity in the White House ... the visibility is high, the pressure is heavy, and the margin for error is practically non-existent."

Booze and Brotherhood

He may have been 32 and seen a lot of the world, but the Robert Pierpoint who walked into his boss's office on day one was about to learn a new lesson; it had to do with how the White House press corps works. CBS News Washington Bureau Chief Ted Koop greeted him with these words: "Pick up a bottle of bourbon and a bottle of scotch to take to the Press Room tomorrow. It's a tradition the first day on the job. You can put them on your expense account." He "wasn't kidding," Pierpoint remembered years later. "So, early on the morning of October 7, 1957, feeling slightly nervous and a bit foolish, I entered the White House carrying two bottles in a brown paper bag."[7]

The Press Room, in those days, he said, was "jammed with worn desks, rickety typewriters, and greasy telephones," with a table and chairs which did double duty as a poker table—details that made a deep impression on younger daughter Marta who, to this day, recalls that "my dad's office at the White House was so small. Imagine three phone booths stuck together with three phones for each of the networks, an octagonal table, and the AP wire." It was tiny, but just a short walk from the White House briefing room and even the Oval Office (the location would change during the Nixon administration years later, keeping the press further away).

Arriving on that first day bearing the gifts of the two bottles, he placed them on the table and left for the lobby, saying to the other reporters that

4. Back Home: Marriage, Family and the White House

Preparing a report from the press room in Brussels, Belgium, in 1975. Press rooms in those days often involved sharing a good number of resources—phones, typewriters, and so on. The somewhat rarefied title of White House correspondent entitled Pierpoint to his own set of reporting tools, including the electric typewriter on the desk.

there were some "refreshments" available in the press room. Gradually, the contents of the two bottles disappeared and it was then that he realized "drinking on the job was apparently no handicap." It softened up the veterans on the White House beat to the point where "toward the end of the day, several of my fellow journalists congratulated me on my new assignment." He reached the conclusion that "if I had not exactly arrived, at least my presence was acknowledged."

Nevertheless, self-doubts sank in. "My journalistic training had been entirely on the job," he recalled, looking back on his White House life. "All of my experience had been overseas, in Scandinavia and the Orient. What concerned me most was my almost total lack of experience of American political life." He sized up his "new colleagues" at the White House as not only more experienced, but also "a shade sharper and a step quicker than any others I had known." Humility setting in, he decided "I simply had a lot to learn, a great deal to feel insecure about, and I knew it."

If he ever doubted it, the "welcome wagon" of the White House Press Corps stood in line to remind him of just how much he had to learn. On his first trip outside the White House he and six other reporters followed President Eisenhower's motorcade in a rented limousine. He was "sandwiched," as he put it, into a rear seat right in front of Merriman Smith of United Press International. Smith was informally known as the dean of the White House press corps. Pierpoint was in awe at Smith's facility with words, "just listening to the ease with which he dictated his lead and first few paragraphs left more than one toughened veteran feeling inadequate." It wasn't long before Pierpoint had his own adequacy to be on the job questioned by Smith.

"We had not travelled more than a few blocks from the White House when Smitty began to harangue me," he wrote. "'Why did CBS think a punk like you could cover the White House,' he said with a sneer." The other reporters turned silent. "Although I was too old—thirty-two—to be a complete novice, I suspected that Smitty was asking a very good question. Furthermore, I respected Smitty and the other men in the car and dearly longed for their good opinion of me." Pierpoint also admitted to feeling resentment and fear, but then realized the man criticizing him was drunk. "I guess we'll just have to see if I can do the job," he said, also thinking "I certainly could not broadcast in his condition."

Later, alone, Robert Pierpoint reflected on what Smith had said. "Drunk or not," he thought, "he had put a finger on the problem: Was I capable of reporting from the White House for a major network?" He had a sleepless night. Soon, however, he began developing some friendships in the press corps. He also began to consider the man who initially taunted him—Merriman Smith—as one who was "above all a brilliant reporter," and he "watched him particularly closely as part of my education." What he noticed most of all was that Smith "asked for facts, details and color that revealed he was thinking far beyond the first paragraph of his story into what we today refer to as background and analysis." Before long, Pierpoint himself would prioritize those elements in his own work.

While the White House "and everything in it awed me," as Pierpoint put it, it was here where he would hone his questioning, writing, broadcasting, socializing, and, yes, even tennis playing, skills over the next 23 years. That journey would carry him through the terms of six presidents, beginning with Dwight D. Eisenhower, already a year into his second term when Pierpoint arrived in 1957, through five additional U.S. presidents: Kennedy, Johnson, Nixon, Ford, and Carter. In the process, his confidence increased incrementally. He needed only to make it through the days of covering the daily activities of a man he called a "remote, almost legendary figure."

The Eisenhower Years

Another lesson the neophyte soon learned was that "politicians, Presidents included, look upon the press as there to be manipulated, if possible, and tolerated at best." This was true of President Dwight D. Eisenhower who, wrote Pierpoint years later, ran the White House using a "military chain of command"—not unusual, given the discipline of a high-ranking military commander. Eisenhower established a few practices for dealing with the White House press corps that were borrowed from previous presidents, but also instituted a few of his own. The president's visitors traditionally went in and out of the Oval Office through a public lobby into which the White House press corps often spilled over (especially if the visitor was someone whom they wanted to interview).[8]

Under Eisenhower, this practice changed. Now, "those arriving to see the President were usually escorted into another room, nearer the Oval Office and out of bounds for reporters." Presidential aides and those waiting to meet with them, however, were "thrown into the lobby with the spillover from the Press Room." Reporters, ultimately, gained the advantage of "such haphazard contact" during Eisenhower's day "when very few top administration aides ever talked to the press in private."

Not only were his aides tight-lipped and aloof, Pierpoint found the chief executive to be even more so. "From the very first day I covered a presidential news conference, I was about five feet from the president, which I found intimidating, to tell you the truth," he later recalled in a PBS interview years later. "He had no idea of what our role was all about ... and kind of looked at us as privates in his army." Eisenhower, he said, would often point at reporters because he didn't know their names.[9]

Pierpoint soon found that he would have very little access to the president himself. "I covered President Eisenhower for more than three years," he wrote, "often wondering whether he knew my name, even though I repeated it once every two weeks when I asked a question at his news conferences as was required in those days. I don't even know whether he ever heard my broadcasts or how he reacted to them." In many ways, it's a wonder that the newly minted White House correspondent had any scale by which to gauge his success or failure in covering this president. "Eisenhower carefully avoided personal contact with most reporters," he remembered. "When I first arrived, for example, I asked Press Secretary Jim Haggerty if I could meet with the President, thinking this to be a normal request, since I was to cover him for the next few years." Haggerty replied that he would try to arrange it sometime. The meeting never happened.

Eventually, there was one reporter with whom Eisenhower did feel comfortable: Larry Burd of the *Chicago Times*. One reason was his skill as a golfer (Pierpoint had no such skill and, after a futile try at becoming adept, stuck with tennis). "Whenever possible, Haggerty put Burd in situations that required a pool reporter," wrote Pierpoint. "The rest of us approved, since Larry got much more from Ike than we would, and since he was also an excellent journalist we knew we would get good pool report from the eighteenth hole."

Despite the distance he put between himself and those reporters assigned to cover him, Eisenhower gained the young Pierpoint's respect. He was especially impressed, he told the PBS interviewer in 1998, that the president, after suffering a minor stroke, went to Europe. Upon his return, he was still having trouble pronouncing words, but nevertheless held a press conference. When asked why, Eisenhower said, "I did it because I took the oath of office—and I decided part of my job was to hold press conferences; if I couldn't do it, I should resign." Pierpoint felt that showed a lot of "integrity" that he would one day find lacking in future presidents.

Eisenhower also instituted what Pierpoint considered to be some positive changes in the ability of reporters to do their jobs. One involved permitting the President's press conference remarks and his responses to reporters' questions to be quoted directly. Under presidents Franklin D. Roosevelt and his successor, Warren G. Harding, reporters were forbidden to quote directly from press conferences. The advantage, Pierpoint always felt (and he wasn't alone), was that the chief executive could deny anything later on, claiming he had been misquoted or the reporter misunderstood his meaning. Eisenhower, or perhaps more accurately his press secretary Haggerty, saw that this could also turn into a situation where reporters could engage in opinion or interpretation of what the president had said. Haggerty had been a *New York Times* reporter pre–White House, and it was Pierpoint's opinion years later that he "initiated the policy that press conference answers could be quoted directly." There was a catch, however. Radio and television were becoming ubiquitous in the White House by late 1957 and Haggerty set up the rule that neither radio nor TV tape could be aired until the portion to be used was cleared.

While this may sound suspiciously like censorship, Pierpoint, reflecting back years later, said, "During the eight years Ike was in office, however, Haggerty made no transcript changes that had major domestic or international implications." Changes were more for image than content. "He rarely intervened," remembered Pierpoint, "and then only when the President's garbled syntax made his sentences almost unreadable." The policy on broadcasting *after the fact* may have been benign, but broadcasting presidential news conferences *live* was an entirely different matter, one that the Eisenhower administration, through Haggerty, rejected.

According to Pierpoint, in his book *At the White House,* Haggerty argued that "what we are actually trying to do is prevent a human fluff that the communist propagandists can use to a good advantage." The talk among reporters, however, was "this President simply could not express himself easily, that under tough questioning he sounded confused and distracted, and that he had a particular fear of television." Pierpoint's assessment: "In retrospect, I think this judgment a little harsh. Ike would have done as well as most presidents in live press conferences, and his genial personality would have been a definite asset."

Pierpoint seems to have been more bothered by the *timing* of Eisenhower's press conferences. In one of the last interviews he gave, in 2011, he said of Eisenhower: "He always seemed to have press conferences at 10:30 a.m. and I had to go on the air at 11 a.m. and sum up what he had to say." He labeled the job "a challenge because Eisenhower was a relatively good president, but he wasn't a good communicator."

These live updates were something Robert Pierpoint learned to master, with the help of what his son Eric called a "trick" involving a small tape recorder. He would write his words, record them, play them back in his ear while on the air and "always manage to stay just a little ahead of hearing himself." It was almost a form of early teleprompter (without the visual prompt) and the skill came in handy when doing an impromptu report from the White House steps.

That skill was nearly put to the test in late November of 1957, when rumors circulated that Eisenhower was ill again. "We felt was something wrong," he recalled. "We had seen the President's doctor come into the White House and the doors were closed. Reporters, sensing a story, began to gather. Pierpoint's pulse quickened. He realized that it was probable he would have to run from the briefing room to get a story on the air immediately. A note from an aide, in "medical jargon" reading "heart evasia," was released (the intent was to relay that Eisenhower had *not* suffered a heart attack—he *evaded* one). With no doctor to confirm the diagnosis, one reporter in the room misinterpreted what he read and yelled, "Is that another heart attack? Is it a stroke? I gotta go on the air and say something. What do I say?" Another yelled into the phone that the president had suffered a "cerebral heart attack." Pierpoint exercised a measure of restraint which would become his trademark. He would later joke that the reporter on the phone who announced the "cerebral heart attack" diagnosis "never recovered."[10]

There was one other incident a few years later from which the president might not have recovered—this one involving a female reporter. The incident, as Pierpoint recalled it, was evidence that "Ike's attitude toward women was not so benevolent." It was 1960, after the Presidential election. Eisenhower took his annual trip to Augusta, Georgia, site of the Masters golf tournament. The usual cadre of White House correspondents accompanied him. Because he was in his final term, the reporters on the trip decided to give him a farewell dinner. Among those in attendance was Anne Chamberlain of *Time-Life*, one of the first women to cover the White House. Pierpoint called her "a liberated woman before the term became fashionable." She was seated directly across from the President. Everything went fine until, Pierpoint recalled, "cigars were passed around and Anne took one." Eisenhower was "clearly offended, and although he never said a word, those famous furrows in his brow were eloquent signals of his shock." Chamberlain, as he put it, "coolly ignored the President's stony silence, but she came in for considerable kidding and even some angry verbal abuse from a few of her colleagues afterward."

His first year, 1957, at the White House was relatively quiet. In fact, Pierpoint would remember Eisenhower as "probably among the least active of the presidents I've covered." One exception occurred in 1958, when Eisenhower sent troops into Lebanon. In July of that year, Lebanon was threatened by a civil war involving Christians and Muslims. Through a series of events involving multiple nations, including the Soviet Union, which threatened the use of nuclear weapons if America intervened, Eisenhower put into play "Operation Blue Bat." In a nutshell, it meant that U.S. troops would intervene to back the pro–Western Lebanese government in power from threats by Syria and Egypt. It was the first time the policy called "The Eisenhower Doctrine" was employed, and it involved nearly 14,000 U.S. troops.

In Lebanon, Pierpoint met a man who would become a lifelong friend. Ed Fouhy was the commander of a U.S. Marines infantry unit in July of 1958. His main job was to run a recognizance patrol out to the central part of the country, on one of its major highways. Because of the obvious photo possibilities, many television journalists tagged along with their camera crews. Pierpoint was among them. "We hit it off, immediately," recalls Fouhy.[11] "Because of his combat experience in Korea, he was much more aware of our weapons, our strategy, our game plan than most of the journalists there." The two were about the same age. Showers were hard to come by in the field, and Pierpoint offered him the use of his hotel room to clean up. "It was just a sort of chance encounter," says Fouhy.

Both were caught off guard at that first meeting. "When I introduced myself, the young lieutenant said, in obvious surprise, 'Bob Pierpoint. You

4. Back Home: Marriage, Family and the White House

are the CBS White House Correspondent. What are you doing here?' I was just as surprised that a Marine officer would know that I had just left the White House assignment to come to Lebanon." In fact, this particular change in assignment left Pierpoint desperately searching for stories. One that he found which stuck in his memory years later was the exact one that united him with Fouhy. Pierpoint had learned from a Marine Corps public affairs officer that "some Marine jeep patrols into the mountains above Beirut were very enjoying their duty. They were being welcomed by Christian Arabs throwing flowers, candy, and even some kisses." Pierpoint recognized that "this sounded like my kind of story." He was told by the P.A. officer to find Fouhy and go on patrol with him:

> As we started up the hill toward the mountain villages, Fouhy explained rather sheepishly that this was not exactly a combat patrol. He said that all the villages we were patrolling were friendly, and there probably would even be some young girls with flowers and candy to meet us along the way. There were! I had spent some time with the Marines in Korea during that war, but this was entirely different. We never heard a shot fired in anger, and it was one of the most delightful days I ever spent with a fighting unit.

Pierpoint had volunteered to go on the Lebanon assignment, even though, as he reflected in an e-mail years later, "the Marines had already landed, there was little or no fighting, and in fact they were met on the beaches by Lebanese peacefully welcoming their 'visitors.' So there was no danger involved in my volunteer 'war correspondent' duty, except for the flight over." "I had been covering the war in Korea, so I was familiar with the military, so I went over there," Pierpoint said in a PBS interview. Besides, he said, he felt Eisenhower's decision to "prop up the legitimate government in Lebanon was very astute."

For someone who was adapting to the quick pace of White House coverage, "the story was pretty boring," Fouhy remembers. "He was very restless in Lebanon because there wasn't much of a story. He wanted to get back to the White House and to his family." Recall, too, that Pierpoint had not only recently begun a new job in Washington, but also was in the throes of being a newlywed *and* a father. Balancing all three—correspondent, husband, and dad—would be a lifelong challenge, made more so by distance. Lebanon, while not under siege, was not a family zone, either.

The Lebanon assignment, though of brief duration, may not have brought Pierpoint many stories, but it did result in a new colleague. The young lieutenant, Fouhy, told Pierpoint he was a recent college graduate and hoped, when he left his Marine Corps duties, to become a reporter. He followed through on that ambition. Ed Fouhy eventually joined CBS

News as a producer, rose to the rank of White House Bureau Chief and, in essence, became Pierpoint's boss. "Believe me, it is wonderful to have a good friend as a boss," he would one day reflect. The two would one day win a prestigious award for investigative reporting, involving another president, Richard Nixon.

The Lebanon experience stuck with Pierpoint as the best of the Eisenhower presidency. Overall, Eisenhower both "impressed and depressed" him. Lebanon may have been in his wheelhouse as chief executive, but "there were a lot of domestic problems he wasn't comfortable with." He faulted the 34th president for not believing that laws were necessary to ensure civil rights. While Pierpoint believed Eisenhower was as disturbed as he was by the actions of those in Little Rock who sought to block school desegregation, he believed that Eisenhower was reluctant to use the power of the presidency. Ike had not agreed with the 1954 U.S. Supreme Court decision desegregating schools, believing that the problem would be solved by "patient good will." Ordering troops there, as he had, became, in Pierpoint's view, "an act of personal courage and integrity."

By all measures, Robert Pierpoint's first years at the White House, from 1957 to 1961, were going well for him, but still Pierpoint didn't feel as if he was measuring up. The Eisenhower years had presented certain challenges, but overall it was a time when, he reflected, "the nation perhaps wanted a quiet president." In an interview just before his passing in 2011, Pierpoint assessed his own performance during his own first "term" as White House correspondent: "I didn't feel that I did a good job, but they kept me on." The work was about to become more challenging and, in the estimation of so many of his former colleagues, Robert Pierpoint was on his way to becoming the new "dean" of the White House press corps. It coincided with a time when the nation was embracing change and life at the White House was about to become anything but quiet.

The Kennedy Years

Back on home soil, Robert Pierpoint rounded out his coverage of the Eisenhower years with a new level of confidence. While Eisenhower's administration taught him much about the White House beat, he shared little in common with the president. Eisenhower may have seemed to some like the patriarch of the nation; mirroring the makeup of the nation, John Fitzgerald Kennedy was more like most Americans, a parent as opposed to a general. For the first time in a long time, the White House was filled with the sound of children. For the first time *ever*, so was Robert Pierpoint's house. That's where Pierpoint's affinity for Kennedy would begin; it became a connection shared with no other president he would cover.[12]

With John Fitzgerald Kennedy's election in 1960 came many changes in how the press could cover the president on a daily basis. Chief among them was something Pierpoint noticed immediately: Kennedy, unlike his predecessor, actually liked the press and enjoyed interacting with them. This came as a surprise to many in the White House press corps. For Robert Pierpoint, the difference between Ike and JFK in this regard was palpable, beginning with how Kennedy handled press conferences.

Less than a week after his inauguration in January 1961, the new president began holding his press conferences on live radio and TV. It was a calculated effort by the new administration to ensure its message got through to the American public. Kennedy's press secretary, Pierre Salinger put it this way: "The fact of the matter is that [at] the time when President Kennedy started televised press conferences there were only three or four newspapers in the entire United States that carried a full transcript of a presidential press conference. Therefore, what people read was a distillation.... We thought that they should have the opportunity to see it in full."[13]

Pierpoint and his colleagues finally got what they wanted: the ability to question the president on all things, foreign and domestic, while listeners and viewers heard and watched. The first event, on January 20, brought out over four hundred reporters, all with assigned seats. Pierpoint had the CBS seat in the second row on the right-hand side. "This was quite different from the old crowded Indian Treaty Room of the Executive Office Building, where President Eisenhower had held his press conferences," he wrote. "There I sat only about ten feet from the President and directly in front of him. He could not avoid me when I rose to ask a question." There was a disadvantage to the new arrangement, however: "But to get President Kennedy's attention in the new setting, I had to bob up and down until he glanced my way. Excitement was high at these early live-televised sessions, and there was heavy competition to be recognized."

Kennedy's live press conferences "were an instant success." For one, Pierpoint found the new president "completely at ease" and "clearly enjoying the combative give-and-take, triumphing in the informal debates much more often than he lost." Pierpoint and his colleagues provided Kennedy with a challenge, while Kennedy didn't always provide them with the information or story they came to report: "Frequently, I came away chuckling over some Presidential thrust or parry, but just as frequently found myself wondering what I, and the public, had really learned." That was the case five months after the Cuban missile crisis when Kennedy was asked if he could provide the number of Russian troops that were removed from Cuba.

As the president waited silently for a moment, a second question—whether he was satisfied with the rate of troop withdrawal—and a third—was there any way to verify troop removal—followed. Kennedy, in a response Pierpoint would later recall as "so simple and disarming," said "no," delivered with a smile.

"That was the president's full response and the official transcript confirms what we all remember so well," he wrote. "At his answer, the audience, packed with tough, hard professional journalists, burst into laughter." Pierpoint, looking back, assessed that Kennedy's response on that day and others "would be hard to get away with now." If it wasn't the measure of the man, it certainly was the charm of the man, namely JFK, that made him a refreshing change from the battle-honed stoicism of Eisenhower—at least to those who covered him in the early days of the Kennedy presidency. One day, Pierpoint would tell an interviewer that, of the six presidents he covered, Kennedy was "the most fun." In part, he believed that stemmed from the president's own background: "He was not afraid of the press. He had been a reporter. He knew everyone in the White House press corps by name and reputation and joked with us. He was comfortable in his own skin."[14]

What Pierpoint saw in Kennedy was, in many ways, a mirror of himself: a man who cared greatly about social justice and social activism. Pierpoint's own activism had been forged during his time abroad, beginning with Sweden and continuing throughout his assignment in the Far East. A close family friend, Mary Silverman, had met Pierpoint a few years earlier, in 1967; she and her husband, John, remained friends with the Pierpoints. They lived next door in Washington and saw the Pierpoint kids grow up, even babysitting the youngest, Marta, when she was seven. "Bob was as Swedish as he was American," she said with affection. "He very much believed in the system Sweden had for its people, in terms of education and welfare." As a result, he developed a very egalitarian view of life and of people. The Silvermans, for example, had no professional backgrounds in common with Bob Pierpoint. Neither was in news, but he found both interesting. It was the way he was off-camera: "always curious about everything" and seeking out the views of those with whom he didn't agree, but from whom he might learn.

Others who saw him socially outside the White House, at home with Pat and the four kids, remember a man who liked having others around to engage in conversation and debate. He loved, they say, the "challenge" of a good argument, whether with his sons Eric and Stan or a Washington politico off duty. The Pierpoints' dinner parties were legendary. "Oh, those parties" is a refrain shared by those who were there. Pat was the perfect hostess, everyone agreed, and Bob was often the instigator, bringing up social issues for discussion around the room. He could get into what one friend called "steaming arguments about ideological issues." He loved a good dinner table, "all talking at once, all talking about their points of view. He didn't care if it was bombastic." Eric would sometimes play the guitar, remembered one partygoer, maybe one of the more soothing sounds in the room. The rest of the time the room could be loud and contentious.

He carefully planned these gatherings, surgically trimming the guest list to ensure that all opinions on a particular social issue would be represented and, if necessary, vigorously defended. He had his own social inner circle—"Pierpoint's people," as one on the inside referred to those who made the guest list. In his day job, he may have been a correspondent at the highest level, but, in these dinner party conversations, "his enthusiasm almost doubled his curiosity," according to a regular guest, former *Washington Post* political columnist Myra MacPherson. "He loved having people around him; he loved the energy." MacPherson, who came to her job, first at the *Washington Star*, from the *Detroit Free Press* in June of 1960, calls the Kennedy years "one of the most exciting periods in Washington.... How different this was from Ike. Kennedy injected the city with the idea that there was news on every corner, young people were coming into the government. It electrified the city." She, too, found that Kennedy's press conferences were "funny and witty; it was a performance more than anything else. That sort of stuff won over journalists. Bob was impressed by that."

It's easy to see why—and he wasn't alone. Kennedy, at least at the outset, became the press's darling. He held 64 press conferences, all of them covered by the three networks, all of them helping his image with the American public, 65 million of whom had watched his very first one on television. Television, after all, had helped Kennedy win the election by reinforcing his quick wit and youthful energy. While many admired his on-camera persona, something more substantive resonated with Pierpoint. Kennedy was "an activist," Pierpoint would one day tell an interviewer, and that's why he had been able to defeat Richard Nixon. "He was willing to campaign not only on changes that needed to come about, but to send to Congress legislation that would bring about those changes." He compared JFK's activism with what he called "Ike's 'leave well enough alone'" approach and concluded "that may be why JFK was seen as such a great president."[15]

Being so close, so on the inside of what he called "the power center" that is the White House put Robert Pierpoint, the correspondent, in a precarious place with Bob Pierpoint the family man. There were times when he knew more than he let on, more than he could tell, at least on television. One of those times came in October of 1962, during the 13-week period that's come to be known as the Cuban missile crisis. It was one the tensest times of the cold war between America and the Soviet Union. JFK ordered a military blockade to prevent Soviet premier Nikita Khrushchev from continuing to build nuclear missile sites in Cuba per an agreement with Fidel Castro earlier that July.

There was a standoff during which the president ordered a Russian battleship to reverse course. Pierpoint knew how close the United States, as a nation, was coming to nuclear war. "If that Russian ship didn't turn around by 3 o'clock on that Thursday ... we really believed were goners," he told an interviewer.[16] The White House had already arranged for the press corps to be evacuated to shelters. Having the knowledge he had and fearing the worst, Bob Pierpoint phoned his wife and told her to be ready to hunker down with the kids. "I knew approximately where it [the shelter] was and I told my wife if that afternoon the situation wasn't resolved, go." He termed it a "very frightening time." Fortunately, Khrushchev blinked first and it was one reason why he came to see Kennedy as someone who had the ability to solve problems that had eluded other presidents who preceded him.

In a 1973 lecture, Pierpoint told an audience in Wichita, Kansas, that John Kennedy "brought a new sense of purpose to America." He saw Kennedy as a man who believed there were too many problems in the United States that remained unsolved. "His style was to try to get the nation involved in problem solving," he said. "He brought many intellectuals into the White House ... and he tried to bring a certain cultural style to a White House function. He tried to stimulate particularly young people in government, to get them involved in problem solving." Kennedy, in short, was, to Pierpoint, about change—someone who "challenged the country to be better ... stir up the country and motivate it." His way of doing so was through politics; Pierpoint's was through journalism.[17]

He felt a kinship with JFK, at least at the outset, but, as time went on, "there was disappointment on his part that Camelot was over," says his friend and colleague Myra MacPherson. Part of that, certainly, was the young president's handling of Vietnam, a war with which Pierpoint, the private citizen, vehemently disagreed. It was one of the topics around the table at those dinner parties, where Robert Pierpoint the journalist would transform to Bob Pierpoint the social activist—a difficult balancing act for anyone in his profession. MacPherson once asked him how he could be on television reporting and be so "middle of the road" when in his private life he was so opinionated. Bob Pierpoint had a simple answer, she says: "He knew what the job was."

Friends and colleagues agree that he took the job home with him every night. For him, "social was work," is the way MacPherson puts it. As the job followed him home, during the Kennedy years it also transformed Robert Pierpoint the White House correspondent into someone whose bankroll of sources set him apart from most of the competition at other networks. At many of his dinner parties, not to mention the ones to which he was invited (and attended), there were Washington insiders, power brokers. He once told his colleague from the *Washington Star* that "you have to be sociable with these people because you get more from them this way." His former boss, Ed Fouhy, says all of it—the parties, the tennis that he would play between his White House duties, often with high-ranking administration officials—made Pierpoint the reporter he became: "He made friends easily and he developed a lot of sources."

Not to belabor the comparison, but Pierpoint was a likable guy, similar to the new, young president he was covering in 1961. In Kennedy, he saw personified much of the hope he had for solving the nation's problems. Like Kennedy, Pierpoint was a complex man who had a life away from the public eye that was often at odds with his "down the middle" image on camera. Unlike JFK, he did not have a dark side, though he was hardly naïve and, therefore, had an inkling of what happened at the White House when the lights were dimmed and the cameras were off.

"As is now public knowledge, JFK liked attractive women, wherever he spotted them," wrote Pierpoint in *At the White House*. He once used that character trait of the president to get a meeting with Kennedy. Another change from the Eisenhower years was that JFK "made it relatively easy to for us to reach his aides: we simply had to call them on the telephone and request an appointment." On one hand, "access to Kennedy himself—at least in a cursory manner—was easy." On the other hand, "a meeting with the President was somewhat harder to manage." Pierpoint had a plan and, not surprisingly, it involved an attractive young woman.

Being around the president on a daily basis, Pierpoint was familiar with his habits, including this one: "Frequently, he would walk up to the prettiest girl in a crowd and strike up a conversation." Pierpoint knew it to be such a "strong habit" that, when the wife of a close college friend wanted to visit him at work and asked if she could meet Kennedy, the question turned into an idea. The woman in question happened to be a beautiful blonde Czech named Eva. On the day of her visit, the president was meeting with a foreign head of state; after such visits he would walk his guest through the White House lobby to bid farewell. Pierpoint "stationed the beautiful Eva and her husband in the lobby." After the foreign dignitary left, Kennedy was en route back to his office when he noticed Eva and turned abruptly on his heels. Shaking her hand, he asked the young woman if she worked in the White House. She replied she was actually visiting her friend, CBS correspondent Bob Pierpoint. The president muttered "something to the effect of 'lucky Pierpoint.'" He then, after putting forth an effort to speak briefly with her husband, "wandered reluctantly back to the Oval Office, visibly disappointed that he could not spend a bit more time with the beautiful blonde in the press lobby."[18]

No one who covered the White House in the Kennedy years could have been unaware of the president's dalliances outside his marriage. Pierpoint certainly was, as he addressed in a 1982 interview.[19] He was asked whether he thought certain details of Kennedy's personal life that "you and obviously many others observed" would today be handled very differently in terms of whether the press would keep such personal matters quiet. "I don't think so," he replied. "We have wrestled with that question since, during the Kennedy era and since then. With almost every president there is an issue of some kind that comes up. One president, for instance, was drinking heavily, and the question was 'Should we publicize that?' And the decision was: If he doesn't stop, yes. But he did because he was put on notice. The children of another president were smoking pot in the White House. Was that to be a story? I decided I wasn't going to get into it because I didn't want to be and don't want to be a gossip columnist. I mean, that's not why I went into this business."

He went on: "Okay, I knew about John Kennedy's, some of his sexual endeavors outside of his marriage, and I didn't report it. And now it isn't really much news to anybody. And even if I had eyewitness information, so it didn't have to be second-hand...I didn't feel that was a kind of story that I would report.... I don't think that that's pertinent to his presidency. On the other hand, he drew a line for a future president, based upon his public moral stances. "Now, Jimmy Carter, there you have a real problem." He said that if he had found out Carter was having an affair, he would consider it a "much tougher call" because Carter had "made a national issue out of his morals.... I'm not sure but that I would have reported that because he himself made such a standard out of his morals and ethical conduct."

In Kennedy's instance, it didn't hurt that "some reporters were among his best friends, including columnist Charles Bartlett, who had introduced him to Jackie, and Ben Bradlee, then with *Newsweek* and later the editor of the *Washington Post*. Going back to his campaign for president, Kennedy astutely cultivated his relationship with the press, carefully learning the names and affiliations of any new reporter who joined the coverage pool and even inviting the reporter to fly with him on the *Caroline*—the Kennedy family's private plane. He would make time to chat with reporters, especially the women, according to Pierpoint. "Sometimes he would ask for our opinions on how the campaign was going, and he seemed genuinely interested in our criticisms. When it appeared that he had a good chance to defeat Richard Nixon, Kennedy began talking about Presidential appointments for our friends and contacts." Specifically, the future president asked Pierpoint about two individuals already working in government—at least one of whom had been in charge of army public relations during World War II. That person, Ted Clifton, Kennedy later appointed as his chief military aide. It was a situation that "worked out well for everyone concerned—including me, since I then had a good source close to the President."

After he was elected in 1960, JFK went on a trip to Palm Beach for a recovery and relaxation stay. Pierpoint was ordered by CBS to switch his coverage form Eisenhower to the incoming president. "Palm Beach was a dream assignment," he recalled. "The November weather was warm and balmy. Each correspondent had a comfortable apartment in the Palm Beach Towers Hotel, with plenty of time for tennis or golf after the light day's work." It was to become a pattern in covering the president. Kennedy's proclivity for meeting attractive women synched nicely with his desire for a good party. Right after the election, he began what became almost a tradition in his relationship with the press, by inviting correspondents and their families to what he called a garden party. It was held at a rented beachfront mansion, where the guests could avail themselves of swimming, playing tennis on the private court, drinking, and dining. Again, for Pierpoint, work and play—professional and social—merged during these times.

Kennedy press secretary Pierre Salinger told the correspondent corps that members of Kennedy's staff would be there and Pierpoint "sensed a unique opportunity to get acquainted with the people who would soon be running our nation." Immediately, he took note of another major difference from the soon-to-be-preceding administration: "Nothing like this had ever happened in the Eisenhower years, and we were all pleasantly surprised." It was the shape of things to come, a new openness that had its purpose—for the nation, but as importantly for Kennedy himself.

Pierpoint's wife, Pat, had remained in Washington, and, while it would be a sort of working holiday, he also sensed that the planned garden party meant "the social scene was too good to miss." He phoned Pat to suggest she get a live-in sitter for the four kids and join him in Palm Beach. She arrived the next day. Pierpoint details how Kennedy flirted with his own wife. Having been introduced to Pat Pierpoint, Kennedy looked at her "with those bright-blue eyes and appraising her from top-to-bottom, he very deliberately said, 'How do you do, Mrs. Pierpoint.'" Then he asked if they hadn't met before. "A sophisticated thirty-five-year-old woman, my wife reacted like a schoolgirl, stammering in her flattered surprise, 'I—I—I don't believe so.'" Pierpoint early on saw Kennedy's game up close, in slow motion, seeing each card as it was dealt. "This incident," he wrote, "demonstrated one of Kennedy's greatest assets—his extraordinary personal charm. He had a quick wit and a self-deprecating sense of humor. His open flirtation with my wife was kidding her and himself, but JFK knew he had a devastating effect on women and enjoyed it to the fullest."[20]

On the other hand, Pierpoint felt that Kennedy, as president, "had great difficulty marshaling press and public support for his specific policies." Specifically, Pierpoint believed that JFK, once ensconced in office, was ineffectual in dealing with Congress, which constantly and consistently stood in the way of his agenda. In contrast to his vice president, Lyndon Johnson, Kennedy had all the charm but none of the influence with Congress. "He started the processes that LBJ was later able to bring about," Pierpoint would later tell an interviewer. Johnson, Pierpoint believed, knew how to get things done. Thus, he came to refer to him, much later in life, as "the great manipulator" among the presidents he covered.[21]

The Kennedy clan around JFK was often as accessible as the president himself—with some restrictions. The First Lady, for instance, was a hard person for Pierpoint to figure out. He once called her, during an interview years later, "a very strange woman" and recounted an interaction he had with her during one of the Palm Springs gatherings. As an aside, such gatherings, once Kennedy was in office, occurred over the Christmas holidays. Correspondents, their wives and families were invited to spend at least part of the holidays with the Kennedys at the aforementioned rented beachfront mansion.

It was on one of those visits, when the Pierpoints were visiting on the day before Christmas, that Robert Pierpoint learned a valuable lesson about Jackie Kennedy. All the Pierpoint kids were there—Eric, Stan, Kim, and Marta, ranging at that time from thirteen to six months. Mrs. Kennedy arrived and was "a gracious and regal hostess," even suggesting that the Pierpoint's youngest, Marta, spend time upstairs in the nursery with John-John, then only a year or so older. She chatted with everyone and Pierpoint was left with the impression that she was interested in the families as individuals. The next day that all changed.

Seeing Mrs. Kennedy in the morning, he simply said, in a cheery tone, "Good morning, Mrs. Kennedy." He got a "frozen stare and dead silence." Twice more that day she ignored him. Pierpoint asked a fellow correspondent, "What happened there?" His colleague replied: "You just got the treatment." Pierpoint said, "I know that, but what happened?" The other man told him: "I never speak to her unless she speaks first. You just never

4. Back Home: Marriage, Family and the White House

Pierpoint at a party given in honor of Jacqueline Kennedy in the 1980s. He had great respect for the First Lady, though he recounted more than once that he found her to be an enigma. At least once, Pierpoint felt he had done the unpardonable at a social gathering by speaking to her before she had first spoken to him.

know what kind of mood she is in." The whole incident bewildered Pierpoint, who, when it came to the First Lady, admitted, "I never understood her."[22] On the other hand, when the events of 1964 occurred in Dallas, Jackie Kennedy's conduct directly after the assassination was something he found "so inspiring."

The president's brother, Robert Kennedy, was also somewhat of an enigma to Pierpoint. He found Bobby Kennedy to be "aggressive, smart, a lot more difficult to difficult to deal with than Jack." For one thing, Pierpoint's view of RFK, in contrast to his brother, was that he was "a lot less diplomatic, a lot less politic than Jack." If you got into an argument with Bobby, he once observed, he was "vicious." Unlike his brother, Robert Kennedy "didn't care if he made a few enemies here and there; in fact, he probably delighted in it." On the other hand, from his vantage point in the Kennedy White House, Pierpoint could see that RFK occupied a central role for his brother: "He was important in that he could say to Jack, 'let's look into this a little further'"—helping the sometimes mercurial president with a measure of analytical balance.

The idiosyncrasies of the Kennedy clan aside, Pierpoint and his colleagues continued to find working conditions at the Kennedy White House a major improvement over the previous administration. For one thing, press secretary Salinger mainly left reporters alone to find their sources and do for themselves. He was there to help, but not to direct, a fact Pierpoint came to appreciate perhaps more than any other about Kennedy's time in the White House. Behind the scenes, however, increasingly all was not entirely rosy between Kennedy and the press. In the spring of 1962, the *New York Herald Tribune* ran a series of editorials critical of the president.

As an example of how impulsive JFK could be, Pierpoint recalled in *At the White House* how the president ordered all twenty-two White House subscriptions to the *Herald Tribune* cancelled. Instead, he ordered the *St. Louis Post-Dispatch,* a paper that generally supported him and his policies. It was a public relations mistake and Salinger knew it. Unknowingly, Pierpoint was targeted as part of the way out of a PR problem. Salinger, the next morning, called him into his office to "chat." Salinger, with a smile on his face, dropped the story about the newspaper cancellation. "But between his casual manner and my general disinterest it slipped by me completely," wrote Pierpoint. Sensing his strategy hadn't worked, Salinger "chatted" with other White House reporters. The cancellation became a front-page story, "Kennedy looked foolish, the White House re-subscribed to the *Herald Tribune*, and I had the good sense to keep quiet about how I had missed the story."

That story was a one-day affair, at best. The story Robert Pierpoint did not miss, the one in which he played a central role, and the one which would in some ways haunt him the rest of his life was still on the horizon. It was the last story he would ever cover involving President John F. Kennedy. It also defined a generation and showed the nation just what kind of reporter Robert Pierpoint had become.

Covering the Kennedy Assassination

November 22, 1963, was an atypical day for Jackie Kennedy. She had spent much of the summer in Italy and didn't like politics, but there she was in Dallas, Texas, shaking hands, smiling, actually campaigning. Robert Pierpoint remembered thinking at the time that perhaps they had resolved their differences since that awkward encounter in Palm Springs. The local newspapers at the time had been very negative about her husband's visit, using headlines in their editorials like "We don't want you. Why are you here?" There were so many anti–Kennedy factions that Pierpoint recalled "[people] were a little nervous." Some of the president's opponents carried nasty signs, though, on balance, he recalled that most were friendly.[23]

The White House correspondents were following the president's motorcade in a bus, at a distance. "All of a sudden, we heard three shots. I wrote in my notebook, 12:30. Three shots," Pierpoint remembered. Some of the other reporters covering Kennedy's motorcade thought the sound might have come from the backfire of a car. "Those of us in the bus argued about whether what we had heard were actually shots or backfires, but I had heard enough firing during the Korean War to be fairly certain they were rifle shots." He says he "then knew something was terribly wrong."

When he and others of the press corps arrived at the Trade Center where the motorcade was to have stopped, they didn't see the presidential limousine. "For minutes that seemed like hours I frantically searched for the press room and a telephone which turned out to be two floors above the main hall." When he called CBS News headquarters in New York, they confirmed Kennedy had been shot. He was told they needed a broadcast immediately. "I said no way. I didn't know anything." He couldn't even get near the president's car, but was kept away by the Secret Service.

Pierpoint made it to the hospital emergency room, which was already cordoned off. He talked with some Secret Service agents and local politicians who had been in the motorcade a few cars behind the president. He was told by them the president had been hit and that it was "very serious." Then, he saw a "blond priest" going into the emergency room. "I didn't know enough about Catholicism to realize that he had gone in to administer the last rites. I asked the priest if the president was dead. He didn't answer."

He finally felt like he had enough information to do a broadcast. He tried everywhere to get to a phone when a "rather stout black lady in a white uniform came up and said to me, 'you want to get to a telephone, don't you.' I said I certainly did. She took me by the hand, led directly through the police cordon around the Emergency Ward and said 'There is a public telephone on the wall just to the left of the corridor.' There was and I grabbed it." He would stay on that pay phone for an hour and a half, keeping the line open, feeding information on the president's condition, as he received it, to New York. His first-person reports, along with those of Dan Rather, were what helped form the basis for Walter Cronkite informing the nation. He spent the rest of his life being grateful to the unnamed nurse who took him by the hand and made his reporting possible, though he never knew her name or met her again.

The pool reporter[24] that day was Sid Davis, a correspondent for Westinghouse broadcasting. He recalls how it was actually Pierpoint's time in the rotation. They tangled over who was supposed to file the story for the other news organizations that day. Davis's boss in New York told him he had to file. Davis resisted, saying, "Pierpoint follows me in the rotation; it's his turn." When the issue was raised with Pierpoint, the response was "I don't want it; you go ahead." A police car took Davis to the airport, where the new president, Lyndon Johnson, was to be sworn in on *Air Force One*. The press was to be there, but only two seats remained—a coin flip would decide between Davis and Charles Roberts of *Newsweek*. Davis declined, so Roberts went. Searching for a phone to give his pool report, Davis saw three payphones at the far end of the field. They were all occupied, one by Robert Pierpoint. "Pierpoint kept talking and talking and I said, for Christsakes, let me do my story." Davis became frustrated because Pierpoint "commandeered one of those three phones" and the others were two or three miles away. Finally, Pierpoint relinquished the phone and Davis completed his pool report just as *Air Force One* lifted off. He always thought that day showed the fiercely competitive side of Robert Pierpoint. There were no hard feelings, just two men doing their jobs, displaying tenacity in the face of extreme circumstances.[25]

For Robert Pierpoint, the dedication and perseverance to his craft on that tragic day should have been the defining moment in his career. Oddly, he never thought so. In fact, he was highly critical of his own reporting—especially on the day of Kennedy's funeral. He was nearby as the slain president's coffin passed by. "That was an occasion when I fell down on my reportorial job," he replied to an interviewer nearly forty years later. "I didn't do what I should have done. As Mrs. Kennedy was walking out with her hand on the casket, which was being wheeled by, I saw the blood on her skirt and the blood on her, down here on her right side and down her leg and down onto her stockings. And I could not report it. It was bad. I should have done it."[26]

Pierpoint, like the rest of the nation, was in a self-described state of shock: "Well, I was live on the air at the time and I just couldn't do it. And later, of course, I regretted that I didn't. I just talked about 'She is leaving now, her hand is on the coffin as it's wheeled out the door and it will be taken to the airport.' But I didn't describe her." It was an omission that haunted him right up to the end of his life. In his final interview, with the *Santa Barbara News-Press* in October 2011, nearly a half decade later, Robert Pierpoint still felt he fell down on the job. He even went so far as to call it his "one bad mistake," and, as his youngest daughter, Marta, put it, "he spoke about it more the older that he got and the more important it became what people thought about it."

He was so fixated on that moment that he relayed his feelings to his granddaughter, Rachel. In the last year of his life, clutching a gin and tonic (with two green olives!) on a sunny day in Palm Springs, he reflected on the omission in his reporting to the next generation of Pierpoints. Reminded that it was okay, that someone else had reported the details of blood on the First Lady's clothing, he wasn't soothed. "But *I* didn't report it," he insisted. "I was not the one who described those images of Jackie, who reported how she looked." His hand was shaking more now. "It was my job to report every detail. What the nurses, what the doctors said. My duty to my country. Someone else did my job. I failed in my duty to my country."[27]

Sid Davis talked with Pierpoint shortly before he died in 2011 and the omission, says Davis, still bothered him. "You had to know Bob. He had great respect for Mrs. Kennedy ... you're in Dallas and you see this beautiful couple, she was out for the first time after her baby had died in August. You put that all together with Bob's background at the White House and I think it was really out of respect for Mrs. Kennedy," asserts Davis. "I don't fault Bob and I told him that on the phone. I felt the same, but I was the pool; if I had left that detail out for the thirty or forty other correspondents my name would have been mud."

Those who knew him best, including his wife Pat, don't find it surprising that Pierpoint would be so hard on himself. "He *couldn't* do it," she stresses. "He would have broken down." He wouldn't have been the only one. The Pierpoint kids were watching at home and, as Eric remembers it, "we had had a maid at that time and she burst into tears and she and I watched the TV for about three days. We saw Bob eventually coming out of the hospital and he was on the phone and he wouldn't talk about Jackie because she was covered in blood and he couldn't talk about it. He was fond of Kennedy, he had followed him around on all of his trips and, boy, that hit him."

It didn't surprise his daughters, either. Kim Pierpoint puts the self-criticism of her dad's reporting this way: "It was probably the most poignant moment in his career. He felt he owed it to the country to report what he knew—the facts as he experienced them." She knew her father as a man of standards and they had come to the fore when hitting closest to home. "He had very high standards for everyone," she says, and that meant "he wouldn't let himself off the hook."

Their dad had been through the wringer that November day, first reporting the assassination itself, then transitioning to the funeral. Later, on the *CBS Evening News*, "I simply recounted from my notes what I had seen and heard that terrible day." He flew back to Washington and there he saw firsthand the impact on his family, somewhat different, but much the same as on other American families at that time. "Early the next morning," he wrote, "I was in the kitchen preparing coffee when our daughter Kim, then 11 years old, came in to say, 'It is pretty bad, isn't it, Dad?' 'Yes,' I said, "it is pretty bad.' Then she added, shoulders slumped, 'I guess we won't be going to Palm Beach again for Christmas this year.' 'No,' I said, 'not this year.'"[28]

The sadness of his child at the loss of a cherished memory was mirrored in Bob Pierpoint's own sense of loss, one that was never fully resolved. The Kennedy assassination and its aftermath became a flashpoint for him for much of his life, in a variety of ways. In 2011, he tearfully relived for an interviewer his anger at the words spoken by the priest at Kennedy's funeral. "I didn't like what the priest said about a time to live and a time to die," he said. "It was not Kennedy's time to die."[29]

Many years later, in 1997, Pierpoint was also angered by references to him and the Kennedy assassination coverage in Walter Cronkite's biography. "It's 3:30 a.m. and I am sitting here in mild shock," he wrote in an e-mail to the book's editor. "Walter has given Rather credit for one of the proudest accomplishments of my career ... what Walter has done is name Rather the White House correspondent and put him inside the emergency ward of Parkland Memorial Hospital ... to this day, I have no idea how much of my reporting was aired directly and how much was relayed to Walter and others to air. But I am broken hearted to realize that Walter thinks it was Rather there."[30]

Later in 1997, he was still upset enough to write a letter on April 11 to Professor Barbie Zelizer of Temple University regarding a book she was writing on the assassination, clarifying his role and Rather's, hoping the earlier mistake wouldn't be replicated. He noted in his letter that when he heard a loud noise from a distance, "I immediately wrote in my notebook '1233 ... sounds like three rifle shots."[31] There's no evidence that either concern was directly addressed, no responses, no letters. But to Robert Pierpoint, that wasn't the point. In a business filled with egos—and even his closest friends and family will concede he, like others in the business, *had* an ego—Pierpoint was setting the record straight, the way he always wished he had when reporting the Kennedy funeral. It wasn't about credit, his closest colleagues say, but accuracy. It simply wasn't right.

This tenacity for the truth, whether he put others or himself under the harsh lens of scrutiny, became the trademark of Robert Pierpoint as a journalist. It was going to be tested throughout the administrations of the next two presidents he would cover, one more than the other. As JFK himself had been fond of saying, the White House was not a good place to make new friends.

The Johnson Years

Where John F. Kennedy's charm separated him from Dwight Eisenhower's militaristic demeanor, "Kennedy's successor had none of this charm. In fact, my first experience with LBJ got us off to a bad start and from then on, it was downhill."[32] That was even before Johnson had become president—back in his days as Senate Majority Leader. Because the CBS Washington Bureau was short-staffed in 1959, Pierpoint was asked to cover Johnson's press conference. In those days, separate press conferences for print reporters and those in broadcast were commonplace. Having listened in to the print reporters' questions, Pierpoint found nothing very newsworthy and decided "to begin a new line of questioning designed to elicit for film the most colorful quotes from the session just held for the print media."

LBJ suddenly turned on Pierpoint, barking, "I didn't agree to answer any questions on that subject." Surprised, Pierpoint informed the Majority Leader that he hadn't agreed to limit his questioning in any way. There was awkward silence. He repeated the question. Johnson began to leave, "angrily claiming I was breaking the rules," Pierpoint recalled. The other network correspondents asked that Pierpoint order his camera crew to stop filming, a request at which he bristled. It seemed there was a "gentleman's agreement" in place that Johnson would not permit TV cameras at his press conferences, but would consent to answering questions after the fact in a nearby TV studio IF the correspondents would limit their questions to certain subjects. "It was a disgraceful situation," Pierpoint felt, "one that would never be tolerated by the networks today, but as the new kid on the block I was forced to agree."

Fortunately for Pierpoint, once he became president, LBJ didn't seem to remember the incident. The reporter in Pierpoint, however, never forgot. It came to him years later, in 1963, soon after Johnson was sworn in. It was in December, with the president flying to New York for the funeral of that state's former governor and U.S. Senator Herbert Lehman. It was the first time Pierpoint had spoken with Johnson since the confrontation with him in his Senate Majority Leader role. Along with two other White House correspondents, he had been invited to have a private chat with the president in his airborne bedroom on *Air Force One*. The four had a drink and had general conversation. As the gathering broke up, Johnson grabbed Pierpoint's arm, looked him square in the eye and said, "Ah'm a good friend of yo' boss, Frank Stanton. Anything Ah can do for you, just let me know. Ah know we're going to get along just fine."

The point wasn't lost on Pierpoint, who described his feeling as "disgusted." As he returned to his seat, the thought popped into his head: "Lyndon Johnson apparently thought I could be bought, intimidated, or both, and it seemed highly possible that if neither could be accomplished, he might try to get me off the White House beat." It was a reminder of how, as Pierpoint would put it on other occasions, "Johnson repeatedly demonstrated this need to be in constant control." He would seldom, if ever, allow many, if any, of his high-level officials to speak with the press. If any broke ranks and answered questions, they suffered what Pierpoint called "LBJ's considerable wrath." Evidence of daily restraints on the press only multiplied. For one, Pierpoint noted how one of Johnson's close aides and fellow Texans "shared his paranoia about the press and was especially adept at contriving ways to harass and restrict reporters." White House switchboard operators were ordered to screen calls to determine if they originated from a reporter or news organization. If so, they were told to ask the caller what he wanted to discuss—before putting the call through. Also, records were kept of the answers provided.

Pierpoint saw LBJ as "a man of extremes," one who "could be as kind as he was crude." Despite being "overbearing, full of energy, like an enormous engine operating nearly out of control," Pierpoint also saw a softer side. "In any mood," he wrote, "LBJ was awesome, especially to children." There was one exception: Pierpoint's own youngest daughter, Marta, then three years old. It was July 1965, and he talked about the exchange subsequently, in both interviews and his personal papers. The press corps was invited to visit Johnson's childhood home, a small farmhouse in Texas. It was full of vintage furniture, some of which was said to be in the president's family. LBJ was playing the genial host, acting like a "kindly school teacher as he greeted wives and children lined up at the entrance to the 'birthplace.'" He spotted Pat Pierpoint holding daughter Marta's hand and decided to invite them both on a personal tour, proudly proclaiming his ancestral story as they walked. Marta was taken with the president's enthusiasm. Then came the moment: LBJ pointed to a high chair in the kitchen and proclaimed it as "Lady Bird Johnson's baby chair" and urged Marta to have her photograph taken in the "baby chair." Mirroring her father's contrarian nature, the three-year-old firmly said, "I'm not a baby." LBJ was crestfallen. Pierpoint described him as "retreating from the scene with a hurt look on his beagle-like countenance."

Despite the Pierpoint family proclivity for not toeing the line, during LBJ's early days in the White House, Robert and Pat Pierpoint were invited to Johnson's social events, once to a dinner for Britain's Princess Margaret, the second on the occasion of a visit by India's Prime Minister Indira Gandhi. President Johnson, Pierpoint believed, considered such social occasions to be a form of bribery, "to be dispensed as favors to the press." However,

4. Back Home: Marriage, Family and the White House 81

the president also received something in return: information. As a variation of the adage "keep your friends close and your enemies closer," Johnson would have a staff member assigned specifically to watch various reporters in social situations and report back to him precisely what they did. Pierpoint was among them, especially in 1966, at the height of the Vietnam War.

Pierpoint once asked a White House aide, a young lawyer who regularly received calls from the president inquiring about a reporter's actions or motives, what LBJ thought of him. He was told the president was upset by some of Pierpoint's recent broadcasts, one especially that suggested important information about the war was being withheld from the press and the public. In it, Pierpoint had questioned LBJ's "lack of candor." The president called the aide into the Oval Office one day and peppered him with questions about Pierpoint and why he had been "so ungrateful, ... after all Ah've done for that boy." Pierpoint took the comment to mean the White House dinner invitations.

As the Vietnam War escalated, relations between the president and the press deteriorated. This was especially true of the relationship between Johnson and Pierpoint. For one, the president knew Pierpoint considered the war to be what he (Pierpoint) called it years later in his book: "a national disaster." The dispute simmered between the two and came to a head during a private luncheon in the fall of 1967. For Pierpoint, it was an awkward time. He knew that LBJ was, to say the least, not happy with him. Throughout their conversation, the president spent time defending his policies and complaining that the press "refused to see things his way."

After the luncheon, Johnson began bragging that the U.S. military was doing a great job "licking the Communists." The North Vietnamese, he said, "have got two hundred thousand people today cleaning up the mess I made yesterday." Pierpoint had heard enough. He had been restraining himself, but now had to speak up. "Mr. President," he said to LBJ, "the North Vietnamese keep saying that if you stop the bombing, they will negotiate a peaceful settlement of the war. Why don't you try it, and then, if they don't seriously negotiate, you could resume the bombing, but with the monkey on their backs?"

It caused what Pierpoint called "a small explosion." Johnson tore into him. "You're just helpin' ma enemies, the Communists!" He then went on to rant against Pierpoint and all those who questioned his policies in Vietnam. Most of them were, in the president's view, reporters, who didn't understand that if the Communists weren't stopped where they were, we'd soon find them on the shores of California. According to LBJ, those who were openly skeptical of his strategy in Vietnam were aiding and abetting

On board *Air Force One*, on the way to Texas, September 14, 1968. President Johnson briefs White House correspondents on developments in the Vietnam War. Pierpoint is in the light-colored suit in front of the president. Others in photograph: Chuck Roberts, far right, Robert Fleming, standing front, Maryanne Manners, right.

the enemy. His face turning red, Johnson then stammered that FBI director J. Edgar Hoover had warned him that there were some "five thousand Communists inside the U.S. government." The room was silenced, the journalists "stunned" by what Pierpoint later considered to be a "disgraceful" statement by a president of the United States. He eventually chalked it up to another attempt by Johnson to intimidate the press. He regretted that, under the rules of the luncheon, he could not report the conversation because it was understood to be off the record.

On another occasion, he and other White House correspondents were invited by Johnson's press secretary to attend a birthday party in the president's honor at his daughter's home. An "embittered" LBJ watched as what Pierpoint referred to as "one of the strangest episodes of my career" unfolded. It consisted of about twenty reporters singing "Happy Birthday" to the president (with a rousing, rhyming chorus of "Happy Birthday, LBJ") and sharing small talk with him and his family. It was 1968 and the party took place during the Chicago Democratic Convention. By that time, antiwar rallies and general protest and condemnation of the president's Vietnam policies had taken their toll and LBJ decided against running for his party's nomination. Far from the convention center, in an ironic twist, here he was at a birthday party with anyone but his friends—in fact, he was surrounded by those he considered to be his foes. Many years later, Pierpoint, in a speech, commended LBJ for deciding against running for reelection. "He felt the campaign in which he would have to run would have turned up so much hatred that, the country would have been so divided, that I think it was to his credit he recognized this and it was probably the right thing to do," he said.

So large was Johnson's ego that Pierpoint felt compelled to question its origins. "I generally viewed [it] as a manifestation of deep self-doubts and insecurity," he wrote. During the Johnson years, Pierpoint saw LBJ abuse reporters as well as his own aides. He was prone to insulting both behind their backs, "sometimes even in their presence." He had a particular method for dismissing those he especially disliked: he would publicly and deliberately mispronounce their names. As an example, there was an NBC correspondent named Ron Nessen, who he would purposely call "Nesson" or "Messon." It became such a regular practice that those who were in LBJ's doghouse had no doubt they were being collared.

On the other hand, where Kennedy had liked reporters and was accessible, Pierpoint found LBJ, at times, to be "almost too accessible." There were periods where he wanted to talk with reporters "by the hour, and I mean literally by the hour and it wasn't so much a dialogue as a monologue." Pierpoint was once invited to lunch with LBJ and assumed there would be two or three of his colleagues there. He also thought that this was Johnson's way of "massaging" them a bit, in order to get them not to report things that Johnson would prefer to have kept quiet. Pierpoint and the president started walking around the backyard of the White House. LBJ then invited him—Pierpoint alone, no other reporters present—to join him for some lunch upstairs in the White House.

They were finishing lunch when Mrs. Johnson came in and cheerfully announced that "today, for the first time we had more visitors to the White House than when the Kennedys were here." LBJ seemed pleased and said to her, "You know I'm kinda tired. What time was it I got into your bed this morning, bird?" Pierpoint couldn't recall her response, but he couldn't forget what came next. "Maybe I oughta take a nap, but I want you to come over across the way; I'm not through talking," the president said to Pierpoint. When the president invites, you follow, and so Pierpoint trudged with LBJ over to the presidential residence. "He just went on and on and on and, meanwhile, he's taking off all his clothes," recalled Pierpoint. "A valet was standing there holding all his clothes and the President of the United States is standing there stark naked." A short time later, after putting

Pierpoint filing a report from Caracas, Venezuela. As part of his duties as CBS White House correspondent, he would cover the president on the road. It's likely that this photograph was taken during a presidential visit by Lyndon Johnson.

4. Back Home: Marriage, Family and the White House

On a press plane, en route to Vietnam, with the rest of the White House press corps. Unlike *Air Force One*, press planes were fairly spartan and quarters were cramped.

on a pair of pajamas and talking himself out, he walked by Pierpoint, en route to the bathroom. Then, LBJ walked back, got into bed and kept talking for another ten minutes. Pierpoint slipped out, finally, but never forgot two things about the interaction: (1) it was a show of what LBJ considered "western hospitality," displaying that he was "just plain folks"; (2) at base, Johnson was a deeply lonely man.

Given his glimpse of the private LJB, it was all the more curious to Pierpoint that the president would actively shun some in the White House press corps while relentlessly pursuing conversation with others. More often than not, those shunned by LBJ were those he perceived to be on the wrong side of the Vietnam issue. For Pierpoint, the topic was always top of mind. During one presidential news conference, he wrote in his reporter's notebook: "Propose increase of troop levels (Vietnam)?" Presumably, that was a question he either asked or intended to ask LBJ. The president's response, which may or may not have made it into Pierpoint's report that night, was evasive. Pierpoint noted, in shorthand: "No discussion today of troop levels.

As you have implied we are scheduled to receive additional troops—would not be proper to discuss."[33]

On numerous occasions, Pierpoint personally witnessed the toll Vietnam was taking on both the nation and the president. He recorded this incident in one of his notebooks. "Teenager hurled himself in front of Pres. Car—50 feet beyond front of Capital. SS [secret service] hauled youth away unhurt—squatted in street with legs crossed—troopers pulled him way while Pres. car proceeded." The teenager was a Vietnam War protester. The situation had been defused. With an eye both for detail and for the humanity of the man behind the office, Pierpoint made a second notation in the same notebook. A short time later, Johnson stopped for ice cream. "Ice cream came from Dairy Queen," he recorded.

More than straightforward documentations of an event, Pierpoint's reporter notebooks were the place where he sometimes recorded his private thoughts on a subject or issue. They sometimes became the basis of a nearly completed script for that evening's news. In a 1968 notebook, he wrote about what he figured to be a bad day for President Johnson. It was on the day then Minnesota governor George Romney withdrew from the presidential race. At the Washington Hilton Hotel, Pierpoint reported the story: "This momentous news will have far reaching effects on the entire political picture," he reported, "especially on the Republican race for the nomination. The ramifications of Romney's withdrawal are tremendous. Richard Nixon, in New Hampshire, is now in effect running against no one." He added, from his notes, the following: "Certainly President J. never expected this—at least not at this time, and will be watching with narrower eyes the effect (referring to the then likelihood of a Nelson Rockefeller nomination) ... Lyndon Johnson would much prefer to run against Richard Nixon and now he may never get that chance He doesn't relish a race against Gov. Rockefeller—but that is a chance he may now have to take."

As a reporter, Pierpoint had the ability to differ with nearly all the presidents he covered on certain matters of policy, but still find something redeeming in them as people. Johnson may have tested that ability, but, when looking back years later, he saw LBJ through a different lens: "One day Mr. Johnson stopped me in the hall at the White House and said, 'You're just like all those Harvard Eastern liberals.'" Pierpoint responded: "Mr. President, I was born and raised farther west and a little south of where you are from. I went to the University of Redlands." He was surprised when LBJ replied: "I know where that is. I worked in San Bernardino when I was 17."[34]

Johnson had been a San Bernardino resident for several months in 1925, working there as an elevator operator. In October of 1964, during his presidential election campaign, he returned to San Bernardino as a crowd of 20,000 gave him a warm welcome. The *Sun-Telegram* reported that while standing on the corner near the Platt Building, where he operated the elevator, President Johnson said, "I got plenty of vocational education running that elevator."[35] In addition, before turning to politics at the age of 24, LBJ taught grammar school, high school, and college. Both aspects of his background impressed Pierpoint, especially in regard to his strong commitment to civil rights—which Pierpoint believed to be "absolutely genuine."

That commitment was, to Pierpoint, all the more laudatory because of Johnson's roots in West Texas where he grew up knowing "practically no blacks." Among his teaching jobs in 1938 was a position in a small Mexican town. "I think he genuinely believed in civil rights," Pierpoint said years later. "He was convinced that without government intervention, blacks would never make progress." The bill he introduced was important enough for LBJ to "twist every arm of every senator and every congressman that he could to get support for it."[36]

Pierpoint personally observed Johnson's behavior toward those outside the U.S., especially those in Latin countries, during his 1968 coverage of LBJ's trip to El Salvador. "A labor of love," he labeled it on CBS radio, noting that the president "seems to have a more easy rapport with the Latins than with other foreigners, perhaps dating back to the time when taught school to Mexican school children back in the 1920s." The report included mention of LBJ's reflecting on how "when I gave up teaching and went into public life, I carried with me the trust students put upon me ... I hope that when you grow up you can go to the University of Texas and I can be your teacher."[37]

It was "the kind of day Mr. Johnson loves, lots of color, excitement, crowds, and fun," Pierpoint observed. When the first family attended mass, "an altar boy kept lifting his robe to snap his picture, with a camera strapped around his neck." Later, in the presidential motorcade, Johnson "stood in the back seat to shout *muchos gracias* ... the happiness and eagerness on the faces of the little children said it all." He didn't neglect mention of the protestors to Johnson's visit, saying the "warm welcome was only slightly marred by a small protest." He noted that eggs were thrown at LBJ's motorcade and a sign read "President Johnson, assassin." Red paint hit the president's car and, combined with the confetti also flying about, "created a gooey, but colorful omelet, quickly removed by Secret Service agents."

Johnson, during his speech, answered the protestors with praise for "important social advances" made by the El Salvadorans as they progressed into membership in the Central American common market. "Bearing welcome gifts, or at least loans, Johnson pledged $65 million in loans," he reported. That included money for transportation and communication networks to improve the lives of those in the region. It was the other side of Johnson, the one Pierpoint admired, as opposed to the man presiding over the Vietnam War. He was able to see—and appreciate—both sides: the man he saw in El Salvador and the one who gave orders to send young Americans into battle in Southeast Asia.

Perhaps more than any other journalist covering the White House at that time, Robert Pierpoint was an antagonist to the man he saw as chiefly responsible for continuing the Vietnam War. Despite the early truce surrounding the "California connection," the two continued to be adversaries throughout Johnson's term as president. It wasn't general knowledge at the time, but the president—through his marriage to the First Lady—owned a number of radio stations, all of them in Texas. In fact, the Johnsons, through a holding company run by Lady Bird Johnson, actually amassed a sizable number of broadcast holdings, the first an AM-FM operation in Austin, along with a TV station, and others in Waco and Corpus Christi. One of them was a CBS-affiliated radio station and, when Pierpoint became especially bothersome at the White House, LBJ tried to get him fired by calling his boss. He also, according to Pierpoint in *At the White House*, tried to get his press pass revoked. Both attempts were unsuccessful.

What's remarkable is that Pierpoint still had respect for LBJ, despite all the tension between them. In part it was the president's stand on civil rights. In part it was the fact that, like him, Johnson had spent time with real people in real places doing real jobs. On balance, Pierpoint pronounced him as "the most qualified of all the presidents I covered"—testimony to the job he did as president, but also recognition that LBJ's fear of what Pierpoint called "free flowing information" was both minimal and understandable compared to the man who would next be president. Richard Nixon, he and the nation would soon learn, was not to be trusted: an eventuality that was so far from the way the 37th president began his relationship with the White House watchdogs.

The Nixon Years

"Johnson's fear of free-flowing information was so intense that Richard Nixon's Presidency came somewhat as a relief," wrote Pierpoint in *At the White House*. "In fact, despite Nixon's previous history of attacks on the media, relations between press and White [House] eased significantly during his first years in office." In those early days of Nixon's administration, the new president even tried to create a better working environment for those covering him. One day, walking through the White House press room, he was "horrified" at the conditions he saw there. He decided the press needed a new home. As Pierpoint saw it, not only was this not the first time he showed concern for the White House press corps—he had once instructed press secretary Ron Ziegler to ensure reporters received comfortable accommodations whenever accompanying him on presidential trips—it was also a wise public relations move. On the other hand, Pierpoint would one day relay to a college audience that he had been among the first of a very few reporters invited to talk with Nixon the morning after his inauguration. "He told us how he removed the wire service tickers and the television sets that were in his office, that Johnson had left there." According to Pierpoint, he then told the assembled reporters that he "wasn't going to worry what you guys are writing about me." Pierpoint's assessment was that Nixon "had arrived at a goal and he was no longer operating from fear, fear of us, or fear of us finding out what he was all about."[38]

The honeymoon between Nixon and the press was short lived. His aides made it known they wanted offices in the White House close to the president, in order to be closer to the center of power. They prevailed upon Nixon to oust the press in order to make room for them. That would have meant moving across the street into what was known as the EOB (Executive Office Building). The White House bureau chiefs protested, arguing it would make the often difficult flow of information from administration even harder. Proximity to power, they argued, was important to their work; so, too, did the presidential aides.

By this time, Dan Rather had not only joined Pierpoint at the White House, but had also, through a series of events that will be discussed in the next chapter, assumed the role of chief White House correspondent. Rather suspected the administration's plan was "the more distance we get between ourselves and these reporters, the better things will be." The opposition from the press grew and, according to Rather, Pierpoint's voice was the most articulate. "He said to Ziegler, if you really want a lot of bad publicity, just keep doing this because it will be a story that runs for days, if not weeks," recalled Rather. "It's the wrong thing to do and, if you're going to do the wrong thing, you're going to pay a very heavy price for this."[39]

Ultimately, due to general opposition, as well as what Rather calls a "sharp, articulate, and insightful" argument by Pierpoint, Nixon relented. He announced he would give up the White House swimming pool, located near the West Wing, and turn it into the new press room. The conversion involved a number of structural machinations, including building a wooden floor above the pool, rather than removing it. The project cost just under $600,000, but it bought a lot of good will for the new president with the established press corps. In contrast to their old digs, the new press area had more phone lines, shelf space, even a recreation area. Things were off to a good start.

For a while, things went well. Nixon even eased a lot of the restrictions previously imposed on the press. Things began to take a turn for the worse, though, when his vice president, Spiro Agnew, attacked the press for their perceived (and in some instances actual) criticism of Nixon's handling of Vietnam. They got even worse when White House police were given orders to keep reporters off the driveway near a portico that protected them from rain, snow, or other inclement weather. The location was central because it allowed reporters and photographers access to those on the president's guest and meeting list as they came and went.

"One of the things you used to do as a White House reporter was the 'driveway stakeout,'" says Eric Engberg, who covered the White House in for Westinghouse Broadcasting in 1972 and eventually became Pierpoint's colleague at CBS. "If the president was meeting with a group of senators or business leaders and there was a willingness to have them speak to the press, you would wait outside the door and you could ask them questions." Engberg recalled how one day in 1973, he was among a group of 15 or 20 reporters, photographers, and soundmen standing in the White House driveway. "While we're standing there, a White House policeman, now called Secret Service, comes out and says you gotta move these cameras off the driveway."[40]

No one in previous administrations had ever done so, and it came as a shock to the assembled media corps. "Knowing how they treated the press with contempt, we thought someone in the administration did it just to show us they had the power and they could just move us around, push around whenever they wanted," says Engberg. Everyone started moving. Everyone, that is, except Robert Pierpoint. To Pierpoint, much like the proposed press room move to the EOC, this became another matter of principle.

"Wait a minute. We're not going anywhere." Pierpoint spoke and his colleagues froze in place. The cop began to stare him down. "This is where we always work, this is where we're going to work, and we're not leaving here until we finish," Pierpoint said to the cop. "I'm not moving this camera. If you try to force me to move, my camera crew will take pictures of it and I will take those pictures and put them in my story tonight and it will make a very nice story of how the press is pushed around at the White House." The White House cop went off, conferred with someone inside, returned, and the order was lifted. The journalists were told they could stay where they were.

To Engberg, it was another example of the burgeoning respect Pierpoint had earned among his colleagues, both inside and outside CBS News. "He was respected by everyone who worked that beat," Engberg says. "He provided the pool backbone. He stood up to these guys. He knew we were just being screwed around with and he made it clear he wouldn't stand for it." Roger Mudd, another CBS colleague who covered Congress during Pierpoint's White House years, put it this way: "Bob was a very tough man to push around and he believed very strongly in the sanctity of news. He believed journalists should have total access and he stood up for those beliefs and represented the best of them."

What made him popular with his colleagues did not always make him a favorite with those he covered. Neither was he a darling to network management. His firm stands on issues of press freedom and fairness would, at times, set him back in the CBS News pecking order. Most of the time Pierpoint's bosses were both understanding and supportive; sometimes they were not. Born of the idea that it was important to speak truth to power, Pierpoint was often the reason CBS news executives' phones rang in New York, with an angry politician on the other end. The 1973 broadcast on a "Double Standard in the Middle East," discussed in Chapter 3, was one, but there were others, including LBJ's calls to CBS News division president Frank Stanton during the previous administration. Beginning with the Nixon years, Pierpoint's unquenchable thirst for truth became a problem, not only to those in and around the Oval Office, but also to his own bosses at Black Rock.[41]

As he developed in his White House duties, he became an even stauncher supporter of journalistic autonomy when it came to judging a story's importance to the audience. "Bob and I shared a prickly nature toward management," says colleague Roger Mudd. "Both of us got the reputation of being a pain in the ass to a lot of people, particularly those above us.... We both regarded the standards of our managers as sometimes inferior to ours."[42] Pierpoint himself put it this way in an interview: "People ask, 'How long did you work for the White House?' And I'll say, 'I didn't work *for* the White House—I worked against them.'" He thought of his role thusly: "Everything is political, so interpretation is probably the most important thing a White House correspondent does. If you just regurgitate what's told you, you're not really doing your job." He called the "end piece," the 15 or so seconds at the end of a report where the reporters wrap up the story while in front of the White House, "so important." "That's really the guts of what it means to be a White House correspondent," he said. "It's the only way you have of saying to the public, 'This is bull—.'"[43]

The relationship between Nixon and Pierpoint did not begin as adversarial, at least not any more than is appropriate between a president and a reporter. Pierpoint, whose reporting would ultimately create so many problems for Nixon, "came to the Nixon presidency clean," according to Dan Rather. "He was open-minded about Nixon and his administration, even enthusiastically looking forward to it." Pierpoint and Nixon shared a California heritage. "Contrary to what the Nixon people believed," says Rather, "there was no deep-seated animus" on Pierpoint's part. He felt there would be new people to cover, a new outlook, and it would be good for the nation.

As time went on, Pierpoint became very concerned about what the Nixon administration was doing and what they were trying to convince people they were doing." Two major instances, principally, caused him to really dislike Nixon. One of them, Watergate, is well known. The other is less so, but it won Pierpoint the first of two Emmy Awards. It involved alleged influence peddling by Nixon, in his prepresidential years, to help a friend secure a banking charter. As the Nixon administration became more ensnarled in both, each became a macrocosm of the White House's smaller, yet daily, attempts to manipulate the press.

"Bob said to me, the first thing they're going to try to do is wedge us," recalls Rather. "They just didn't just dislike the press; they hated it." Pierpoint's prediction was correct. "Sure enough, they did," says Rather. "They'd hand a few stories to Pierpoint and a few to me and try to divide us. Bob would say 'they're at it again; here they come. But the harder they tried to make this wedge tactic work, the less successful it became." Rather credits Pierpoint with sensing what was going on and cluing him in. "Bob was absolutely rock solid, I would say 'cold steel' in any attempt to divide us."

Nixon tried to establish what he called the "Western White House," moving the entire administration there for virtually the entire summer each year, beginning in 1968. The press was housed in Laguna Beach, a pristine area of beaches and beauty. "Bob was very helpful," says Rather, by reminding him and other reporters that "it's easy in the sun and the long blonde beaches of California to lose your edge." It was a cautionary note to "keep your focus, keep your discipline."

It would take both focus and discipline to withstand what can only be interpreted as animosity directed at him by the president of the United States. It began during a situation Pierpoint described as "a minor incident that created a major conflict." It was October 1973. Watergate-related pressures were building on Nixon. The result was the president attacking the press during a news conference, calling their reporting "outrageous, vicious, distorted, frantic, and hysterical." He was especially vehement about what

4. Back Home: Marriage, Family and the White House

he said were lapses by television news reporters, although he added, oddly, "I am not blaming anyone for that."

Pierpoint was unsure of which specific television reporters had raised the president's ire. He said years later he thought Nixon might have been upset by a story a competitor at ABC News had aired a few days earlier. It dealt with evidence of a kind of presidential "slush fund" in Florida held by Charles "Bebe" Rebozo's bank. It was the tip of an iceberg that also led Pierpoint and bureau chief Ed Fouhy to launch an investigative report stretching from Key Biscayne to the White House and win both an Emmy. From behind the presidential podium, Nixon, Pierpoint sensed, was beginning to boil.[44]

It was his turn next to ask a question. First he noted that the president seemed "angry." He then pushed Nixon to be specific in his accusations. "Mr. President, you have lambasted the television networks pretty well," Pierpoint began. "Could I ask you, at the risk of reopening an obvious wound, you say after you have put on a lot of heat that you don't blame anyone. I find that a little puzzling. What is it about the television coverage of you in these past weeks and months that has so aroused your anger?"

What came next provoked what Pierpoint termed "shock and dismay" among the assembled press corps. Looking directly at Pierpoint, Nixon replied: "Don't get the impression that you arouse my anger." Thinking quickly on his feet, Pierpoint continued: "I'm afraid, sir, that I have that impression." The next move was the president's and Nixon took sarcasm to a new high. "You see," he said, eyes still fixed on Pierpoint, "one can only be angry with those he respects." Pierpoint, "astounded by the quiet ferocity of his attack," sat down. The president turned to the next questioner, but then abruptly broke off mid-answer to address Pierpoint. "Let me say, too," Nixon began, "I didn't want to leave an impression with my good friend from CBS over here that I don't respect the reporters. What I was simply saying was this: that when a commentator takes a bit of news and then, with knowledge of what the facts are, distorts it, viciously, I have no respect for that." Nice try, but the damage had been done.

When he got home that night, he asked his wife, Pat, if the White House had called. Pierpoint thought an apology from the president might be forthcoming. It was not. He later learned two revealing facts from a source inside the administration: one that Nixon's daughter Julie and son-in-law David Eisenhower expressed to the president that he had made a mistake; two, that the president's remark was, as Pierpoint suspected, directed specifically at him. The series of reports on the *CBS Evening News with Walter Cronkite* made Nixon furious. It wasn't the ABC story that had bothered him, but subsequent investigative work by Pierpoint and

Fouhy, focused on an eleven-month probe suggesting a too-cozy relationship between the president and Rebozo. Their findings were that nothing specifically illegal had taken place, but there were some "questionable banking practices" resulting from Rebozo's friendship with Nixon.

Pierpoint had developed a source who worked for the federal government in a low-level place, according to Ed Fouhy, who produced the series of reports. The source was outraged that Rebozo was getting favorable treatment in banking decisions because he knew Nixon. "We staked him [Rebozo] out, followed him everywhere, and gathered our facts," says Fouhy, adding that "it was very hard to get anyone to talk." Eventually, Fouhy and Pierpoint got their story, one that was considered significant enough to run for three consecutive nights. The series of reports, while they attracted Nixon's fury, would probably not have gained attention without the president's outburst, since there were so many other Watergate-related "scandal" stories coming from the White House at the time. In fact, Fouhy called it a "one day wonder kind of story." Nixon's implosion had helped by giving the story a shelf-life well beyond its expiration date.

The story received amplification through other media, based less upon its content and more as a result of the press conference fireworks. Adam Clymer of the *Baltimore Sun* reported the Nixon-Pierpoint exchange on October 27, 1973, in an article titled "Vicious Stories Attached." He wrote:

> During a nationally televised news conference, Nixon engaged in a "long blast," saying "I have never heard or seen such outrageous, vicious, distorted reporting in 27 years of public life. I'm not blaming anybody for that. Perhaps what happened is that what we did brought it about, and therefore, the media decided they would have to take that particular line." Then, one television news correspondent, Robert Pierpoint of CBS News, who has been reporting frequently on Mr. Rebozo's banking interests, asked what it was in the television reporting that had made him angry. The President replied with a satisfied smirk: "Don't get the impression that you've aroused my anger. One can only be angry with those he respects."[45]

The following Monday (the contentious press conference had taken place on a Friday), Nixon's speech writer, Patrick Buchanan, appeared on the *CBS Morning News*, along with Pierpoint and Dan Rather. "I think, Pat, I'll have to ask you," began Pierpoint to Buchanan, "I'm still in a bit of a state of shock at that vitriolic attack on the news media. I have to assume it wasn't directed at me personally, although I happened to be the immediate object of it." As Buchanan looked away, Pierpoint persisted: "Just what is it in specific terms in the last few weeks that has so aroused the President's anger—and I think it's obvious he was angry, despite his denial." Buchanan replied: "Well, the first thing I think we ought to consider is the mood in the East Room on the night of the press conference. I don't think it came through on that camera ... the mood there was really like Sunday afternoon in the Tijuana bull-ring, in my judgment, and I thought, in that mood, the President expressed feelings that he had gathered over a period of time."[46]

"Television Turns on Nixon" was the headline of an article by writer Robert Kunter, who praised the banking story: "Robert Pierpoint's first report on favorable treatment for the Rebozo banking group required several days digging and seven minutes of air time, and it scooped the print press, which disdained the story until Congressman Wright Patman began an investigation—giving the papers a fresh lead." The article began a lively debate, prompting a letter from Frederick Taylor, managing editor of the *Wall Street Journal*. "Mr. Pierpoint's report was a fine one, and I don't like to knock a television news exclusive, since the medium has so few," wrote Taylor, in a backhanded compliment, "but I'm afraid Mr. Pierpoint's report was neither the first, nor did it scoop the print press. His report appeared on the network news Monday night, October 15. That story, by Stanley Penn, appeared under a three-column headline in the *Wall Street Journal* of Monday morning, October 15, and was available to our readers some 11 or 12 hours before Mr. Pierpoint's broadcast."

Kuttner replied that "Mr. Taylor is partially correct in that the *Wall Street Journal* did run a brief story on page 32, October 15, which contained part of what CBS had that night." On the other hand, he wrote, "The CBS story was substantially more detailed in several other respects, and had obviously been in preparation for some time. My points were: (1) This was a remarkable example of the power of television to perform enterprise reporting, which should be done more often. (2) The print media were slow to credit a rival medium, and tended to downplay the scoop by dismissing the story."[47]

Aside from the debate over who did what when, the reverberation of Pierpoint's tangle with the president kept the story alive. Ironically, it came at a time when the White House was shifting its strategy in dealing with the news media. According to Ed Fouhy, the Nixon administration had actually been consciously *trying* to get on television, especially, to show the nation its future was in good hands, following tension over the cold war and the Cuban missile crisis. Nixon was supposed to look like a strong leader and, Fouhy says, he was urged to be on television to suggest the security of the U.S. was assured. "He had PR people like Bob Haldeman," Fouhy recalled, "telling him he needed to dominate the political dialogue every day and that meant you had to be on TV."

Nixon's jousting with Pierpoint didn't help him look either secure or in charge. It was atypical for him to engage a reporter at close range in combative terms. The entire episode was also atypical of how Pierpoint handled himself in presidential press conferences. While he was tough, he generally avoided confrontation. As his colleague Eric Engberg put it, "Unlike Rather, Pierpoint would have been offended by a personal confrontation with a president in public," adding, "That wasn't his style." On the other hand, his tenacity could lead to unexpected confrontations. One occurred with another Nixon—Julie Nixon Eisenhower—when one day during the Watergate investigation she was sent out to talk to the press.

The idea was to help take some of the heat from Watergate off her father. It didn't work. Engberg recalls that "some genius in the White House thought 'we'll send her out and the press won't beat up on her.' So, she goes on and on saying her dad is a wonderful guy, doing great things for the country, and so on." At that point, says Engberg, "Bob said, 'I have just one question, which is why are you here? The issues facing your father are matters of public importance and they are issues that he should be here talking about.'" According to Engberg, Julie Nixon told him she was "disgusted" with his attitude.

When reflecting back on those times, Pierpoint once commented that "such tense confrontations were not unusual during the Nixon years." In fact, the specter of threats by the administration to get certain reporters fired, begun for Pierpoint during the LBJ years, became more realized under Nixon's reign. They were no longer threats and they weren't just centered on a single reporter. As much as he hated going to management for any reason, there were times during this period when he—and especially his colleague, Dan Rather—needed CBS's support. Many CBS affiliates around the country, as the network's correspondents became more quarrelsome during the Watergate years, began to complain that local advertisers were unhappy. The words Pierpoint used were "they thought we were too consistently antagonistic." Networks need affiliates, but for some time CBS brass kept the wolves at bay. Agnew's attack on all the networks, not solely CBS, during a broadcasters' conference in 1970 didn't help. He charged that the network news organizations were against the Vietnam War and had formed a conspiracy to derail Nixon's best attempts to deal with the war.

Next came a planned strategy to put pressure on network White House correspondents by directly contacting network executives to complain about coverage of the war and the president. At CBS, it had begun years earlier when there were rumors of White House loyalists contacting both CBS Chairman William S. Paley and news division president Richard Salant to urge removal of certain dissident on-air voices. This happened in tandem with a steady drumbeat of dissatisfaction from the local affiliates. Pierpoint learned later that one local station owner, in 1973, had organized a scheme to get Rather fired from the White House beat. By then, CBS management had elevated Rather to the "number one" position at the White House, leaving Pierpoint in a back-up, number two role. Eric Engberg, now retired from CBS News, calls it a "typical CBS turf fight." Rather maintained in an interview that he and Pierpoint worked "hand in glove" in those days, but Engberg and others saw it differently. "The chances Bob could get on the air were nothing. Rather was going to get on the air every night. Bob was left to do a secondary role, which I know grated on him." This all occurred during a time when Salant was out as CBS News president and Bill Small—a Rather devotee—was in power.

Another colleague from that time, Jim McManus, verifies that Small was neither a friend nor a fan of Pierpoint's—and the feeling was apparently mutual. McManus, a radio correspondent for Group W (Westinghouse) broadcasting recalled a time when he stood up against the exclusion of radio journalists from traveling as the pool reporter with the president, including on *Air Force One*. McManus suspected it was part of a "deal" between Ziegler and network executives to marginalize the broadcast corps. One day Nixon press secretary Ron Ziegler announced that he—McManus—would be the "surprise broadcast pool reporter" on *Air Force One*. McManus was insulted because it was a one-time offer and then everything would return to the way it had been. As he put it, he "refused to follow the White House's orders."

Pierpoint defused the situation by immediately volunteering to be the pool reporter on the flight to California. Later, McManus approached Pierpoint and thanked him "for his recognition of my position." He also couldn't resist, he said, "telling him it was his own boss [referring to Bill Small], by then a vice president in New York, who was part of the discriminatory deal with Ziegler. What came next was surprising to McManus. "In an instant, his voice rising to an angry pitch, Bob Pierpoint snapped at me, 'My boss is not a very nice person!' And he turned his back." According to McManus, "it was my first clear recognition that Bob carried a deep hostility toward Bill Small and that he was not afraid to make it known." More importantly, said McManus, it showed "he was not a party to discrimination, against even his competitors."[48]

Despite what some saw as his decreased role, Pierpoint came to Rather's aid when the bosses' support of their number-one guy began to waver. Probably more because of the principle than any personal feelings he had for Rather, Pierpoint supported him with management. According to Rather, Nixon aide John Ehrlichman personally went to CBS headquarters in New York and tried to get him fired. "Bob Pierpoint stood tall for me. He could really make an argument. He spoke up for me privately and publicly," says Rather. It was the "measure of the man," he believes, that Pierpoint did so, stating the obvious reason that letting Rather fall would have elevated Pierpoint to the number-one position at the White House. What Dan Rather didn't know, couldn't have known, and didn't become clear until years later was that Pierpoint's head might also have been on the chopping block. The same source that told him about threats against Rather "refrained from saying they were also trying to eliminate me from the White House beat, but that was a safe assumption." Ultimately, both men would be reassigned from the White House to other beats, but, so far as anyone can tell, not due to outside pressure.

Pierpoint never lost the bad taste left by Nixon's attempts at intimidating journalists. Still, his notebook entries show a concerted effort to view the president in a human light. Typical is one entry that, in the midst of the dark days of Watergate, lends a humorous element to the president's day. He jotted the following: "Pres. gets back about 2:30.—Having some bridge repair work done—put off for about 10 yrs. Had temp. work done in NY—(2 teeth knocked out in college basketball). Sked: building bridges this AM—less difficult than building bridges in other areas." Then this: "Had TV set sound on so he can follow the Ohio State Game (May have to be checked in month or so)."

During the Watergate investigation, Pierpoint made these notations in his notebook regarding Nixon's refusal to turn over certain materials to those investigating the burglary. He sat down with then White House press secretary Ronald Ziegler and asked about "efforts to set forth factual materials and comments by the Pres.—to touch on some of main issues that have been raised." "Why now?" he writes. "Various charges directly involving the Pres. in W[atergate]—in all cases hearing—this sets forth Pres. version—Need to prevent certain disclosure of certain (sensitive) materials." He was aware that many had much to lose in the investigation. "Many on W.H. staff not avail—since themselves under investigation," he wrote. "Pres. intends to go into this further in very near future."

As an illustration of how closely family and the White House beat necessarily had to coexist and accommodate, each to the other, are personal notes written in Pierpoint's reporter notebooks, one in particular during the Nixon years. In a note, presumably by Mrs. Pierpoint to their older daughter, is written: "Kim—have gone to get Dad at WH—he has to leave for Miami—back by 1." It's signed only with a frowning face at bottom. In another, Mrs. Pierpoint writes to their son Eric: "Would you please find time to tie up the newspapers in bundles and take them to the recycling center.... Remember to water plants, feed gerbils, etc." It's testimony to just how much the family of a White House correspondent, in those days especially, had to chip in at home.

There was the time when Pierpoint had to leave his 10th wedding anniversary dinner party at the behest of Bill Galbraith, one of the network's assignment editors. He insisted Pierpoint had to stake out FBI director J. Edgar Hoover's house. It came about because Rather had done a story on the *CBS Evening News* stating that Nixon intended to fire Hoover. Gilbraith told Pierpoint by phone that night—October 3, 1969—that he had been ordered by CBS News Washington Bureau Chief Bill Small (who later became the network's news president) to head over to Hoover's house, where he and Nixon were having dinner. Pierpoint resisted. "And I said, 'Wait a minute. That's not my story. That's Rather's story,'" he recalled in an interview with former colleague Roger Mudd years later. "And he says, 'Small says you're to go out there anyway.' I said, 'Bill, I'm celebrating my 10th wedding anniversary with a group of friends.' Galbraith calls Small again and Small orders me to go out there or else. So I had to leave my dinner party on my 10th wedding anniversary and go out there."[49]

As it turned out, Small's instincts were correct: "I did an interview with Nixon in which he denied the whole story, said he was supportive of Hoover and that played on the morning news and it played on the next evening's news but it was Rather's basic story which he hadn't checked." While he had resented the intrusion, he had corrected the record and that had always been important to Pierpoint. On the other hand, so was the family gathering he had been forced to leave. The next morning he complained to the other White House reporters about what had happened and one of the newspaper reporters, not understanding how television works, said "I don't understand why they called you out to do this. What's the point?" Pierpoint's reply: "I'll tell you what get out of it, you get a ruined evening."

As time went on, Pierpoint came to doubt everything that came out of the Nixon White House—even something as innocuous as the count provided for those receiving the president's annual Christmas card. In a note he made on the unveiling of the White House Christmas card by Mrs. Nixon—a "4" × 6" Hallmark"—he records and notes that the official mailing, says Mrs. Nixon, is "40,200 persons she described as 'friends,' but, in parentheses, he writes Staff Dir. Says 37,000."[50] It may seem humorous on the surface, but it shows that when it came to Nixon, Pierpoint took nothing for granted.

As much as his dislike for the president grew, he held the first lady in high regard. Pat Nixon, he believed, had been put in an untenable situation through her marriage to Richard Nixon. "It was a tragedy," he once told an interviewer. "I knew Mrs. Nixon from Whittier High School, where she was a teacher and excellent with the students. I felt sorry for her in that relationship." That wasn't the only regret he had related to the Nixons. His father, Charles Pierpoint, had been a staunch Nixon supporter, even helping to raise money for the president's campaigns.

When Nixon was in Orlando, he made the now infamous statement "I am not a crook" to a group of 400 managing editors from the Associated Press. Defending his public service record, the president maintained he had never strayed, ethically or legally. It was November 17, 1973, and shortly after the speech, Charles Pierpoint phoned to get his son's opinion. "I told him 'Yes, Dad, he is a crook, and he is going to have to resign or he will be thrown out.'" It wasn't an easy pill for his father to swallow. "My dad didn't like what I said," recalled Pierpoint, but he, of course, turned out to be right.[51]

He was even prescient enough to see the end coming for Nixon, while giving a speech to a college audience at the height of Watergate. Nixon, he said on that December night in 1973, "may very well be driven from office." He quoted polls at the time showing the president's approval rating below 30 percent (taken, he noted, just before key minutes "showed up missing" on some White House tapes). "The president may be riding out this particular storm, but he faces a long winter of discontent," Pierpoint told his audience. "It's very hard for a weakened president to deal with either a domestic or an international crisis." He found it sad to see a "president under such an assault ... much of this, of course, he has brought on himself." The blame, as Pierpoint saw it, was Nixon's choice of the people with whom he surrounded himself. "He made the mistake of isolating himself from the political mainstream," he said. "The White House has become a kind of mythical kingdom ... that simply doesn't belong in a democracy."

The end came for Richard Nixon on August 9, 1974. Four months later, in the *Tampa Times*, Pierpoint admitted his personal dislike of Nixon to reporter Sara Schwieder. "I had a strong personal dislike of the man," he said in response to a question from Schwieder. "Day after day, week after week, I saw him doing things I thought were dishonest, leading the American people down the primrose path."[52] Still, he couldn't help admiring the part of Nixon who, with Henry Kissinger's help, had made "remarkable progress" in dealing with Russia and China. Some might say uncharacteristically, the two presidents he found most similar were Kennedy and Nixon. "While that may seem strange to some," he once said, "they were both very introspective and both were focused on foreign affairs."

The Watergate years were taxing for all who covered them, Pierpoint included. He never included his reporting of Watergate among his proudest moments, citing instead the Kennedy assassination and, somewhat surprisingly, the Johnson administration, the latter mainly because of his coverage of the Vietnam War from the White House steps. Dan Rather, he graciously maintained, "had the biggest impact" among those in the CBS White House Bureau during Watergate. "He had the dramatic flair for making everything perfectly clear that this was a major travesty, a danger to our society and a danger to our way of life and that Watergate was full of crooks."

Nixon's resignation might have been the only time in his reporting career when Robert Pierpoint would not have been minded being wrong. It also marked the second time when a wave of relief came over him for the promise of a new administration, headed by a man who he considered, along with his wife, Betty, to be "two of the nicest people that ever lived in the White House."

The Ford Years

Gerald R. Ford was a popular Republican congressman, who fit the bill in terms of sharing Richard Nixon's conservative beliefs, when he was appointed vice president in the wake of Spiro Agnew's resignation in 1973. Agnew had been Nixon's point man, a surrogate bulldog when the president wanted to attack the press. By contrast, Ford was a genial guy, easy to get along with, someone who reporters liked, despite their opinion that he was ineffectual, first in Congress and then in the Oval Office. Part of that perception was real: in twenty-six years serving in the Congress only one significant piece of legislation had been passed under his sponsorship: the highly unpopular call for the impeachment of Supreme Court justice William O. Douglas.

While he meant well, his first action as president was to make another unpopular move—the pardoning of his predecessor, Richard Nixon. In what Pierpoint called "a memorable speech," Ford declared that the nation's long nightmare of Watergate was over. The attempt to heal the country's wounds was right-minded, thought Pierpoint, but actually resulted in further dividing the nation, "creating a partisan controversy and causing the Republican party even more severe losses than they had expected in the 1974 Congressional elections."[53]

Pierpoint once observed that "personally and politically Ford never aroused much passion from the public." Despite that, he sensed an authenticity in this president that was often lacking in others. "What you saw was what you got," is how he put it in an interview. "People underestimated him. I overheard a conversation between two top Republicans saying Mr. Ford wasn't smart enough to be president. They were wrong." Still, he labeled Ford's presidency as "generally lackluster" and suffering from "the same lack of new ideas that marked his congressional career." His one "big idea," according to Pierpoint, "ended up as a disaster."

It was in response to an epidemic of swine flu that took hold in different parts of the country in 1976. The threat was that it would spread and become increasingly deadly. In response, Ford assembled the White House reporters, telling them a widespread inoculation program using a new vaccine would soon begin. Pierpoint's skepticism kicked in. "Brief reflection reminded me that the target date for completing the inoculations just happened to coincide with the finish of the presidential campaign," he wrote, adding, "It did not seem to me that the timing could be purely coincidental." On his first broadcast, for CBS radio, he pointed out the coincidence. He then got a call from the CBS bureau chief in Atlanta (site of the federal Centers for Disease Control) who relayed that the CDC did not support the inoculation program. While some in the scientific community believed everyone should be inoculated immediately, others, a sizable number, doubted the vaccine's efficacy against swine flu.

That night, on the *CBS Evening News*, Pierpoint did a story saying there were those in the know who had serious doubts about whether the proposed vaccination program was "medically sound" and suggested it "might have been politically motivated." Predictably, the White House was "incensed." Pierpoint received calls from several top aides who accused him of being too cynical. Ultimately, his reporting was vindicated, at least in terms of the drug's safety and efficacy. The vaccine was determined to cause paralysis in some people, which caused millions of Americans to shun the program. It failed.

Pierpoint learned there was one major difference (probably more than one, but in this instance a major one) between Ford and his predecessor. "Although my broadcasts probably had some effect on the public's antivaccine attitudes, neither Ford nor his aides held a grudge. Their reaction was typical of the Gerald Ford White House, reflecting the president's good-natured ability to roll with the political punches." Gradually, while there were some Nixon holdovers, Ford brought in more of his own people, ones who reflected the same attitude. As a result, Pierpoint found that "the Ford White House was a pleasant place to work in." The congenial atmosphere was bolstered, he felt, by a certain quality Ford had that other presidents lacked: "Gerald Ford genuinely liked people, even reporters."

The feeling appears to have been mutual. While the president did occasionally exchange barbs with some members of the White House press corps, for the most part Ford's brief time in the White House was marked by a calm détente between the executive branch and the fifth estate. Outside the White House, an incident occurred during a Ford road trip that reminded Pierpoint of an event over a decade earlier. It was in San Francisco in 1976 and brought back memories of Dallas, Texas, in 1964—right down to the familiar sound of gunshots ringing out.

Ford had been speaking at the St. Francis Hotel and was in the process of leaving for the flight back to Washington. Pierpoint and Bob Schieffer, who by then was also a part of CBS's White House press contingent, were the only two from their network on the trip (normally there would have been three; there's no explanation for why the third correspondent, Phil Jones, did not make the trip). Schieffer was at the local CBS affiliate preparing to do a "cut-in" (also known as an "insert") for the evening news. Pierpoint was hurrying to finish his radio pieces so he could leave to follow the president's motorcade to the airport. Scheduled departure time from the San Francisco airport was 3:30 p.m.

Pierpoint assembled his baggage, typewriter, and so on. As he walked out the hotel's door he could see the motorcade coming around the corner. Just then, he heard a familiar sound. There was a haze of smoke, what he at first thought were exhaust fumes. "Then I noticed an acrid smell," he wrote, well remembered from the Korean War, and heard a woman say 'I think someone shot at the President.'" He saw a San Francisco police officer nearby and asked him if shots had been fired. He replied that they had and added: "I think someone fired at the President." Pierpoint asked if he had been hit. "I don't think so," was the cop's response.

Just then, a bystander, a man Pierpoint described as "chunky, shabbily dressed ... in his thirties," spoke up. He told the officer something had hit him in the stomach. That something turned out to be the .45-caliber bullet fired at the president that had ricocheted off a building. The force hadn't been sufficient to cause the man harm, but the bullet was telling of an assassination attempt. The police officer took the bullet, while another told Pierpoint that authorities had a suspect inside the hotel.

Pierpoint had all he needed at that moment. He ran back into the hotel, hit the press room, and grabbed the nearest telephone. What he didn't have among the facts running through his head was whether President Ford had gotten away uninjured—or even alive. Not wanting to rush to air, he searched for a Secret Service agent or press aide to confirm the president's condition. He found a deputy press secretary and asked if the president was okay. The aide was reluctant to talk, partly because he wasn't certain of all the details, and partially because he wasn't sure what he should say. Pierpoint persisted. "Someone shot the president, I know that," he pressed. "What I want to know is did he get away in the motorcade okay?" The other man nodded. Pierpoint picked up the phone to New York. By now, the other reporters who hadn't left with the motorcade to the airport were hovering around Pierpoint, asking what he knew. He told them: "When I get New York on the phone, you'll hear the story as I broadcast it."

First, he did a bulletin for CBS radio, then, because the incident also happened during the *CBS Evening News* broadcast, Walter Cronkite interviewed him live on TV. The Associated Press put out a bulletin crediting him, saying, "CBS News correspondent Robert Pierpoint had reported that an unknown assailant had fired a shot at President Ford who ... Pierpoint reported ... had escaped unharmed." The suspect arrested was later identified as Sara Jane Moore. Pierpoint, both exhausted and exhilarated, stayed the night and caught a commercial flight back to Washington the following morning.

While demonstrating his highly competitive nature, Pierpoint also displayed his immovable insistence on accuracy. It was a hallmark of his reporting that many of his colleagues say separated him as a journalist from others, Rather among them, they say, who would go with a story before having all the facts pinned down. Fair or not, the perception among those who were closest to Pierpoint at CBS was that he was a stickler for being right before being first. Moreover, this incident, among others, distinguished him in the minds of colleagues as being professional, despite the competitive pressures of network news.

At the time, Westinghouse Broadcasting was a player in terms of providing national news coverage to its string of owned and operated stations. They, like the "big three" (CBS, NBC, and ABC) operated a Washington bureau, where Eric Engberg served as their reporter. He was there that day when the Ford assassination attempt occurred and remembers Pierpoint as being collegial with the others who were around the hotel press room that day—once he got his story on the air. For those who hadn't heard, Pierpoint came back into the room and said "guys, someone just took a shot at the president," recalled Engberg. "People rushed over to Bob and asked him what he knew about this and he said he'd gone down early to get on the bus to go back to the airport and there he heard someone in the crowd yell out 'someone shot the president.' He went over to a person who said 'I have a bullet that bounced up, it hit the ground and bounced up.'"

Engberg remembers it as a moment of "professional camaraderie" that he had seldom seen before—or since. "I've thought back to that incident a lot," he says. "If such an incident had happened today, I can't think of a person who would do that, because of the competitive pressures. Bob represented an age when reporters helped each other. There was a lot more cooperation in those days." He might have added cooperation *and* compassion.

There was the time when Engberg lost his job at Westinghouse, the victim of his employer closing its Washington bureau. It, too, happened during the Ford administration. "We were flying back from wherever Ford had made a speech, on the press plane, maybe 40 minutes from Andrews, when I hear Pierpoint get on the plane's PA system. 'Ladies and Gentlemen, I want to make a brief announcement that travelling with us today is Eric Engberg, a fine reporter, and, because Group W is closing its Washington Bureau, he's going to be out of a job. Let's all wish him well.'" To Engberg, that was Pierpoint's human side.

It was not only what his friends and associates say made him stand apart from others in the same position; it was also what Pierpoint liked the most about Ford as a president: his humanity and humility. Even if he was not the greatest president who ever served, Pierpoint saw him as a good and decent man. As he put it, "despite a faltering and a heavily Democratic electorate, this quality brought him breathtakingly close to defeating Jimmy Carter in 1976." Because he never held himself above others, Pierpoint found the next president he would cover—the last president he *did* cover in his twenty-three-year stint at the White House—as a person whose "self-righteous air" prevented him from becoming as good a president while in office as he became after leaving the office.

The Carter Years

Jimmy Carter had a lot of problems when he came to the White House—at least that's how Robert Pierpoint saw it. "He had a lot of ties to Georgia, was a creature of Georgia politics, didn't have any experience in Washington ... if you make enemies out of Congress during the campaign and after the campaign, you're probably not going to be very successful," he told an interviewer, reflecting back on the Carter years. As an example, Pierpoint cited the first bill that ever came across Carter's desk to sign. It contained funding for thirty different western water projects. Carter studied it and decided none of them should be funded. "He may have been right," said Pierpoint, "but he didn't know western politics. If you want to get into real trouble in the west, veto a water rights bill. He didn't realize that."

The Washington outsider image Carter so carefully crafted during his run for president worked to get him elected; it did not work with the Washington insiders he offended before even setting foot in the White House.[54] It didn't help that, once in office, that "self-righteous air" cited by Pierpoint alienated politicians. One of his first social invitations to a group of Democratic congressmen was to "tea." As one put it to Pierpoint, "He invited us down for four o'clock tea. And you know what he served? Tea!" The image of a good Baptist teetotaler annoyed many on Capitol Hill. It wasn't destined to endear him to the press, either. Remember the bottles of whiskey Pierpoint himself had been instructed by his boss to bring reporters as a peace offering from the new guy? Given his own views about his Baptist upbringing, it couldn't have played well with Pierpoint either.

Still, that was surface and Pierpoint fairly quickly recognized that "Carter's problems ran far deeper." Realizing long-term goals didn't come naturally to a man who "seemed unable to persevere with other politicians well enough ... always moving off abruptly in another direction," Pierpoint saw Carter as someone who was good with slogans—"I will not lie to you" and "America deserves a government as good as its people"—and used them to override the nation's despair over Watergate and the Vietnam War. However, once he acquired power, Carter, thought Pierpoint, didn't know how to use it.[55]

With the Carter years came more changes in the CBS News White House Bureau lineup. Pierpoint, who had been the de facto number-two man to Dan Rather, now faced another new face. Bob Schieffer and Phil Jones both arrived when Ford replaced Nixon; Rather headed to London. Now came Ed Bradley, who knew the Carters from his earlier reporting days, and the CBS brass thought he would bring an inside edge to their White House coverage. Pierpoint told Roger Mudd years later that Bradley was probably right in assuming he occupied the number-two position to Schieffer, with Pierpoint himself now in the third slot. "I don't know that we had a hierarchical arrangement," he told Mudd, "but he was the guy we had to check everything with because we didn't know the Carter people."[56] In any case, Bradley's stay was short—a few months, then back to New York and, ultimately, the chestnut of becoming a *60 Minutes* correspondent.

It was during this time, perhaps because he saw so much indecision by those in power at the White House, that Pierpoint began to tire of the changing faces in CBS's White House ranks. It was also during this period that he told his bosses he was tired of training others who would then surpass him on the job. He even threatened to quit on several occasions, but stuck with the job. Walter Cronkite personally implored him to stay. What

Pierpoint began to see during the Carter years was a tendency for network producers to assume a larger role than ever before, often questioning the judgment of the correspondent covering a story. He experienced this firsthand, he told Mudd, during the earliest days of the Carter administration.

"I was sent down to Plains, Georgia, after Carter was elected," he recalled. "Ed had gone off on vacation. He needed time off. I took over. Rick Kaplan was the producer." Kaplan, who later became Cronkite's producer on the *CBS Evening News*, enjoyed a long career at ABC, and spent time as the president of CNN years later, was someone Pierpoint had never met. Carter held his first press conference. "There I was, sitting down in front," Pierpoint told Mudd, "and I guess I asked a question or two and, as soon as the news conference was over, Rick comes up to me and says, 'Now, here's the way I see the story.'" Pierpoint replied: "Rick, here's the way I see the story. He was kind of taken aback, but he took it graciously. We worked it out."[57]

During this time, Pierpoint, who was well into his fifth decade of life and entering his third decade at CBS News, was tiring of what he began to see as the network slacking off on standards and expenses. In a rarely heard, yet revealing audio tape, he complains that his report has to be redone multiple times due to poor transmission quality. That November, in 1976, he was covering the Carter transition at a southern luncheon, "the main topic: the reorganization of government." Pierpoint experienced difficulty getting the feed of his radio report back to Washington. On the tape, after the report, is heard one side of a conversation with a remote producer asking Pierpoint to redo his report by "trying to get closer to the microphone."

Pierpoint, good-naturedly, balked. "That's the best we can do when they won't have a technician come," he tells the producer on the other end. "You might mention it would help with the quality if the radio people would send a tech." There's a pause. He continues: "I'm serious, though. We're trying to do this on the side and television doesn't do things on the cheap and I don't see why CBS radio should either. They're never going to get quality out of us being our own technicians." It's evidence that radio news was being relegated to a second position to television in the 1970s. It also is indicative of how standards in general were becoming subservient to profit margins. That, plus a lack of accountability, had begun to grate on Pierpoint—a product of the Murrow days when the motto for correspondents was "whatever it takes, do it" and "whatever resource you need, you have it."

If nobody else was going to take a stand, Pierpoint was. "Well, if somebody would just let the top people know that. The trouble is everybody tries to protect all along the line, instead of sending in a bad quality piece and saying 'this is what you're getting.'" He urged the producer to "put in a little note saying ... put it this way, say Pierpoint says the quality would be much better if you send a tech down. Maybe that'll help, but I doubt it," he laughs.[58]

His comments that day were, in some ways, seminal in pointing to how the world of being a White House correspondent was in transition. Part of that transition was the growing differences between radio and television. Some of it signaled important changes going on, not only in Washington politics, but in the politics of broadcast journalism, especially television news, during the Carter years. "In those days, the producers were not quite as strong as they are now and the correspondents were still the guys who decided what the story was," but the balance was shifting toward producers.

In a strange kind of way, the power over his work that Pierpoint was fighting to retain was mirrored in the power he saw the president of the United States progressively losing when dealing with the Congress. Lyndon Johnson certainly had that power and wielded it at will. On the other hand, "Carter's inability to wield the powers of his office was noticeable even before he moved into the White House." It was most apparent to Pierpoint during the time between the 1976 election and the inauguration, that period when the new president was attempting to get his cabinet appointments approved by Congress.

Carter put before Congress the name of Theodore Sorenson, a former JFK aide, to head the CIA. Sorenson had helped him during the campaign. The choice ran afoul of the Select Committee's Democratic chairman, Hawaii's Senator Daniel Inouye. Instead of standing up for his appointee, Carter backed down. When asked by Pierpoint and others if the president-elect would insist upon the Senate approval of Sorenson's appointment, Carter withdrew his name. It caused embarrassment for all involved and caused Pierpoint to speculate on what Lyndon Johnson would have done in the same situation.

For one, Pierpoint concluded, LBJ would have been certain that he had the number of votes in the Senate for his appointee's approval before publicly putting his name forward. Then, if he received resistance, Pierpoint could imagine LBJ picking up the phone and applying pressure—including the not-so-subtle suggestion that certain favors might be withdrawn. In the specific instance of Inouye, the idea that certain military bases in his home state of Hawaii might find a new and finer home in, say, Alaska.[59]

Covering Johnson, Pierpoint had seen this kind of power wielded all the time. "That's the kind of power a President has," he wrote, "and that's the kind Jimmy Carter never understood or never used. For some reason, Carter strongly disliked confrontations." As another example, he pointed out that, in 1979, the president wanted to fire Bella Abzug as his head of the women's advisory panel. He called her to the Oval Office, they sat and talked for quite awhile, and Abzug then left, telling reporters the meeting had gone well, that she and the president had settled their differences. As she was holding the briefing, a minor Carter aide slipped her a note. It said to see Hamilton Jordan, Carter's chief of staff, immediately. When she complied, Jordan told her the president wanted her resignation.

Pierpoint saw his inability to be up front, either with Congress or his own people, as a character flaw in Carter. He was unable to manipulate the former and incapable of candor with the latter. "Jimmy Carter seemed unable or unwilling to play politics with the Congress and, therefore, had serious trouble getting through some of his most important legislation, at least in the form he wanted it in," wrote Pierpoint. Combine that with what Pierpoint saw as a "streak of hostility ... the way his steeley-blue [sic] eyes would transfix questioners with a cold glint when he did not like their questions," and Pierpoint was among several colleagues who began to miss the Ford days. As he had once said of Ford, he was not the greatest of presidents, but "what you saw was what you got"—and he did have experience with the Congress.

Carter gave his press secretary, Jody Powell, more than a few headaches and Powell, in turn, could cause some of his own for reporters. Once, at a Carter rally in Philadelphia during the 1980 primaries, Carter committed a faux pas that caused the White House press corps to dash for their typewriters and telephones. Secretary of State Cyrus Vance had resigned in the wake of objecting to Carter's ill-fated plan to rescue the hostages in Iran. In the midst of a town meeting, where ordinary citizens could ask questions, Carter, as Pierpoint put it, "lashed out at Vance ... most unfairly," shocking reporters. Powell did his best to repair the damage by telling reporters Carter hadn't meant it, but the dam had burst.[60]

Powell spent a fair amount of time doing his own lashing out when a story didn't please him. "We had a lot of run-ins with Jody Powell," Lesley Stahl, now a CBS *60 Minutes* correspondent, said in an interview. Stahl joined the CBS White House bureau in 1979. "I pick up the phone one day and it's Powell. He screamed at me, a raging tirade, venomous and horrible. I didn't want anybody in the newsroom to know I was nearly in tears." The one person in whom she confided was Pierpoint. "The next day I told Pierpoint. He told me about a time when Jody had called him when he was at a dinner party and yelled at him about a story he'd done." Pierpoint told her he handled it this way: "I just held the phone away from my ear and waited until he yelled himself out."[61] Pierpoint's advice was appreciated, especially when dealing with Powell—a man he called both "quick-witted" and "quick-tempered."

In some important ways, Pierpoint saw the people around Carter as the embodiment of the hostility he sensed in Carter himself. In 1980, when Carter sought reelection, Pierpoint carefully watched the incumbent's demeanor in his debate with Republican nominee Ronald Reagan. The polls showed the two running close, making the debate critical for Carter. "That night, the President clearly tried to keep his temper under control," wrote Pierpoint, "which, in this case meant keeping the anger out of his voice, face, and eyes." In Pierpoint's opinion, "he did not quite succeed." Television, the medium that had once sunk Richard Nixon in his debate with JFK, claimed another victim: "Carter shot hard, vindictive looks at his opponent, which the television cameras clearly picked up."[62] Reagan, a master of camera technique, cast a smiling glance in Carter's direction, delivering the now famous line, "There you go again." Pierpoint saw it as a personality contest that Carter had lost.

As a result, voters denied Carter a second term, affirming Reagan in a landslide victory. For Pierpoint, the Reagan win "brought to the White House a new and untested commodity—a former movie actor, an advocate of public-policy positions sometimes regarded as extreme, and a former governor with no foreign-policy experience." At the time, Pierpoint wrote in his own book that "covering the Reagan Administration promises to be anything but dull." It wasn't a statement that would be tested—at least by Pierpoint. Carter was the last president he would cover. In over twenty years at the White House covering six presidents, he had seen many changes. Politics certainly had changed. So had television. But there was always tennis.

5

Back Row: Tennis, Television and Politics

At first glance, the three topics—tennis, television, and politics—might not appear to share a lot in common. In Robert Pierpoint's life, the three had a strong connection, each to the other. For one, the political battles among those who worked at the White House were not limited to presidential aides or appointees. Pierpoint discovered that television, as it evolved, also became a political battleground between correspondents. Tennis, a competitive sport, helped him stay on his game with White House insiders, even if he often was on the back court with CBS management.

To begin with tennis, Pierpoint wasn't alone, though he was among the few, who considered tennis to be a part of his job at the White House. "I have to confess I like it better than golf—which in the Eisenhower era was almost a professional requirement," he once wrote. One thing he had against golf as opposed to tennis was how the former was played at a long distance from telephones. "It was impossible, while on the links, to to keep up with the constant phone calls that plague a network correspondent covering the President," he added. "Being fetched by the club pro in a golf cart, or having to jog all the way back to the clubhouse from far out on the course after someone delivered a message saying I was wanted on the phone, upset everyone playing with me. So I turned to tennis; at least there was always a phone near the tennis court."[1]

A friend, George Ostrom, recalls how he once invited Pierpoint on a fishing trip—fishing being Pierpoint's other great passion—at a time when he hadn't "had a vacation for as long I can't remember." However, Pierpoint called him, saying, "George, I don't think we are going to be able to go fishing together because somebody in New York is trying to call me and they probably want me to go someplace right now." Ostrom's reply: "What if I could get you 30 miles from a telephone?" Proximity to a phone was all the persuasion Pierpoint required. "You're kiddin'," he said, at first. "Oh!, you're not kiddin'. Could we go right now?"[2]

When Nixon moved into the White House, his tennis acumen became a huge boon for Pierpoint. His fellow Californians felt a strong affinity for the game, and so Pierpoint found it "became a good way to maintain contacts." He had played on the White House courts a few times during Kennedy's administration, but Nixon's people—those like press secretary Ronald Ziegler, chief of staff Alexander Haig, secretary of state William Rogers, and H.R. Haldeman—all played tennis. He even became "an occasional partner" to Haldeman in the pre-Watergate years. Even through the Watergate days, he continued playing with Ziegler and Haig. It's one major reason why, as then–bureau chief Ed Fouhy put it, "he developed a lot of sources, even during the Nixon years, when it was difficult to develop sources. He would bring his tennis gear and that helped."

"He was well above the league of most of the people in the White House press corps," Sid Davis says of Pierpoint's tennis skill. Davis, a former Westinghouse White House correspondent who rose to become a vice president at NBC News, knew Pierpoint during the Kennedy years when both covered the events of that fatal day in Dallas. "He was very athletic, very social," Davis said of Pierpoint in an interview. "We were in the Bahamas one night, travelling with Kennedy," he recalled, "and Bob phoned me in my hotel room and said, 'I'm having an asthma attack, would you take me to the hospital?' He would have these periodic coughing spells, but they never kept him from playing tennis." Charles Roberts, a correspondent for *Newsweek* back then, was one of his favorite opponents. "They were fierce competitors," recalled Davis. "I heard you didn't want to play tennis with Bob Pierpoint if you weren't good. He wouldn't play with someone who wasn't as good as him anyway."

Just how important was tennis in the power game of White House politics? An article from the time in *Tennis* magazine recounts how President Ford had to "fire two highly regarded holdovers from the Nixon administration" in order to open up two top jobs on his national security team. It came after the high-level shakeup involving Henry Kissinger (who was downgraded). It also meant Donald Rumsfeld would move to the Pentagon. "At 4:20 p.m. Kissinger left. Why didn't Rumsfeld also leave? Because President Ford likes to unwind after important conferences by playing tennis and he needed Rumsfeld for a fourth at doubles." The article goes on to say, "Some close observers of the White House contend, only half joking, that it was no accident that the two big beneficiaries of that

October 'massacre'—Rumsfeld and Bush—were both tennis players. Ford had played with both of them, one Presidential aide notes, but never with the men he fired. 'Men who play tennis together usually work well together,' the same aide adds, shamelessly adding the old church slogan about people who pray together."[3]

On at least one occasion, his White House tennis routine crossed the line with the news division bosses at CBS. Because so much of the press corps' time was spent either in San Clemente or Key Biscayne covering the president, Pierpoint fell into the habit of attending press briefings wearing a tennis shirt and shorts. If news from the briefing didn't require a television appearance, he, along with his fellow correspondents from the other networks, would simply do a radio spot and then head to the courts without having to change. Two competing correspondents—ABC's Tom Jarriel and NBC's Herb Kaplow—began the practice of bringing a dress shirt, sport coat, and tie to the briefings. They could then, if needed for television, put the top half—the shirt, coat, and tie—on with the tennis shorts on the bottom, out of view of TV viewers. The cameramen were in on the deal and knew never to shoot their correspondents below the waist. It worked well, until one day in 1973.

On a Saturday at Camp David, Pierpoint was doing his job, working on a television piece for that evening's news, and looking ahead to a tennis date immediately following with press secretary Ron Ziegler. In between, he had agreed to have some photos taken for a book about the Washington press corps. Its author, a former newspaperman, had already interviewed Pierpoint. He simply wanted a few pictures to accompany the book's text. Sure, said Pierpoint, forgetting that not all cameramen were aware of the need to keep the shot above the waist. The rest was predictable, though the fuss it caused unforeseen. The writer, "properly," as Pierpoint put it, asked for permission to shoot the photos. Pierpoint agreed and, as he did his on-camera piece for the night's news, the cameras clicked, catching the full body image of Pierpoint, microphone in hand, wearing his jacket, shirt, and tie and ... tennis shorts on the bottom.

"My superiors were far from pleased," wrote Pierpoint, of what has now become perhaps the most famous and lasting photograph of him from those days, "apparently feeling that tennis shorts, a jacket, and tie do not provide a dignified image."[4] Even worse, so far as CBS management was concerned, was the fact that the photo was used on the cover of the book and, later, in newspapers. CBS News vice president Bill Small even demanded that Pierpoint sue both the book's author and its publisher. Pierpoint told his bosses they could sue if they wanted to, but he would not. Small, who considered the photograph "demeaning," also pressed the idea that it had been used illegally, since neither the author nor the publisher gained Pierpoint's permission to publish it (or so he thought). Unknown to his boss, Pierpoint had signed a waiver. He got off easy. Small backed down when confronted with the idea that CBS would have to do the suing. Pierpoint called it "a lucky bluff on my part."[5]

It wasn't the first time, nor would it be the last, that Pierpoint locked horns with network brass. Some of the disputes dealt with journalistic principles. Others dealt, simply, with the direction in which television—always a "cosmetic" business compared to radio—was going. To some extent, by the Kennedy years and, certainly by the Nixon years, Pierpoint found himself becoming one of the old guard, Murrow's boys, relegated to the back row of correspondents. In the front row were the newer, younger, more "telegenic" correspondents, those who looked good on TV and knew how to both appear and sound convincing. The tail end of the 1970s and the entirety of the 1980s became the age of coiffure over substance, delivery over meaning. Dan Rather became the symbol of what CBS wanted, first in a correspondent, and, later, in an anchorman. Affirmative action brought female correspondents, including the very blonde and very attractive Lesley Stahl, to the White House.

Pierpoint, who had once been in first place as CBS's White House correspondent, or at the very least shared that spot with veteran newsman George Herman, saw his fortune drop from number two under Rather, to number three behind Ed Bradley, and, finally, as the backup to Stahl, a woman he helped train and who had none of his contacts or institutional memory—at least not upon arrival. Television, a medium which he had done his best to learn along the way, was never as natural to him as radio. Television was fast becoming not only the dominant medium, but the *only* medium to which Americans turned for news. In addition, it was also becoming ratings driven and more competitive than ever. The competition, always acute between networks, had now turned inside. A pecking order among CBS's correspondents had begun. One could argue it had long existed, dormant beneath the surface, but Pierpoint's current bosses—especially Small—hand selected "his" ideal correspondents, many of them cut from the cloth of Rather, not Murrow.

In a metaphor for the fierce competitor he was on the tennis court, Pierpoint, behind in points, became locked in a battle just to stay in the match. The politics of that battle rivaled anything he had seen going on behind White House doors. Insofar as he felt the American people stood to lose more than he did, the stakes seemed equally high. Though he had covered many politicians, he could never become the politico Rather was—nor did he want to be. And he wasn't the only one. By the Carter administration, the entire definition of what a television news network correspondent is, was, and should be had drastically changed.

Many others found themselves in the same "back row" as Pierpoint, but few had either the tools or the experience to fight back; then again, even fewer carried much of the negative baggage Pierpoint had begun to carry with CBS management. Some of it was personal. Most of it was just business. Journalism, once separate and distinct from the broadcasting business, now *was* the business. CBS news honchos panicked when their perennial "star," Walter Cronkite, was threatened in the ratings by the duo of Huntley-Brinkley at NBC. Their response: create a hierarchy of those who were good on TV and those who weren't.

The "A List"

Call it being in the "back row" or off the "A list." Either way, a de facto caste system emerged in the 1980s which left CBS's correspondents in no doubt as to where they stood with management. Former CBS legal correspondent Fred Graham was there and chronicles the era in his book, *Happy Talk*. According to Graham, in the post–Cronkite era of the *CBS Evening News*, began an emphasis on lighter, frothier stories that were the antithesis of what Pierpoint and his colleagues in Washington produced. "Between 1972, the year when I joined CBS, and 1984, when infotainment was on a roll, the number of stories done by correspondents in Washington was cut almost in half (from 614 stories in 1972 to 349 in 1984)," wrote Graham. The shift in priorities at CBS News had, said Graham, a "corrosive effect," an especially "demoralizing impact on those who had gone to work there to practice journalism."[6]

It came to be known, according to Graham, who was there throughout this period, as "the purge of the old and ugly." That may sound extreme, but Graham's observations are corroborated by many others who worked under then CBS News president Van Gordon Sauter, who oversaw the period between Cronkite and Rather. Much has been written about how "Sauter's tenure at CBS News included one of the most bitterly unhappy periods in that division's history, with many layoffs and a collapse of morale. At one point in the mid–1980's, several of CBS's most prominent correspondents and producers, shocked at the continued decline of CBS News, offered to buy the division away from CBS." Graham saw that "soon after the coming of Sauter, the 'Evening News' picked an 'A list' of correspondents, those favored to appear regularly on its newscast. Those not chosen included such old timers as Bob Pierpoint, Ike Pappas, Marya McLaughlin,

Jim McManus, Robert Schakne, and the dean of the CBS correspondents, George Herman."

Herman had been at the White House, with Pierpoint, throughout the Eisenhower and Kennedy administrations. It never really was clear if either possessed the title "chief White House correspondent," but at the time it doesn't appear to have been an issue. Herman was someone Pierpoint greatly respected and admired. The two had worked together in Korea and, in fact, Pierpoint had succeeded him as Far Eastern Bureau Chief. He once told a fellow Washington colleague he considered Herman to be both a friend and mentor, both in Korea and at the White House. "He took me as an academic and turned me into a reporter," is the way Pierpoint put it.

After the so-called A list was put into place, Herman rarely, if ever, appeared on the *CBS Evening News*. The network gradually tried to occupy him with early morning or late night stakeouts or doing interviews for other correspondents' stories. Herman protested that this was the demoralizing equivalent of being fired without cause; CBS relented, but also assigned him to on-air radio duties or middle-of-the-night TV appearances. This was only the beginning of the hurt Pierpoint would feel, as he saw his valued colleagues and friends sent to the back row of correspondents, not just physically, but politically. It only got worse, Graham insisted, once the transition to Dan Rather on the *Evening News* was complete.

Rather had his own "A list," said Graham, and Pierpoint wasn't on it: "Bob Pierpoint became a victim of double-jeopardy: at fifty-seven years of age he was getting long in the tooth and there was bad blood between Rather and him." The "bad blood," according to many besides Graham, began when the two worked at the White House. Herman and Pierpoint had been CBS's White House correspondents for more than a decade when Rather arrived in 1964. Before and after, Pierpoint had become fed up with what he saw as management tinkering with the White House beat. A big Pierpoint supporter, CBS News president Richard Salant, was replaced by Murrow's once right-hand man Fred Friendly. Pierpoint's impression of Friendly from their brief, earlier relationship in Korea was of a man who was "tough" to deal with. He was reminded of that when he was called in and told more changes were in the offing. He could stay or go, his choice, but change would happen either way.

Pierpoint had endured the triumvirate that now included Rather, but Friendly decided to assign a new face, Harry Reasoner, to the White House. The move was prompted, at least in part, by the anchor team of "Huntley-Brinkley" on NBC overtaking CBS in the evening news ratings. Reasoner was seen as a rising "star" in the CBS news pantheon, a "big name," thought Friendly. Rather, in an interview, said of Reasoner's hiring at the White

House, "It was a shock to Bob." The bigger shock came when Reasoner didn't work out, was reassigned to New York, and back came Rather to White House duty in 1966. Back to number two went Pierpoint.

Graham's story is that Pierpoint "was a solid reporter who had served CBS with distinction in a number of assignments—including the second slot at the White House back in 1966, when CBS put the hard-charging Dan Rather on the beat as number one. Pierpoint let it be known that Rather came on a bit brash, and Rather spread the word that Pierpoint was one of his least favorite people. Fifteen years later, when Pierpoint failed to make the A list, nobody was surprised." Rather's story differs. While not acknowledging the existence of an "A list" at CBS News during his tenure as lead anchor, he will say there were circumstances that disadvantaged people like Pierpoint.

"I think it's true in this sense," says Rather. "He came into electronic journalism when radio was still prime. Television didn't become the dominant thing at CBS News until the late 50's, even the late 60's. Bob was a transition figure, if you will. He was hired by people to do radio, but learned TV." Suggesting that Pierpoint was seen more as a radio guy, Rather's take is that "the people who were running CBS corporate said, 'Look, we have to retool. One of the reasons we think Huntley-Brinkley has overcome us is that they're television people; we're stocked with radio people. We have to find younger people who show talent, or at least promise, to be television correspondents." In other words, Rather attributes the falling fortunes of the Pierpoint era correspondents more to the times than to politics.

Others disagree. "I think Bob's primary problem was Dan Rather," says Phil Jones, in an interview. Jones worked alongside Pierpoint and Bob Schieffer for CBS News at the White House. Jones had come from covering the Ford campaign, Schieffer from the Pentagon. Both were part of a more harmonious cohort of CBS White House correspondents. The coming, going, and then the return of Rather continued the problem. "He had become an expert on the White House beat and, all of a sudden, they bring in Dan Rather," observes Jones. "He didn't go public with his unhappiness with being number two to Dan, but he expressed it within the CBS ranks. Dan didn't feel the vibe that Bob Pierpoint was on his side. That's hard to do when you have someone who's number one, number two, number three. It's body language, especially in that small space you work in every day."[7]

Pierpoint was "a very careful and very thoughtful person," according to current CBS White House correspondent Bill Plant. "That put him in conflict with people higher up than him and with some of his associates, with people like Mr. Rather." They were two very different kinds of reporters, said Plant. Rather "was willing to take a flyer on a story, go out on a limb; he was more of a cowboy." In contrast, "Bob did everything by the book. There were people, probably including Rather, who thought his standards were too rigorous," Plant concluded.[8]

Lesley Stahl, who joined the CBS White House brigade after Jones and before Plant, felt it too. "He was number two to Dan Rather and I never knew whether he was more upset with the bosses or Rather.... When I was assigned, I did know he was very upset at being number two again, especially to me, someone who was very inexperienced." Similar to Rather, she saw the decisions being made more for the sake of television than journalism. "I think it was unfortunately more what our bosses came to see as what was successful on television, whether it was good looks or a deep voice."

The two views may not be entirely incompatible. While viewers may not (and ought not) to detect the politics of network television news on-air, politics exist, as in any organization. In this instance, Pierpoint and his colleagues from the Murrow era may have fallen prey to them, but the changing landscape of the television medium also most certainly played a role. Phil Jones likened his friend Bob Pierpoint's on-screen presence to that of another journalistic icon, Eric Sevareid: "Bob was a little more formal, more straightforward, and in his presence standing before the camera. I think some of the management thought he was a little stiff on-camera." The technique he mastered to prevent looking down at his script—the aforementioned taped recorded words replayed in his ear as he spoke—was a boost and a bane. "It was terrific for eye contact," says Jones, "but probably didn't serve Bob well for his overall on-camera appearance. It made him look stiffer, because he was listening to himself."

Sid Davis, one of Pierpoint's friends, who also worked for a compet-

CBS News White House correspondent from 1957 to 1980, Pierpoint, seen here in the 1970s, was among the older guard of correspondents who fell out of favor with management toward the end of his career. The result was a transfer assignment to the State Department and then to the magazine program *Sunday Morning*.

ing network, saw Rather as the major transitional figure in a new movement at CBS News, where "the culture was kill for a story. You were under tremendous pressure. They were tough taskmasters." It was a different kind of pressure and spawned a different breed of correspondent. "The glamour really came in from Texas," said Davis, ostensibly referring to Rather. "The older correspondents were World War II vets; they'd been in Normandy and the Far East. They'd had their baptism by fire and they weren't afraid of anything." By contrast, Davis believes television stressed the "cosmetic" over the experience. "You gotta have that look. You gotta have that voice. Pierpoint didn't have 'balls on his shoulder,'" a reference to the stereotypical deep-voiced correspondent.

Rather is also correct in pointing out that Pierpoint himself was a "transitional figure," in the sense that the business of television news had transitioned not only from radio to television, but from public service to profit. Pierpoint was, understandably, not on board with the decisions being made, but especially the motives behind those decisions. "This was difficult for Bob," says Rather. "He'd been hired by Ed Murrow. He was by any measure a distinguished CBS news correspondent, outside of an anchor position the most prestigious position in network news." Today, Rather rejects the idea that Pierpoint was relegated to the "back row" of correspondents at CBS. "He never considered himself a back-rower. I never considered him a back-rower. The longer I knew him, the more I respected him," Rather says.

Respect was a commodity, along with friendship, that Robert Pierpoint never lacked. That's probably why, when he finally had enough of CBS's political game, he did something characteristic of his life and career. He spoke up. This time, though, was one of the rare occasions when he did so publicly. It had the impact of a lion's roar. At first, it was heard in the corporate offices of CBS as more of a low growl, the kind that comes just before an imminent attack.

Fighting Back

By 1980, Robert Pierpoint was a man barely hanging on to his White House post. His sources remained intact—by all accounts he still had more sources than anyone in the job or who ever held the job—but he still was mired in the third spot behind Schieffer and Stahl. When the top CBS execs, principally Fred Friendly, initially told him of Rather's return, he was asked what he wanted to do: did he want to stay at the White House or be reassigned? Pierpoint responded that he wanted to stay. At the time, he didn't know that the steady parade of changing faces would continue to the end of his White House days. With the Ford administration came Schieffer and Jones, then, in the last two years of the Carter administration, Lesley Stahl.

While Cronkite was in the CBS anchor chair, Pierpoint had an ally, which meant his stories continued to make the evening news—the most coveted spot of the broadcast day. "Walter liked me for my ancillary stories," he recalled in one of his last interviews.[9] In particular he cited the Bebe Rebozo banking scandal reports. He also made air on weekends when Roger Mudd was on the anchor desk. The coming of Bill Small, seen as "Rather's guy," Rather's ascension to the anchor desk, and the advent of the "A list" (and a subsequent "A+ list") for correspondents all led Pierpoint to more radio and less television air time.

At one point he was ready to hang it up, leave CBS, retire. He told Sandy Socolov, then White House bureau chief and a friend from days in Tokyo, that he wanted out. He told Socolov, who told Cronkite, who phoned him almost immediately. In the interview with Roger Mudd years later, he recalled Cronkite saying "Bob, we need you to stay at the White House and train Lesley. I think she's going to be okay, but we'd rather have you there." Pierpoint told the venerable Cronkite: "Walter, I've had it. I've done this for so many years, and I just don't want to train somebody else to be a White House correspondent." He felt he had already trained too many people and Stahl—nothing personal—was the last straw. Cronkite offered a pay raise, at least 40 percent, and with kids in college, Pierpoint thought that "was pretty darn good." By all accounts, his included, the Stahl relationship worked out well. "She didn't know where the Ladies Room was, but she's a hard worker and she did very well and I enjoyed it, actually, working with her," he told Mudd.

The money didn't buy Pierpoint's silence, however. The inner turmoil at CBS News attracted the attention of the *Washington Journalism Review* (now the *American Journalism Review*) whose reporters smelled a story. They made phone calls and no one on the inside would talk, for fear of retribution. One reporter reached Pierpoint, who, not surprisingly, opened up. He was quoted as saying that CBS was committing a blunder by pushing aside the experience of their older correspondents for a younger, more TV-friendly staff. He told the *Journalism Review*: "WE are being shoved aside and we hope that the quality of CBS News is not being shoved aside with us."[10]

Those who worked with and around him say the fact that Pierpoint could survive having what many in the top echelons of CBS management no doubt took as an attack on their judgment is testimony to his value at the network. Even in the changing days of TV news domination, those who ran the network were savvy enough to realize everyone on the air in one of their most visible positions couldn't be new to Pennsylvania Avenue. As his fellow White House correspondent during the Ford years, Phil Jones, assessed the situation: "He was never really in danger of being taken out of the White House, I don't think. His value as a correspondent to the CBS presence was registered in high places, even though he was doing radio primarily at this time. I don't think the management, although they had become uncomfortable with him, ever thought of taking him completely out of the White House."

In fact, Robert Pierpoint's days as a White House correspondent were near an end in 1980. The time had come for a move, after 23 years on a single beat, tenure unheard of in the annals of modern broadcast journalism. His next assignment took him not so very far from the White House: five minutes and under two miles away. There, too, he would follow in a strong tradition of journalists and utilize many of the sources he carefully cultivated over his career. It may not have been his favorite move, but, by most estimations, it led to some of his finest days.

Moving Forward

Toward the close of 1966, when Dan Rather was brought back to the White House and Harry Reasoner went back to New York, Rather became CBS's chief White House correspondent. It was in the middle of LBJ's elected term. Even Rather was surprised that, when given a choice to stay or go by Bill Small, during Small's tenure as bureau chief, Pierpoint stayed. "How much could a man take," was how Rather put it an interview, but added: "Bob was not a complainer. Bob was a doer. He was a very forward thinking person." What Rather didn't know at the time was that Pierpoint was already negotiating to leave the White House beat on his own terms. It wasn't by any means a surrender; whether at tennis or network politics, friends and former colleagues maintain Bob Pierpoint didn't know the meaning of the word "surrender."

Because he believed strongly in the role of the White House correspondent as a conduit of information and knowledge in a democratic society, Pierpoint recognized his diminished role wasn't serving either journalism or democracy. Plus there was this: a producer on the *Evening News* had been candid with him, saying of the relationship between Pierpoint and the management, "They are down on you because you have said things that have caused this company problems." He was reportedly told that, in his current role at the White House, he would no longer get on the *Evening News*, so long as another correspondent could do the story.[11]

Since he'd covered politics for so long, Pierpoint knew politics when he saw it, in or out of the White House. His friend Sandy Socolow, Cronkite's producer, had a potential solution. Two well-respected network correspondents, brothers Bernard and Marvin Kalb, who had covered the U.S. State Department for decades between them at CBS were now moving to NBC. Socolow asked Pierpoint how he would feel about moving over to the State Department. Pierpoint thought, "That's good." He had covered the State Department on and off early in his career, in fact just before being assigned to the White House and, as he put it, he "knew the routine." It turned out to be a good move. For one, "it was a hell of a lot easier," Pierpoint told his colleague Roger Mudd. For another, he "didn't realize how tired I was at the White House assignment until I got to the State Department."

The timing was also fortuitous. It was at the same time Edmund Muskie because Secretary of State. Muskie was a friend whom he knew very well. When Reagan replaced Muskie with Al Haig, Pierpoint was again in a good position. He knew Haig well because the two had played tennis during the Nixon years, everywhere from Hong Kong to the White House. When Haig resigned and was replaced by George Schultz, Pierpoint had another great moment. He found his way back to the *CBS Evening News*. Rather, having succeeded Cronkite as its anchor by this point, interviewed Pierpoint on the broadcast on the reasons why Haig left the Secretary of State's post. Pierpoint's take was that Haig had gotten a bad image due to his "take charge" attitude. Rather, Pierpoint told Roger Mudd, "had his own theory and it didn't square with mine and from then on I couldn't get on the Evening News." Again.

It was unfortunate on a number of levels. First, a major void was left when the Kalb brothers stopped covering State for NBC. Second, Rather himself had acknowledged Pierpoint's experience as "an advantage" in covering Washington. Ed Fouhy, Pierpoint's former White House bureau chief, their ties going back to the Korean days, was one among many who thought the Pierpoint reassignment to the State Department was a great move. "I was delighted," says Fouhy, "he was doing it. Marvin Kalb had left for NBC and left that a huge void, one that Bob filled ably and with distinction."

Despite that, Pierpoint's insistence on standards once again haunted him. By now, he was critical of what television news was becoming, not out front, but behind the scenes. He disparaged the shorter length of pieces on the *Evening News* and the infiltration of entertainment values in the guise of news. "Pierpoint was always conscious of standards," said current

CBS White House correspondent Bill Plant. "He stood up for them. That, too, got him in trouble toward the end of his career at CBS." As a result, his State Department years from 1980 to 1990 were interspersed, beginning in 1984, with reporting for a Sunday morning news program that, at the time, was not highly regarded by CBS management. "He was assigned," said Plant, "to *CBS Sunday Morning*, instead of reporting for the *Evening News*." It was a kind of news Siberia. "If you were reduced to being on there, it would be seen on the inside as being sent into exile," was Plant's recollection.

When the *CBS Sunday Morning* assignment hit, Pierpoint must have felt like he was being banished to a kind of elephant's graveyard. He no doubt expected to be surrounded by dead or dying correspondents. "I have a vague memory," said Lesley Stahl, "that he really didn't think he'd enjoy it, but I think he was surprised that he did." Mary Silverman, a close family friend, concurs. "When the pieces on the evening news became so short, that's when he realized how much he enjoyed *Sunday Morning*. He got to do longer pieces on subjects that interested him." They involved travel, often to his favorite parts of America, including Montana, Yellowstone, and Yosemite. He could engage his passions, doing feature stories on fishing, his second biggest love, next to his family and tennis. The only time Silverman recalls Pierpoint being uncomfortable was when he had to do a story on Charles Kuralt, the legendary CBS newsman (and host of *Sunday Morning*) when it was disclosed he had another wife and family (in addition to his known wife and children). "That was really amazing to him," said Silverman, "and it hurt him to have to report it."

In 1990, the direction in which television news kept moving—away from public service journalism toward what he saw as profit-driven drivel—plus his own "outsider" status with CBS, made Pierpoint think that maybe it was time to go. In the phone interview with Roger Mudd, he called it "a relatively easy departure." In the last year of his reporting at *Sunday Morning*, he was called in by a CBS executive and asked if he wanted to retire. "What I knew because I'd been part of the deliberations between the union and CBS was that if they fired me I'd get a $130,000 bonus, whereas if I quit voluntarily I didn't get that." Not sure, said Pierpoint, saying he'd think about it. He was still pretty able to do the job and might stick around awhile. Finally, the executive offered the $130,000 bonus if Pierpoint would retire. "I said, bingo," recalled Pierpoint. "If I get the bonus, I'll retire, and I did."

Interestingly, he never really did. In so-called retirement, he continued to write and to speak, both at colleges and universities and on cruise ships, where the CBS cachet helped keep passengers rapt with attention. One

Sharing a light moment with legendary CBS news correspondent Charles Kuralt in the control room of *CBS Sunday Morning* in the 1980s. Kuralt was the original anchor of the show, once considered in CBS circles as "news Siberia." Pierpoint once told a friend that one of the most difficult stories to do was the one for *Sunday Morning* on the discovery, after Kuralt's death, that he had two separate wives and families, neither of whom knew about the other.

thing he didn't do was hang around Washington. Instead, he headed back to California. There were those among his inner circle who say he missed the White House beat, the proximity to power, the social life that accompanied both. Author Myra MacPherson, a close Pierpoint friend, believed "he missed it." She says he would call and talk about the news, which was one of his "rituals." There were parties when Pierpoint returned to town, occasionally, a reminder of the old days. But he would get restless, never wanting to stay.

Instead, he and Pat lived in Southern California during most of the retirement years, also keeping a vacation home in Montana, just a few miles west of Yellowstone National Park. There, they caught up with friends they knew and had maintained, from their earlier lives together in California and in Washington, D.C., and in Maryland—in addition to many he knew primarily from his years in Stockholm and the Far East. Former colleagues like James McManus say he was steadfast in his desire never to look back at his CBS career. As late as 1997, McManus e-mailed Pierpoint, proposing that he (McManus) set up a website and invite old "comrades" from the

White House press corps to join an on-line colloquy on journalism, politics, foreign policy, and so on.

"Bob immediately said he would not join," recalled McManus. "I remember clearly that he said he was more than seventy years old and he would rather not return to news-driven writing—even as an unpaid volunteer without deadlines. And, to underline his idea of keeping busy in retirement, Bob invited me to come west for a visit and enjoy the good fishing near his place." All of this McManus took as characteristic of a man who had put down the pen in favor of the (fishing) rod. "It seemed clear to me that he had put his career and his excellent work behind him."

That synchs with the way his White House colleague Phil Jones remembers Pierpoint left the Washington limelight and with what he told Jones about retirement. "He said, 'Phil, when you retire, get out of Washington. Get out of it because for 25 years you've been in the middle of it and you retire and you're going to wake up in the morning and no longer be a part of it. That's going to drive you nuts.'" Jones said it was good advice. "As I look around at the former correspondents who stuck around Washington, I think that's true. They get very frustrated." His words inspired Jones to come up with his own mantra for retirement: "If I leave with my hide and my pride, I've won." By that standard alone, Robert Pierpoint had won.

6

After the White House: Casting a Critical Eye

In many ways, his long career in broadcast journalism—four decades—provided a voice to the once asthmatic boy whose youthful survival mandated quiet and solitude. It's not surprising that, while he didn't find it difficult to give up the "job" of network correspondent, he would never surrender that "voice." Robert Pierpoint, after 1990, was able to spend more time engaged in activities he had pursued his entire working life: writing and speaking. He would present lectures on college and university campuses, including his alma matter, the University of Redlands. Of course, while he was a working CBS News correspondent, there were certain constraints placed upon what he could and could not say publicly. Despite that, on numerous occasions, he would speak openly—and even critically—about politics, religion, and business.

Even before his retirement, Pierpoint would take on controversial topics in public forums, risking the ire of his bosses. In 1963, he approached the topics of religion and civil rights head-on during an alumni address at the University of Redlands. Titled "Civil Rights, the John Birch Society, and the Christian College," his speech ran the risk of offending many within earshot and those farther away in CBS's New York corporate offices. "I work in a profession where public speech is a way of life," he began. "Yes, it is a frustrating way of life for those like myself who have strong opinions and would like to express them in public." He went on to say it wasn't his job to broadcast his own personal judgments on the day's news, though he told his audience they should have no doubt that he possessed "admittedly strong views."[1]

That was just the warm-up. Next came a gentle remonstration of his employers at CBS, one so gentle that its real meaning could almost be lost. "This is not necessarily a complaint against the networks or the Columbia Broadcasting System, which employs me," he said. "The owners of CBS long since ruled that news correspondents are to express their beliefs from the facts, and to avoid personal opinion ... editorializing, if you will. Within the industry there is continual heated discussion among those who favor allowing editorial opinion to be broadcast versus those who advocate dedication to that other, elusive goal: objectivity." It is clear from what comes next that Pierpoint had his own doubts about the plausibility, if not the possibility, of true objectivity.

His mentor, Edward R. Murrow, once famously eschewed objectivity in situations where social justice compelled a single side to a story. In Murrow's instance, it was the death camps at Auschwitz. Having seen and experienced the stench of death firsthand, Murrow pronounced the idea of reporting both sides to a story like the Holocaust, which true objectivity requires, inane. It's likely that, as in many other ways, Pierpoint picked his battles over social issues in forums outside the confines of CBS—most often in small places, speaking to small audiences, usually at colleges or universities. If the idea was that their words would remain confined within the walls of academe, both Pierpoint *and* Murrow were very mistaken.

Murrow, too, had once delivered a speech in Birmingham, Alabama, during the time of the Korean War. Deciding that he could no longer support the war, he told his audience that U.S. involvement in Korea was a mistake. "If we decide, as we did three years ago, that Europe is our primary interest, and that, militarily, Korea is of no strategic importance, then there is no reason why we should not pull out of Korea lock, stock, and barrel," he said. Murrow had never spoken out against the war, either on his evening news broadcast or *See It Now*. The fact he did so reverberated beyond the lecture hall, into the *Birmingham News*, and then onward to other media outlets nationwide. CBS was not pleased. On the other hand, as one Murrow biographer put it, "platforms like that in Birmingham offered an opportunity for him to get off his chest—as an individual—what he did not feel was appropriate for a CBS correspondent."[2] The Birmingham speech would come back to haunt Murrow and is seen by many scholars as the start of a decline in his corporate value to the network.

Pierpoint's strong social conscience, firmly implanted during the Stockholm years and those spent in what he saw as a more egalitarian society in Asia during his bureau chief days, led him to take on topics outside the realm of his daily reporting duties. One was the responsibility he believed journalists had to take a stand against oppression of various groups in American society. His speech that same evening in Redlands was the beginning of a long journey in which he, like Murrow, would point out that some actions are so blatantly wrong that they must be criticized by those privileged to have a public voice.

That's exactly what he did when it came to what Pierpoint saw as the growing influence of right-wing groups like the John Birch Society on American education. In that first of many speeches he would present at his alma mater, Pierpoint coupled the group's influence with what he termed "a deep crisis in the field of race relations." Pierpoint called it "a crisis completely of our own making" and one "in which we are being forced to live up to principles which we have all thought and claimed we believe in ... religious principles, moral principles, constitutional principles." Despite all the "reasoned talk and fine speeches" and the promise of a better life for "Negroes" in America, Pierpoint saw the pace of change as proceeding too slowly. One of the great social revolutions of our time, he told his rapt audience, could lead to bloodshed.

At the same time, the John Birch Society, said Pierpoint, was adding to the racial, social, and economic division in American society. He saw their political agenda as a "puzzling, evil influence." John Birch Society followers, he asserted, "practice their political arts in private ... secrecy and fear and intimidation are their weapons." His greatest concern was how groups like the John Birch Society branded as communists those with whom they disagreed. The idea that such a group could secretly infiltrate both the American political and educational systems Pierpoint found abhorrent.

He certainly knew this was not the customary role expected of a network television news correspondent, nor was it probably what many in the audience expected to hear that evening. Pierpoint showed again how he could stick to the facts in public, and still nurture his own views in private (while his speech was in a public forum, the University of Redlands is a private institution). When doing so, he often took on topics he believed to be of compelling social importance. Often they dealt, as did the Redlands speech, with race or inequality. Sometimes they directly confronted religion, as in a 1997 commencement address at Sonoma State University.

Pierpoint told the assembled graduates he didn't expect they would be friends by the end of his talk, but that journalists shouldn't be in a popularity contest. He extolled the virtues of the First Amendment. "A free press has responsibilities," he said. "It must keep the public informed, and it must do so with both accuracy and fairness. It must do so even when the public does not care, even when the public does not wish to be informed or does not like the information." In a quote from Ed Murrow, he said the ultimate role of journalism was to "make 'em itch," — "them" meaning those in power who wielded their power with arrogance.

At this point, whether it made them itch, his speech certainly rubbed many in the audience the wrong way. He discussed what he called the "increasing danger to our freedoms from the religious zealots of the right." He went on to criticize the motives of a judge who wanted to begin jury deliberations with a Christian prayer as what he called "another recent example of the pernicious influence of religious zeal." Pierpoint maintained there was nothing wrong with a private belief in religious principles, but told his audience those beliefs had no place being displayed or required in a government office or a judge's chambers. He also expressed disapproval of prayer in public schools. That raised the ire of many, leading to letters to the editor of the local paper, the *Press-Democrat*.

"I had heard from a person who attended the Sonoma State graduation ceremonies that Robert Pierpoint's speech was an anti–Christian diatribe," read one letter. "His last summary paragraph shows he has no idea of the role religion has played in making America great."[3] Another reader wrote: "There is a special irony in the comments by Robert Pierpoint and his almost vitriolic attack against Christians. He accuses them of attempting to deny him free speech, while using a platform from which the liberal left has fought to prohibit any use of prayer or the mere mention of Christ."[4] Another wrote: "If Mr. Pierpoint is disturbed by the display of the Ten Commandments in a judge's quarters in Alabama, how then does he live with the display of these same commandments on the wall of the Supreme Court's own chamber? The use of official prayer at the opening of each session of the Supreme Court, Congress, and the first Continental Congress must cause him extreme discomfort."[5]

In fact, institutionalized religion did cause Pierpoint a great deal of discomfort. As a strong believer at an early age in social justice, he was constantly disappointed that religion didn't, in his view, help correct the social and economic inequalities in American society. As a reporter, day in and day out, he covered those in Washington who fought for equal rights and lamented that so many others uncritically followed the more passive path of organized religion. It wasn't any one religion, just religion in general. Even while he felt it was his responsibility to bring his kids to church in Washington, he still argued with ministers. On one occasion, he went head to head with a Unitarian minister, recalls his son Eric. "What do you know that could change my mind?" is how Eric remembers his father putting the question to the clergyman. Whatever answer he received didn't change his mind. "In terms of the religious thing, he pretty much jettisoned it out of his bones," recalled his son. Eric Pierpoint was with his dad at the end of life and had this discussion: "He said to me, no ministers, no references to God. This is the way I want it."

His views on religion, mercifully from a career perspective, seldom made their way into his journalism, save the 1973 commentary on the Middle East discussed in Chapter 3. It, together with the two speeches above, were his sole public pronouncements on how religion's place was outside of politics—a view common today in most settings, but one which prompted vitriolic responses from those who saw Pierpoint as a godless man whose opinions were forged outside the realm of mainstream America at that time. For Pierpoint, this must have been satisfying on a number of levels. First, it fulfilled what he saw as the role of journalism: making people think, forcing them to challenge their beliefs and assumptions. Second, he loved a good fight.

It's important to point out that Pierpoint, whatever his beliefs and politics, spent much of his time after the White House not simply speaking about social issues, but actively engaged in effecting change. This was especially true in Bodega Bay, the community where he and Pat settled in 1999. Neighbors in what has been termed an "exclusive" subdivision were pushing for a ban on vacation rentals. They were tired of hot tub parties at 2 a.m. and trespassers on their golf course and pushed an amendment to the rules, which would prevent new home buyers from renting out their homes. "We would like it a little calmer," is how one Bodega Bay resident put it in a local newspaper article.[6] Pierpoint, on the other hand, was out to raise hell—again. As with his dissension on organized religion, he was trying to make a point. "If you take away people's right to rent, you're taking away property rights," he told a reporter. He added that he supported homeowners who rent out their houses part time until they can afford to move in full time. "It makes for diverse community," he said. "I don't want to live in a community of all wealthy old people."

And there was the time the Pierpoint kids recall their dad opposing the rules at a private country club in Bethesda, Maryland, near their Washington home. The Kenwood Club, at the time, refused to admit blacks or those of Jewish faith. A committee of like-minded members banded with Pierpoint to petition for a change in the rules. "There were protesters in front of the entrance. I went and stood with them," recalls Pierpoint's son Eric. "They had picket signs. Dad was always bringing tennis buddies to the club. When this slap in the face happened, he went on the warpath."[7]

The group eventually hired an attorney to research the matter and advise them. In order to implement the legal solution brokered, Pierpoint convinced Carl Rowan, a friend and fellow journalist who was African American, to join him on the tennis court the following Sunday. "I am pleased to report that on the Sunday morning when Carl appeared at the tennis courts, every one of the players shook his hand and made him welcome," he wrote long after the issue was resolved. "A few days later, I and the family resigned from the Kenwood Country Club. We recognized that a majority of the members resented our actions, and we would no longer be comfortable there."[8] Given that the club had become such a large part of their social lives,that could not have been easy.

Being a contrarian sometimes wasn't easy either, but it was a role Robert Pierpoint came to embrace with poise and dignity—a voice far from Washington that still had the power to stir the consciences of others, his former colleagues at CBS and the other networks included.

Biting the Hand

An emergent pattern throughout his public and private writings shows Robert Pierpoint's strong disappointment in what he saw journalism—broadcast journalism in particular—becoming. Again, his views had a good deal to do with how he remembered Murrow taking on the industry's power brokers in general and those at CBS in particular. He often criticized the industry in which he had spent a lifetime. His strong opinions were never stifled during his White House years, but they became much more frequent and vehement upon retirement. For the most part, Pierpoint became increasingly disillusioned by the ownership of broadcast networks—CBS, especially, but really all the networks, with the possible exception of the then fledgling CNN.

Even after his time actively covering the news ended, friends say that, at first, he never missed watching the *CBS Evening News*. Family friend and fellow journalist Myra MacPherson recalls how it was one of his rituals, a way in which he took measure of the day's passing. "No matter where he was or who he was talking to, Bob had to watch the news every night," she says. "There was a rigidity to his daily life. Every night he would say to Pat, 'Let's have a drink,' and then put on the news." Those same friends, when they would talk by phone or see each other in person, saw that desire to watch the nightly news diminish to the point where he would no longer watch at all.

It didn't happen overnight. In a 1974 speech Pierpoint gave at Oregon's Linn-Benton Community College, he told the young audience that "only the top of the news is covered in broadcasting," adding that "it's deplorable, a shame if people get all the news they think they need to know from watching just the evening news on television." In particular, he assailed the networks' reluctance to fund investigative reporting, a genre of broadcast news that had brought him and Ed Fouhy one of his two Emmy Awards. "Investigative reporting takes a lot of time and manpower," Pierpoint said. "Are news organizations willing to put the necessary manpower into it?" he asked, then answered his own question: "I'm not convinced they are."[9]

During a question-and-answer period following another speech a year earlier, in 1973, Pierpoint had foreshadowed this same dissatisfaction with how investigative reporting was being neglected. "I'll tell you very frankly, and this gets into the complexities of the profession I'm in, that investigative reporting is a very tough thing in TV. For one thing, it's very tough to tell a story with documents and so many stories deal with people who don't want their names used or their pictures shown on television," he said. "In broadcasting, every hour you spend on investigative reporting is an hour that keeps you off the air that night." His own Emmy winning story on the Rebozo banking scandal took ten months to investigate and complete— and his absence on-air had the potential to rile his bosses. "The company gives you a pat on the back and then says, 'Gee, we haven't seen you in the past ten months. Where have you been?'"[10]

Over the next 25 years, Robert Pierpoint's concerns over what he saw as the deterioration of television news continued to multiply. They reached new heights in 1998, during the much-referenced interview broadcast on KRCB-TV, a California public television station. Over two nights, Pierpoint took on the powers-that-be in a conversation that compared today's television network owners to their predecessors. By comparison to the years during which legendary CBS chairman William Paley ran the network, Pierpoint found CBS News a "pale shadow" of its former self. It was the shift from family to corporate ownership, one Pierpoint saw as typified by an emphasis on profits over people. "We went through a period of CBS where we were sold from the family that essentially controlled CBS news, to an ownership headed by Tisch," said Pierpoint, referring to CBS CEO Laurence Tisch, who ruled the network from 1986 to 1995.

Pierpoint deplored the changes brought to the network once referred to as the "Tiffany" of television news. As a Wall Street investor and billionaire, Tisch, Pierpoint believed, thought of news as just another commodity, to be traded at a profit. "Tisch cut back on expenses. CBS entertainment had always paid the costs for CBS News," he told an interviewer. "Tisch considered that the news division didn't pay its own way," and so, cut costs. "Quality was cut because we didn't get the ratings. Instead of telling the public what we thought they should know, the standard became telling the public what they want to hear." The result was more "soft" news, leading Pierpoint to say of CBS News that "generally speaking, it isn't on top anymore."

Asked about the strengths and weaknesses of how television and other media cover the news, Pierpoint replied that "about half of it now is infotainment ... the better newspapers are going to last, but I'll tell you what I believe is happening ... I think the Internet is replacing both television and radio." In a very prescient comment given the time in which he made it, Pierpoint made the prediction that "perhaps in ten years from now, more people will get their news from the Internet than from radio or television." Son Eric Pierpoint confirmed that, in his final years, his father really lived his prediction, turning to the Internet for his own daily news: "He liked it because it was quick; he could research things."

Another part of the problem in network television news, as Pierpoint saw it in 1998, was the closing of news bureaus around the globe. CBS, in particular, had cut its number of foreign bureaus to three. That caused Pierpoint to extol the virtues of CNN, which had expanded its international coverage, along with its number of bureaus in other countries. "Rightly so, they scoop the other networks," he told the PBS interviewer. "CNN is probably the preeminent news organization in this country." When watching broadcast networks in his later years, it was ABC or NBC, not CBS, though, he told the interviewer, "it hurts me to say that."

"A lot of the frustration Dad had was over budgets," said his oldest son, Alan. "It wasn't just the content of the news, though that certainly bothered him, but the lack of money spent on coverage." He often would tell his adult children that "we don't have the two or three gatekeepers we used to have who helped pick what was important for the audience to see and hear." With all the news sources we had then and the even greater number we have now, Alan says his father didn't believe the public was being any better served. Again, Alan Pierpoint confirms that the man who had been, throughout most of his a career, a company man "wouldn't watch CBS because he was disgusted with the depths to which TV news had sunk."

In another prescient remark made by Pierpoint during the PBS interview, he pointed out the danger in having correspondents replaced by those who only do commentaries and analysis. Recall that was around the time that FOX News Channel and others developed a roster of those who, in the words of one such commentator, "opined" on the news, rather than reporting it. Some of them were also employed by the noncable broadcast networks; he pointed out George Stephanopoulos on ABC and any number of military affairs or national security "experts" who took over the role network correspondents once occupied. "News anchors now very seldom give you anything other than very bland opinion ... you almost never hear anything worth listening to in any way," he said. "They don't want to take the chance of offending anybody on any given subject," which he called "an unfortunate attitude." His conclusion: "The networks are afraid of losing even a few viewers."

Asked if he thought we would ever see the likes of an Edward R. Murrow again, Pierpoint's response was characteristically direct, addressing the question as much from the perspective of the medium as the man. "I don't think that television is ever again going to rise to the heights that radio did during World War II with Murrow and his boys," he replied, adding, "I'm not sure television has ever reached the height that radio did during World War II. Television has never been quite that good." The reason: "Television has almost always been too concerned with ratings."

The ratings race was one more example of where Pierpoint, in retirement, couldn't hold his tongue. "He would speak his mind without filtering it," said daughter Kim Pierpoint. The filtering often fell to his wife Pat. Over the two evenings he was interviewed in 1998 on that PBS station, Pat Pierpoint was at home, awaiting his return. There was no filtering. His former bosses, if told, were no doubt initially pleased to hear him say that so many Americans still received most of what they knew about national and international affairs from the nightly newscasts. His caveat could not have pleased them at all. "The only problem is they're not getting as much information," he said, suggesting the networks had abdicated their principal duty to inform. Pierpoint viewed the fragmentation of the audience into so many channels and sources as actually diminishing the skilled and experienced journalist's role at a time when it is more important than ever.

He had an ally in former CBS colleague Roger Mudd, whose opinions on the deteriorating state of television news mirrored Pierpoint's. "I sort of resent the way the three networks regard news, the way they have taken this precious commodity the nation needs to stay informed and don't use it to tell people what they need to know," said Mudd, who also ran afoul of network politics, first during his CBS stay and later at NBC. "The competition, the deregulation of television back with Carter and Reagan ... now the audience has gone somewhere else, to cable, computers, and all of that." Mudd called it "fighting a commercial mentality on the one hand, and a disinterested audience on the other."

"It was a different age," is how current CBS White House correspondent Bill Plant put it when asked about the "then and now" of TV news. "There were only two news cycles a day and television was very important in helping the White House set an agenda." The White House, he said, could also exert a measure of control over a correspondent's message. "That meant that, in both instances, news in 1971 was what we said it was." Now, he points out that the message is not limited to television, radio, or any other medium. "People have access to much of the same information correspondents do via newswires, etc. on the Internet." He agrees with the premise that the new technology makes the role of a White House correspondent, in many ways, even more important now than in Pierpoint's day. "The responsibility is even greater," said Plant, "when you have to be the one accurate voice in the middle of the muddle of voices available."

That was precisely the point of Pierpoint's outspoken criticism of his own medium. It was not merely a longing for "the good old days," but a concerted, thoughtful reminder that standards are important, that journalism without standards isn't journalism at all. The duality of the increased availability of news is that it doesn't necessarily mean Americans *receive* more news. Pierpoint and his colleagues at the networks had become accustomed to being held accountable for the news they reported—and basked in the societal importance of that role. "We all felt a great sense of accountability for anything that went on the air," is how former CBS correspondent Phil Jones put it. That Pierpoint saw as the antithesis of the journalism he saw on network television in the late 1990s and into the 21st century.

There's little evidence that his sometimes barbed criticism of the medium in which he worked was held against him by management. However, there is at least one instance where the increased conglomeration of media outlets worked against Pierpoint. He was trying to get an article published on one his favorite topics aside from politics. The timing was not fortuitous. It came in 1977, during the height of Watergate. Pierpoint submitted an article to *Field and Stream* on the topic of his greatest pastime (other than tennis): trout fishing. The editor, Jack Samson, wrote an apology telling him that, though the magazine had bought the piece, they had ultimately decided not to run it. "Two things kept us from running that piece, even though we bought it: Your references to Nixon and his trips would not have contributed to the well-being of a hell of a lot our readers during the ensuing Watergate hassle; so we held-off to see what would happen. What happened, again obviously, didn't make any references to Tricky Dicky any more palatable. We didn't want to edit your copy too much so that nobody knew what you did for a living."

A second reason was given: "While *Field and Stream* is owned by CBS, we try to refrain from reminding our readers of the fact as much as possible—even though our ownership is printed at the bottom of the contents page. CBS-TV News (documentary) did an atrocious documentary a couple of years ago called 'The Guns of Autumn,' of which I am sure you have heard. It so infuriated every sportsman in the country (and cost CBS about a million bucks in lost advertising revenue) that they literally boycotted *Field and Stream* advertisers and we lost a bundle of subscribers and newsstand buyers. We have been trying to forget that damned documentary ever since. So you will understand my reluctance to run a story by a CBS newsman—even though I know you are pure and unsullied, as are all good wire service TV newsmen."[11]

The fact that an editor would admit to being cowed by fear of an another advertiser boycott must have made Pierpoint's blood boil. If so, he didn't show it when writing back. While "disappointed," Pierpoint wrote on July 8, 1977, that "I understand the situation. Having been a reporter for lo these many years I had forgotten that sports reporting is really entertainment and hints of anything serious might be an intrusion."[12] There's no subsequent reaction recorded from the magazine's editor; the criticism could not have been well received.

The *Field and Stream* incident illustrates another area where Pierpoint focused his energies, both while actively working at CBS News and, afterward, in his retirement. He used the pulpit he had as a network correspondent to point out the kinds of conflicts of interest he had experienced as an employee of a media corporation that owns other media entities. It was just one area where Robert Pierpoint saw a growing gap between power and responsibility, influence and ethics. Some of his proudest moments came, not on television, but offscreen, writing and speaking what he believed to be the truth about the job that to him had never been a job at all; instead, he saw being a journalist as privilege and was annoyed by others who didn't see it that way.

Ethics and Journalism

Anyone who knew Robert Pierpoint will tell you he didn't criticize just to criticize. His sometimes harsh appraisals of the journalism profession always had a point. As much as any journalist of his generation or since, he had a strong ethical orientation—and he was disturbed, at times, when others around him didn't share an appreciation for the power at their fingertips. He became increasingly conflicted over the delicate balance between press freedom and accountability.

In the College of William and Mary alumni magazine, Pierpoint published "A Defense of the Fouth Estate," adapted from an address he delivered in March of 1979 at the annual banquet of the Society for Collegiate Journalists.[13] "During and after the Watergate scandal, the press has enjoyed a revival in public esteem," he writes. "Thanks in large part to those two outstanding reporters from the *Washington Post*, Bob Woodward and Carl Bernstein, journalism has again become an acceptable, even popular craft. But one wonders how long this sudden surge of respectability will last.

Unfortunately, the unresolved ethical issues of journalism allow us to complicate our own problems with the public. One of those is the troubling issue of privacy."

He goes on to ask, "How much of what a reporter may learn in the pursuit of his duties does the public have a right to know?" He refers to Woodward and Bernstein's book, *The Final Days*, in which they "mention two incidents I personally believe would have gone better—at present—unreported. One sentence deals with Mrs. Nixon's confidential talks with her doctor about her relations with her husband, and the other reveals a bit about her private drinking. Some critics raise objections to other facets of what is—in my view—overall a remarkable and valuable contribution to history. But those two small disclosures do bother me."

It has been addressed previously that Pierpoint was hardly alone among the Washington press corps in knowing about the sexual indiscretions of another president—Kennedy. This presented, in many ways, the ultimate ethical dilemma for him as a reporter. Pierpoint, as we've seen, liked Kennedy and respected his efforts at change—though he thought LBJ was better at actualizing that change. Still, he was aware that the issue of "privacy" in this particular instance—the steady parade of mistresses through the White House—was especially "troubling." It was a tendency in JFK which Pierpoint had experienced—and written about—as early as 1962.

On that occasion, he and an Associated Press reporter were among those covering the president on a Palm Springs trip. They were the only two to witness the following: JFK with a woman on his arm who was not Jackie Kennedy, getting into the back seat of the presidential limousine and just then, the light inside the car went out. Just before it did, the two reporters were able to distinguish "a brief glimpse of his young friend just before she disappeared into the president's arms." Later, when the two emerged from the limo's back seat, the president's sister, pulling up alongside in her car, shouted, "Come on, Mildred." They then observed the young woman "disengaging herself from the president of the United States."

As Pierpoint reflected later, "Mildred posed an immediate problem." He was the pool reporter on this trip and had to decide "whether or not to include this incident in the report I would file for all other correspondents to use in their own stories." It was an unenviable position in which to be placed. "As far as I knew," he wrote, "nothing like that had ever been reported about the president, and to do so seemed to invade his privacy. On the other hand, Kennedy had made little effort to conceal his activity ... and I felt that perhaps I should pass the account on to my colleagues and let each of them decide what to do." Enter the age of modern politics and the ever watchful eye of the news media—television especially. It would become a timeless ethical dilemma, one debated to this day. On this occasion, Pierpoint reported nothing about Mildred, although he wrote in 1981 that "I might report a similar incident were I to witness it today."[14]

The issue still bothered him years later. In a 1982 interview with Sheldon Stern of the JFK Library, he responded to a question about JFK's marital infidelity this way: "Okay, I knew about some of his sexual endeavors outside of his marriage, and I didn't report it." He continued: "And now it isn't really much news to anybody." He told Stern the issue wasn't one of reliable information. "I had eyewitness information, so it didn't have to be second-hand.... I didn't feel tht was a kind of story that I would report.... I don't think that's pertinent to his presidency." On the other hand, Kennedy had never boasted publicly about his own morality and admonished others for their lack of moral character. Another president, Jimmy Carter, would have led to a different decision. He said that if he discovered Carter was having an affair, he would consider it a "much tougher call" because Carter had "made a national issue out of his morals…I'm not sure but that I would have reported that because he, himself, made such a standard out of his morals and ethical conduct."[15]

Pierpoint was constantly concerned about the potential for ethical problems to arise from cozy relationships between those in power and the press. "A very difficult ethical question is just how close to sources of information and objects of his news coverage should—and can afford to—get." He recognized that "at some point, it is impossible to determine exactly when or how public officials may become friends to be protected rather than covered." It was especially an ethical minefield for Pierpoint, who, as noted, often played tennis with White House power brokers and numbered people like Warren Christopher, who served as Deputy Attorney General in the Johnston administration and Deputy Secretary of State during the Carter White House, as friends. The Pierpoint children remember Christopher as always being close to their dad. "They played tennis a lot," says oldest son Alan. "He was a sort of presence in our lives, even if we seldom saw him."

Christopher, whose friendship with Pierpoint is well documented, wasn't alone in that category of being social with the man who might be called upon to cover him. As stated, he played vigorously on the tennis courts with most White House press secretaries, as well as high ranking aides like H.R. Haldeman. Myra MacPherson, the Pulitzer Prize–winning journalist who counted herself among Pierpoint's nonpolitical friends, says she once asked him about the conflict of interest in playing tennis with those he covered. "Myra," he told her, "you have to be social with these people because you get more from them this way." Still, Pierpoint recognized that "lines are difficult to draw."

In *At the White House,* he wrote that "the adversary relationship is necessary and proper during the give-and-take of press briefings, but does this mean the Press Secretary and the correspondent must keep at arm's length at all other times?" He also asks, "what about the President himself? How much camaraderie should a president permit himself with the press corps?" Pierpoint recognized it wasn't a new problem. "This problem has plagued White House correspondents, dating at least from the times when Harry Truman strolled into the Press Room for a few rounds of poker. The reporters couldn't turn Truman away, any more than today they can resist an invitation to a White House function. We never know when the president may drop some nugget of news."

As pointed out earlier, Pierpoint was exceptionally savvy—some might use the word *sly*—when integrating his working life with his social side. The parties with the family on home turf were as much a form of "work" as being in the White House briefing room. That was especially so for a man who didn't observe, as one of his former producers put it, "banking hours." It was all work. He knew it and expected those on the other side of his coverage to recognize that the "lines," though difficult to draw, were always there. Colleagues and friends say that a press secretary—even a president—who took Pierpoint for granted after a social invitation or a tennis match would soon realize their mistake. Pierpoint's questions could become interrogations in a camera's flash. Any semblance of friendship would evaporate amid the journalist's need to ferret out dishonesty.

No doubt it was one reason Pierpoint became incensed by the idea that all reporters, when put in a given situation, would behave in exactly the same way. In an early draft of the 1979 speech, to college journalists at the College of William and Mary, Pierpoint wrote of Spiro Agnew, someone who "liked to imply that this similarity of viewpoint constitutes some kind of conspiracy ... as if a group of journalists daily gather in a basement somewhere in NY to decide such issues as whether the war in Vietnam is a mistake and should be ended or Richard Nixon is a crook and should be run out of office." This monolithic view of journalists as uniformly following the same marching orders seemed, to Pierpoint, both naïve and ridiculous: "That is today as ridiculous as when Agnew first made the charge ... but, it is true that when competent journalists are given the same general facts they will usually come to the same general conclusion, just as most competent doctors, given the same symptoms, will usually come to the same diagnosis of the ailment."

Television news, especially, presented ethical issues for Pierpoint. He was constantly aware that in journalism at the time there existed a sort of caste of respectability based upon whether one was a print or wire service reporter or worked in broadcast. He saw the distinction as coming from a failure to recognize important differences between those who toiled in local television news and those who, like Pierpoint, worked at the highest echelons of the profession. "My experience has been that the closer one gets as a broadcast journalist to the centers of national power, the less one is judged as a broadcaster and the more as a journalist. Most top national news broadcasters closely resemble in knowledge, responsibility, interest, and outlook their colleagues in the written media."[16]

Beyond public respectability, television's power to influence a story—for better or worse—was a concern Pierpoint had dating all the way back to his earliest days reporting in Korea. "He was very concerned about the potential of television to be a manipulated medium," says his son Alan. His concern wasn't just that television could *be* manipulated by others—politicians, principally—but also that journalists could engage in self-manipulation of the images audiences see. Recall that Pierpoint had his start, like all those who signed on with Murrow either during or after World War II, in radio. His first taste of television, ironically, came at the request of Fred Friendly, Murrow's producer, and the bequest of Murrow himself.

It was a story that Pierpoint had inadvertently done for radio while a stringer (see Chapter 2). He had spent the evening with Fox Company in the trenches and his spring-motor-operated tape recorder (which required cranking every seven or eight minutes to keep it running). During an incoming artillery attack, he ducked for cover but left the recorder on. What was captured captivated both Friendly and Murrow. Thinking he was a failure because "anyone could hear how nervous I had been even before that short round had gone off, and how badly shaken I was afterward," Pierpoint still sent it off to Tokyo for shipment to CBS. He knew that Murrow, who had been in Korea himself only on three occasions and only for short stays, was looking for any kind of tape he could find for the radio broadcast he and Friendly pioneered called *Hear It Now*. His estimation was right. A few days later he received "a warm congratulatory cable from them thanking me for my report, which they had featured as a young war correspondent enduring his baptism by fire." Friendly and Murrow focused on the "drama" of the situation. So began, for Pierpoint, the ethical question, again still discussed to this day, surrounding the role of dramatic material in factual news reports.

Murrow and Friendly asked Pierpoint to "repeat my performance with Fox Company—but this time with a television film crew." The idea was to recreate the drama of the original scene, but with pictures. As documented in Chapter 2, Pierpoint raised objections—it was nighttime, no light, and the original position of Fox Company had shifted away from the frontlines—all to no avail. The crew shot foot after foot of film depicting the soldiers in the field, firing their weapons, all of it in cinema vérité style, stressing the visceral, visual experience of the battlefield. It was, for its time, what a CBS News president would demand of all evening news stories—a "moment" viewers would remember and talk about long after the story ended. Though he had misgivings at the time, the young Pierpoint was getting another kind of "baptism"—one in how television, as another journalist once put it, aimed for the heart, not the head.

To accommodate the new medium, Pierpoint fudged at least one aspect of the story. "I never actually *said* we were on the front line, but it looked real." He asked Murrow and Friendly to make clear that the story did not take place near any actual combat, "but somehow the visual drama blurred that point." He had what he called "the dubious success" of being on the very first broadcast of *See It Now*, and became "a temporary hero to Murrow and Friendly." For a time he blamed Friendly for putting him in the position of crossing an ethical line; however, "on fuller reflection, he knew that Murrow had seen the film, had worked on the script, and had final control over the program." It was the first, though not the only time Pierpoint would be let down by his role model. As one Murrow biographer put it, "Pierpoint, as a young, idealistic journalist to whom Murrow was a demigod, was disappointed."[17]

He was never "quite comfortable" with the idea that his first success in television simultaneously involved an initial failure in ethics. "I had learned a valuable lesson," he wrote. "To cover the same stories as did radio, television, in certain circumstances, lent itself to staging." He recognized that the newer medium had to distinguish itself from radio and one important way was through the use of pictures. The visual image was on its way to primacy. Radio had been the medium of World War II. Once Americans got a taste of not simply hearing, but *seeing* the war, there was no turning back. Radio continued its dominance of CBS airwaves throughout the Korean War, but its status within the broadcasting industry was destined to decline.

It was an unleashed monster that would consume its parent, radio. Murrow, Pierpoint, and all of this generation were about to learn that nothing would stand in television's path to media domination. It was "a far more viscous substance than print or radio," is how one observer put it. Pierpoint began to see, as did Murrow, that "the television camera was not neutral, that it did not simply record, but intruded upon, even provoked behavior." When redoing the Fox Company story, he had many willing accomplices.

The soldiers themselves, lured by the fleeting fame television promised, did everything possible to please the lens, as a Murrow biographer put it: "Since the virus of television had also begun to infect the GIs, they happily fired off their weapons for the *See It Now* cameras."[18]

It's ironic that the same man—Murrow—who stood for so many principles of sound, ethical journalistic practice, was also the man who could approve the use of what we would today call a "dramatization" in the guise of reporting. As television's power and influence grew, so grew Murrow's concerns about the medium, culminating in his famous speech before broadcasters at the Radio Television News Directors Association in 1954. Sparked by the cancellation of *See It Now* due to sponsor pressures and low viewership, Murrow again used an off-air forum to speak his mind. The problem this time was that he was speaking to the very people who controlled the air upon which his career breathed. While few knew his intentions, he told the assembled broadcasters they had lost their way in search of profits and pleasing the audience. In words that resonate to this day, he criticized the networks for profit pandering and said of television: "This instrument can teach, it can illuminate; yes, and it can even inspire. But it can only do so to the extent that humans are determined to use it to those ends. Otherwise, it is merely wires and lights in a box."

The words hit hard, no less so when they relayed the problems of radio—"that most satisfying and rewarding instrument." He spoke of a time when radio was "proud, alert, and fast." Radio had already begun to shrink its newscasts to five minutes. When Murrow asked a network executive why the newscasts had shrunk to so little time, he was told that it was because that was the most amount of time it was possible to sell. "If radio news is to be regarded as a commodity, only acceptable when saleable, then I don't care what you call it," said Murrow, "I say it isn't news."[19]

In so many ways, the fate of the medium in which Pierpoint and others (Murrow included) had cut their teeth reflected the fate of its finest practitioners. As television "took over" (a variation of a phrase Pierpoint used as a chapter title in *At the White House*), stories that didn't have pictures, that lacked visual impact, were relegated to radio, along with the reporters who told them. As one account of the history of CBS News put it, correspondents became separated into those who were "good broadcasters" and those who were "good reporters." It was deemed better to be a "good broadcaster," meaning that, on a number of levels, you were good at television.

As TV news progressed (some from that time would say regressed), Pierpoint and others saw their fortunes dwindle in proportion to the need for pictures in every story—even if those pictures were hardly representative or, worse still, totally unrepresentative of the facts. As Roger Mudd, one who fit the mold of "good reporter," put it, this dependence on pictures was another factor in relegating some correspondents to lower class status. "The only time I can remember the rule, the dependence on pictures, was lifted, was during Watergate, when you didn't have to have pictures to tell the story," says Mudd. "As a viewer, you were looking at correspondents telling the story. Producers had to bite the bullet. They had to say 'just put him on camera.' The pictures rule went right out the window. Nobody was any the worse off for it."

Recognizing television's addiction to pictures, politicians became increasingly adept at planning, indeed "staging" events for the networks' cameras. Pierpoint was aware, as all White House correspondents at the time had to have been, that speeches were timed, photo opportunities were created, and stories devised to capture the new medium's power in delivering the broadest audience possible. Eisenhower began it early, by devoting "increasing time and attention to this new medium," as Pierpoint put it in his memoir. Kennedy exhibited what Pierpoint called "a perceptible favoritism toward television," even over the print giants. Through his press secretary, Pierre Salinger, he created special opportunities for the TV networks, adorning their stories with strong and pleasing visuals. The most obvious example was Jacqueline Kennedy's 1962 televised tour of the White House. It represented, referring back to Murrow's nobler use of the medium, an opportunity to teach, illuminate, maybe even inspire.

Pierpoint had nothing against television, although, like those who came from the radio generation, it might not have been his choice to migrate to the newer medium. On the other hand, he recognized its potential to do great good by better informing the public. The ethical issue for him, as for many, became how far does a journalist go to get great pictures for his story? Does he "buy" them? Does he exchange favors for them? In the absence of any strong visuals, does he "create" them or ignore the story altogether? He saw the use (or misuse) of visual images as presenting a continuum of ethical problems for journalists. His thinking, in part, was a product of then CBS News president Richard Salant, perhaps the only CBS News executive for whom he ever had a modicum of respect. Salant headed CBS News twice (1961–1964 and 1966–1979). He reigned during the Cronkite era and decreed that the evening news would not fall prey simply to placating the audience with visuals devoid of information.

Salant wasn't a journalist; far from it, he was a lawyer by education. When he was made president of CBS News by CEO Frank Stanton in 1961, his rise saw an elevation in standards. He more than tripled the budget of CBS News, more than doubled the employee count, and expanded the evening newscast under Cronkite from 15 to 30 minutes. Beyond that, as one historian put it, "Dick Salant's contribution to CBS News that was defining itself in the unfolding television age was something infinitely more valuable: He gave it character."[20] Part and parcel of Salant's leadership was a philosophy with which Pierpoint agreed and a management style under which he prospered. Salant's aim was to make the CBS Evening News the broadcast of record—the television equivalent of the *New York Times*. That meant pictures were important but subservient to content, and the entertainment values that Pierpoint feared encroaching upon television news were kept at bay. Salant put it this way in a memo: "It is my strong feeling that our news judgments must turn on the professional judgments that we can come to on what is important, rather than what is merely interesting."

That one phrase, stressing important over interesting, was pivotal in terms of separating what CBS did as a news organization compared to what its parent company did in the realm of entertainment. "To be merely interesting" was the "lowly aim of the rest of television, of prime, where it is entirely proper to give most of the people what most of them want most of the time." He told his staff that, instead, "we in broadcast journalism cannot, should not, and will not base our judgments on what we think the viewers and listeners are most interested in." That must have been music to Robert Pierpoint's ears. Whatever ethical problems he was beginning to detect in the spillover of entertainment values to television news were resolved ... for the moment.

As evidence, on the night in 1977 when Elvis Presley died, the CBS Evening News was alone among the three networks in not leading with the story. Instead, Cronkite led the newscast that night with a Watergate story. There was no 30 or 60 minute "instant" special on the rock star's life and death that night. The nation's future won out over an entertainer's fortune. In fact, during Salant's reign, most nights the Cronkite news was dominated by what Pierpoint and those of his generation would think of as "real" news. One night in particular, all but one story on the evening news came from Washington, the only exception a Watergate story that, for some reason, was based in New York. It was Cronkite's power itself—an old traditional wire service guy who picked stories based upon what the wires considered important that day, rather than what would drive ratings—that helped keep what some within CBS considered the barbarians outside the gates. Salant was his ally. Pierpoint was a part of it, but so were others who would later be shunted aside—Sevareid, Moyers, Herman, names that defined the tradition some younger voices within CBS News saw as upholding a boring style of television that was fast becoming outdated.

Pierpoint didn't see it as a "new" versus "old," a "gray beard" versus "barely of age to shave" dichotomy within the ranks. He did see that using criteria like "having good pictures," being a "good-looking correspondent," or creating an interesting story instead of finding the interest in a good story created ethical issues beyond an "A" or "B" list of correspondents. Under Salant's time at CBS, it must have been easy to believe, as Pierpoint perhaps hoped to, that people like he and his colleagues would be "safe" from obsolescence. Instead, as we saw in the last chapter, changes on the horizon would move into place a form of TV news that persists to this day, stressing style over substance, compelling visuals over cogent reporting. The politics of CBS from the 1970s to the 1990s have been well explored and documented here earlier, and in many other places; the impact on Pierpoint, specifically, was a near overnight revision in the values he and others had learned at the knee of Murrow. It came in the form of a man who had more experience in sports broadcasting than news. His name: Van Gordon Sauter.

The intent is not to put Sauter at the center of a movement that singlehandedly destroyed the medium of television news, but he was, with or without intent, a player in its decline from what it had been at CBS—a proud resource founded on the backs of Murrow and his "boys"—to another holding in the portfolio of a huge corporation. To Pierpoint, the ethical issue became what happens to the role related responsibility of journalism when the primary goal is to make money. Much has been written about Sauter, but his primary place in *this* discussion is that he brought to CBS News in 1986 the entertainment values Pierpoint so deplored in television news. The so-called doctrine of moments, to which all CBS News employees—correspondents, especially—were expected to adhere preached that stories were to look, sound, and, at all times, *be* interesting to the audience: the very antithesis of the Salant philosophy. Every story was required to have a "moment"—a line, a picture, a person, whatever it took to evoke emotion in the audience.[21]

Pierpoint had been born into journalism in a different age, bred by a different sire, and baptized in the ways of war—a war involving life and death, not ratings. He had been, within the correspondent ranks of CBS, a sort of VIP, invited to the yearly "roundups that Murrow himself would hold for those in his circle at his New York apartment. It always took place between the Christmas and New Year holidays and involved poker and drinking. Murrow, an inveterate smoker and a strong drinker, would hold court. "When Ed spoke, everyone else was silent," said then CBS correspondent Marvin Kalb. Correspondents tested their story ideas on Murrow, not on focus groups, and, if Murrow agreed it was a good idea, everyone bought into it. There was no research, no audience testing, just the belief in a good story's worth.

"He could put away a third of a bottle of scotch while we sat and talked," recalled Pierpoint to Murrow biographer Joseph Persico. Pierpoint could never recall Murrow getting drunk, not in the falling-down sense, but sometimes his speech would become slurred. As the night went on, Murrow would listen less and less and "pontificated more when he drank." Still, Pierpoint would not have minded. A.M. Sperber, who interviewed Pierpoint numerous times for his Murrow biography, characterized the relationship between Murrow and Pierpoint as "easy." Pierpoint had been "one of the charmed circle, the kid from Southern California who had begun in broadcasting stringing as a student, which was enough for Murrow." Their connection to each other was "relaxed, big-brotherly."

Alas, the relationship turned in the early 1960s, when Murrow became too much of an itch for CBS executives to scratch. Instead, they did what executives sometimes do to solve a personnel problem: they kicked him upstairs. He became a quasi–news manager himself, a role he deplored because it took him out of the field and, for all intents and purposes, out of front-line journalism. Sponsors, affiliates, and the changing times for television all led up to the fateful day in 1961 when Ed Murrow left CBS, an institution where he said in his farewell speech his heart would always be, for a job in the U.S. government, specifically the Kennedy administration. In failing health and with a broken spirit, he phoned his then colleague at CBS, Howard K. Smith. "That boy has offered me a job," he said to the other newsman. "That boy" was Kennedy. The job was chief of the U.S. Information Agency, known in most quarters at the time as the U.S.'s propaganda arm. USIA was a foray out of news and into what journalists might charitably call public relations. Smith, who had heard rumors that Kennedy was going to offer the job to Murrow, told him he should take it. Never mind, he said, about the idea that Murrow might have to eat a lot of his own words said about Kennedy. CBS brass also urged him to take the job, all the way up to chairman and CEO William Paley.[22]

The appointment had a strong and lasting impact upon Pierpoint because his next meeting with Murrow presented as large an ethical challenge as the one in Korea years before. It took place in Washington. Pierpoint went to see Murrow about a source who told him the U.S. was using chemical defoliants in Vietnam and causing harm to human life. The source, known to Pierpoint (and Murrow) from a story he once did for *See It Now*, slipped Pierpoint an envelope containing highly confidential reports. The source, he reminded Murrow, was a marine captain who had gotten in great trouble back in Korea for appearing on television criticizing military brass. All he wanted this time, the source told Pierpoint, was for Murrow to read the report and give his reaction. Murrow said he would.

After a few days passed, Pierpoint got a call from Murrow, asking him to come by his Pennsylvania Avenue office. When he arrived, Murrow had a very different demeanor from in the past. He told his protégé, Pierpoint, that he'd read the report and was opposed to any warfare that wiped out people's food supplies, especially innocent people. The source hoped Murrow and then Assistant U.S. Secretary of State Averell Harriman would back him. Murrow declined. Pierpoint decided to let it go, figuring he'd return the envelope, having done what he'd promised. In retrospect, Pierpoint told Murrow biographer A.M. Sperber in 1986, he always had regrets, feeling he hadn't acted ethically. "I never did a story on it until much later, when the defoliation came out and I knew much more about it. I probably should have done a story at the time."[23]

Pierpoint fought a number of inner battles, beginning with the turmoil caused by seeing the news division he helped build disintegrate before his eyes, at the same time he saw his mentor, the great Edward R. Murrow, dissolve into a government bureaucrat. The first was a battle he could not win, at least not on CBS soil. His knowledge, experience, and expertise all gave him judgment, but his stories were castigated and rejected outright as "boring." Part of it was the new mandate that all stories—even those coming from Washington that dealt with policy matters—had to feature not a correspondent relaying what he knew but a so-called real person emoting about the impact the story had on him and his loved ones. For example, in telling a story on a proposed farm aid bill, it was no longer allowable to stand in front of the White House and inform the audience about what it contained, how it would help, its deficiencies, and setbacks. In the Sauter age, correspondents were told to head to the heartland to talk with a farmer and get his views, however representative or biased, and present them as "truth."

Pierpoint would have found ethical issues with doing so, on many levels. First, who's to say that the farmer, however sympathetic to the audience, is representative of those in his position? Even if so, what assurances does the audience have that he really understands what the bill is about? Even then, is he for or against based upon its merits or simply as a result of his own self-interests? These are all questions that began to turn reporting into an ethical quagmire for Pierpoint. If he were going to be doing feature stories anyway, if that was the only way he could get on the air, then he figured *Sunday Morning* was the place to do it. And so he did, as his last assignment. In the process, he helped build respect and cachet for a news program that had begun to gain a loyal and intelligent audience at the same time the luster of the *CBS Evening News* was tarnishing. Cronkite's departure hadn't helped, but neither had Rather's ascension to the anchor desk and the division it brought among CBS's cadre of correspondents.

Pierpoint, no doubt thankful on some levels, was out of the fray. He reported stories from places he loved for an audience that still cared about journalism, as did Pierpont himself. A speech he gave at the Montana School of Journalism illustrates how he never lost all optimism. Even in the midst of his battles with CBS for airtime at the White House, Pierpoint found reasons to be hopeful about the state of journalism. Both the world and television news were in the midst of tumultuous change in the 1970s, but Pierpont engaged in what he called "an impassioned, opinionated, and thoroughly subjective defense of that American institution known collectively as the press." He also talked with his audience about an "almost instinctive fear of reporters" by politicians and suggested "that some of this bad image is due to the fact that we are doing a good job."

He was aware that there were an increasing number of journalists for whom the craft of journalism was laced with bias—the very existence of which Pierpoint conceived as an ethical breach. Referring to reporters who "use the needle as a professional instrument even more than the pencil," he suggested "for them, the needle may work, but it has not helped the image of the profession." Continuing, he writes, "I believe in objective reporting. I disbelieve in subjective reporting. There are writers today, printed particularly in the underground and so-called avant-garde journals, who make no pretense at objectivity. In fact, some scorn it, as their work shows." In a passage that long predates the current debate surrounding a definition of "journalist," he concluded:

> They are, of course, not reporters. Their efforts are not to inform but to propagandize—not to make people think, so much as to make people run in the direction the writer points. It is true, as these advocates of causes claim, that there is no perfect objectivity. It is true that the very selection of the facts to include in a story is a subjective process and much so the interpretation of those facts. But that does not excuse the reporter from the burden of fairness in presenting his story. Any reporter worthy of the title must attempt to get as many of the pertinent facts as possible and arrange them in as fair a manner as he can. His interpretation may not necessarily align with the facts, but that is up to the audience to judge.[24]

That same audience, Pierpoint believed, often deserved better than they got from television news. Those of the Murrow generation saw journalism as a public trust. As the 1970s rolled into the 1980s, Pierpoint saw an increasing trend toward betraying that trust by presenting "a story that will look like news, even if it is not." Coupled with that was the establishment of a "star system" at the White House—one that began with Rather, but continued throughout his final days with CBS. "At times network executives even seem to use the White House as a casting couch for correspondents," he wrote in 1981. "It is hard to tell just how people destined for anchor positions and stardom are selected." He was critical of the trend, but not cynical enough to suggest ability was completely ignored. "Importance is obviously placed on writing ability, knowledge, dedication, and other basic journalistic skills," he wrote in *At the White House*. "But much has to do with appearance. A television newscaster must *look* intelligent and authoritative, as well as sound that way." The cosmetic side of television news was at full throttle: "It helps a male television broadcaster to be handsome and to dress well, and a female to be pretty and to master the art of coordinating makeup and clothes."

Was this an ethical issue for Pierpoint? Perhaps, but only to the extent he feared cosmetics would win over substance. Actualizing Richard Salant's worst fears, this new emphasis on visual attractiveness veered toward giving the audience something interesting to look at, as opposed to something important to think about. "In December of 1979, for example, CBS, NBC, and ABC each had a pretty blond woman covering the White House. They are all very competent reporters, but their attractiveness is hardly a coincidence." In a moment of great self-awareness, he wrote that "while the standards of appearance may not be so high for the networks' male White House correspondents (I freely admit that I was not kept on the job for my figure or handsome face), I know of at least one excellent reporter who was removed from his White House assignment because a network executive did not like his looks." That was *one* male reporter. Pierpoint couldn't count the number of female reporters who never made it as far as the White House because their looks didn't capture the attention of network news executives.

While Robert Pierpoint was raised during the so-called Golden Age of broadcast news, it was only "golden" for some—white males. As former CBS news correspondent Deborah Potter once put it to an all-white male panel at a journalism conference: "It wasn't a golden age for me, because I wasn't there." Pierpoint was a product of the exclusive "boys' club" of TV news, especially where the White House was concerned. Remove UPI's Helen Thomas (and that's not to diminish her importance or impact) and the White House press corps was, for decades, testosterone laden. When women made strides into the "club," it must have been on some levels difficult for Pierpoint to embrace. On others, however, he saw their entrance as good for journalism. After first proclaiming that women covering the president have "added both beauty and dignity to our group," he suggested that journalism would be the better for it.[25]

It must have been a difficult transition to make—not just for Pierpoint, but for all those men, mostly white, who had the White House as their sole domain for so many years. As a father who raised two self-proclaimed "feminist" daughters, however, he could not have objected. To do so would have been to cross his own ethical principles. Beyond that, he would have had to face Kim and Marta, not to mention Pat Pierpoint. Ultimately, their opinion came to matter more than that of any transitory corporate executive. Whether the opinion of others in his work sphere mattered or not, Robert Pierpoint—though not always happily or willingly—passed on a legacy to many of the most influential people in television news today, both male *and* female.

7

Last of Murrow's Boys: A Journalist's Professional and Personal Legacy

"He was a player and I was a kid," is how Susan Zirinsky, then in her twenties, described her first meeting with Robert Pierpoint. It was 1972 and she was a part-time production clerk for CBS News, not exactly high in the corporate pecking order. On the other hand, Zirinsky went on to work as a producer at the highest level on most CBS News broadcasts and is currently executive producer of *48 Hours*. She describes the experience of meeting Pierpoint at an impressionable juncture in her journalism career as "a first peek behind the curtain," giving her a glimpse of the inner workings of the White House that exceeded her expectations.[1] According to Zirinsky, Pierpoint knew far more than he told.

That was the reason, when asked by Pierpoint to work as a researcher on his 1981 book, *At the White House,* Zirinsky leaped at the opportunity. She calls her mentor "one of the early reality correspondents," who sensed there would be public interest in "things people knew about, but didn't talk about." Chief among them, she adds, are Pierpoint's stories about JFK having women in the White House; that surprised her because, as a young woman herself during that time, she had never heard about it.

Her work on Pierpoint's book entailed using the *Reader's Guide to Periodicals* to fact check his work, ensuring its historical accuracy. Pierpoint was "obsessive" about accuracy, getting everything right, what she calls a "detail guy." It's a description that resurfaces in any conversation involving Robert Pierpoint. In this instance he wanted Zirinsky to ensure that his own "historic memory" wasn't at odds with "historic reality."

She felt that, as a young person in the business, she was "in very elite company." To her, Pierpoint was "a reporter's reporter"—someone who was so delighted to be where he was, so flourished in the work he did. She recalled having a conversation with current CBS News White House correspondent Bill Plant that took place one day at the 2012 political conventions. He said to her "I'm just glad to be part of the party." That reminded Zirinsky of Pierpoint. "That was Bob, too," she said.

"He was part of a time in journalism, an era when it was pure, when you built relationships," is Zirinsky's take on why so many of his colleagues, then and now, respect Pierpoint's work. "It was inspiring to me as a kid to see the amazing politics that go into being on the inside of the White House. Sometimes, I felt like I was in a secret society and Bob brought me into it."

"He was always good natured, friendly, and well disposed to those, like myself, who were new and green," recalls the aforementioned Bill Plant. Plant came to Washington at the end of 1976, meeting Pierpoint in the latter years of his time at the White House. He agrees with Zirinsky that standards in news reporting were primary for Pierpoint, but also says the veteran newsman had a great sense of humor. Plant recalls an evening spent at a D.C. restaurant, soon after coming to Washington, when he went to dinner with Bob and Pat Pierpoint. The fare was Italian cuisine. The restaurant was fairly snooty and banned butter from its tables, using only the purest olive oil. Pat Pierpoint, in collusion with Bob, called Plant aside and slipped him a tub of butter she had brought with her. She asked him to put it under his coat. When they all sat down to dinner, out came the butter and, says Plant, they each rebelliously and surreptitiously substituted butter for olive oil, something they laughed about. It was typical of Pierpoint debunking what he thought of as silly affectations.

Eric Engberg, the former CBS News correspondent, learned some serious lessons from Pierpoint, many of them related to having a strong work ethic and being a hell of a writer. It's well known that Pierpoint never failed to take and act upon late-night phone calls from the CBS assignment desk. "One of the things he did a lot of during his White House years was he would get the call from the news desk at 11 p.m. saying AP is reporting the White House is going to do such and such tomorrow morning. Now, he's gotta use the phone to confirm a *Los Angeles Times* story or a *Chicago Times* story and he's gotta sit down and type up a script."

At least once, that caused a family problem. Those were the days of having one phone line in most American homes, with one phone number. When Martin Luther King was assassinated, Pierpoint was waiting at home for the call from CBS giving him his assignment. Unknown to him, son

Eric was on the phone with his girlfriend for a long, long time. Eventually, tired of wondering why the call didn't come, Pierpoint cornered the culprit. It would be a moment that, years later, in typical Pierpoint fashion, he and the family might laugh about. At the time, though, Eric Pierpoint says, "it wasn't pretty."

Pierpoint found nothing amusing about bad writing. In fact, along with so many of his other colleagues, Eric Engberg says he never met a better broadcast writer. In particular, "nobody was ever as good at doing radio reporting," he says. "You could take any of his thousands of radio scripts and hold them up to today's journalism students as a model." It's a point with which Phil Jones, another White House colleague, agrees. "Professionally, he was one of the most succinct broadcast news writers I've ever known," says Jones. "He had this ability because he came up through radio to television. Back in those days, radio spots were a minute and you had to be able to tell all of the story within that time."

On a personal level, Jones says, "the one big thing I learned from Bob Pierpoint was having friends. I have never known one person who had more friends, real friends." Jones spent many a presidential road trip with Pierpoint and recalled one of his colleague's regular practices. "A day or two before we were scheduled to fly back to D.C., Bob would say, 'I'm going to drop off and go see some friends.' I watched that develop over the years and I determined why he was able to have so many friends. It's a very simple formula: he worked at it." According to Jones, "that's what made him a potent journalist."

Current *60 Minutes* correspondent Lesley Stahl knew Pierpoint since 1972 and the two worked very closely together at the White House starting in 1979 or 1980. "I have never known a reporter with more integrity, more decency, more honesty, more commitment to the craft and the rules of the game," she says of her former colleague. She is candid about how Pierpoint was always there if she needed him, but volunteered little that wasn't requested. "He didn't in any way go out of his way to help me ... if I ever needed help, I had to ask for it ... and, if I asked for it, he provided it." Looking back, she says she could understand why he was "uncomfortable in that role,"—meaning the role of showing her the ropes. "He had a hundred times more knowledge, depth, and sources than I had when I got there," she says.

Stahl knew she was stepping into a job way over her head at the time, but credits Pierpoint with teaching by example. "I learned by observing the way he reached out to people, how to make the right phone calls by watching and listening to him, where you had to go as a White House correspondent to get a story—whether it was someone in a government agency or on Capitol Hill or someone who had been in a position previously." One thing that made a deep impression was that Pierpoint's sources always called him back. "If he called someone at a high level, people who were in positions of power at the time, people who had been in power, they'd always call him back."

Sometimes, when she'd screw up, Stahl remembers feeling like Pierpoint was "a kind of father who was disappointed in me." But, she says, a father who never yelled. In fact, Stahl, with others, affectionately recalls his sense of humor. "What an absolutely infectious laugh he had," she says, adding "he was terrific to be around." Overall, "he was impeccable with me. He was kind and generous. I adored him." And there's this personal debt of gratitude: "I could not have covered the White House if he had not shown me ... he was a man of great integrity and high principles. You can take that to the bank."

A legacy is an elusive concept—hardly discernible during a man's life, often embellished by others after he dies. Many of his professional colleagues over the 40 years spent in journalism help provide a perspective. There's agreement that Robert Pierpoint's contribution to the field of journalism ranks with the greatest. James McManus put it this way: "For a news reporter, perhaps especially for a broadcast journalist, a 'legacy' is a sometime thing. Walter Cronkite left a legacy—without a doubt—of clarity and honest effort that established a remarkable connection with his audiences. He was not trying to create the image of a celebrity. He loved his work and to be seen as a journeyman worth his salt was more than enough." McManus is not alone in placing Pierpoint at the same level of achievement. "I believe that also was true of Bob Pierpoint. He looked *through* the camera lens right at you and told you in plain English what he believed you should know. First and foremost, in the matter of both men, they believed they were handling facts that added up to truth."[2]

While so much of Robert Pierpoint's legacy is tied to his professional achievements, it is also intricately linked to a personal legacy, a family life that made him the journalist he became and remained to the end of his life. Stahl, for one, remembers being in close quarters in the recording booth at the White House press room when Pierpoint would be talking to his wife on the phone.[3] "You're so close to your booth mate, so I could hear his conversations," she says. "I knew he adored her," she adds, referring to Pat Pierpoint.

In a business known for tearing apart relationships and family life, Pierpoint was not unique, but perhaps rare, in sustaining the role of patriarch in an intact family. As his lifelong friend Myra MacPherson put it, "parents who are journalists who have broken families are legion." That wasn't Bob Pierpoint. While "the travel works against parenting," MacPherson saw Pierpoint as someone who carefully guarded the sanctity of his home life, in part through establishing firm routines, in part by making Pat and the kids a part of everything he did and most everywhere he went. While he may have, at times, resented the role of playing "parent" to a string of newly arrived, wet-behind-the-ears novices at the White House, he fully embraced the role when raising his four kids.

No one is good at everything and any authentic appraisal of a life must include the person's shortcomings along with his nobler attributes. In Robert Pierpoint's instance, there was one major area in which he did not excel: keeping secrets about how he felt on an issue—some might say he couldn't keep his mouth shut about things that bothered him. There's a sense among those who knew him best that it was a trait standing in the way of his career advancement at CBS. On the other hand, it became characteristic of a strong, unwavering belief in certain principles that he brought home to the Pierpoint children every night. He made no secret of who he liked and who he didn't, at and away from work. He didn't dislike many people, but when he did, it was based on principle, not pettiness. Most of his fiery opinions were reserved for politicians. All four Pierpoint children—Alan, Eric, Kim, and Marta—remember meeting many of their dad's friends, on the tennis court, at one of Bob and Pat's Washington parties, or at the issues-driven dinner table. The Watergate period was especially "tense," says youngest daughter Marta. "We would talk about it every night at the dinner table." The uncertainty of how the situation—"the consternation that caused, the questions that caused"—would be front and center every night over dinner, as Marta Pierpoint remembers it. "I remember thinking, 'my God, let something happen.'"

He left his children a legacy of having been introduced to so many people from so many walks of life—as well as the ability to form their own opinions about them. Some of those around the Pierpoint household were famous, others simply interesting to Pierpoint. His friendship with the late Warren Chrisopher has already been touched upon. It was a large part of Pierpoint's social life, one about which the Pierpoint children, as children are wont to do, formed opinions. Christopher and his dad were "opposites," says the oldest son, Alan. The former diplomat and U.S. Secretary of State was "quiet," while "Bob was all over the place." The author James Michener was also a lifelong friend who existed on the periphery of the Pierpoint children's world, again a quiet kind of guy compared to the boisterous Pierpoint.[4]

It would be hard to argue that one side of Pierpoint's personality wasn't ego-driven, but those who knew him say there was equally a down-to-earth side. The two seemed to be in balance, with the fulcrum being his life away from the microphones and cameras. "After he left the business," wrote friend and author Myra MacPherson on her blog soon after Pierpoint's death, "he peppered friends with his daily opinions about the latest in politics and the media, looking forward, not back." He once told MacPherson that "no way did he want to stay in D.C. as someone who 'used to be Bob Pierpoint.'" Because, she writes, "he knew how quickly they forget in Washington," he went back to California, "lectured, salmon fished in Alaska and trekked through Montana, running into the many real friends he had made there." He had, in the California home, his "Ego Wall," as MacPherson called it, a collection of photos of himself with presidents and celebrities, his awards, and so on. But, she wrote, "he didn't have an ego. At least not a damaging one. He was as much interested in hearing what others thought as listening to his own voice."

When she was in her 20s, MacPherson was married to a sportswriter who was, shall we say, well-coiffed. He did some television spots and always dressed and looked the part. She remembers Pierpoint good-naturedly—for the most part—exchanging verbal jabs with him about the amount of time he spent on his looks. "He was quite contemptuous of the blow-dried types," she says. "He just didn't care that he didn't look beautiful, that he wasn't one of the pretty boys."

It was an indelible part of Pierpoint's personality that, as Phil Jones has pointed out, helped make him such a "potent"—some would use the word "consummate"—journalist. He never backed away from a chance to engage others, no matter how smart or sometimes how foolish he believed they might be. He shared a great deal in common with some, but also was open to others with whom he had no apparent common interests. Often, he enjoyed conversing with those whose ideas and ideology clashed with his own. Peggy Moore knew Pierpoint through her late husband; the two had met as far back as Korea when Bill Moore was offered a Rotary Club scholarship to study abroad. She would often put together dinner parties where Pierpoint would regale the Moores' guests with stories of the news wars and opinions on social or political issues. "He was a great storyteller," she says. There were guests there who could hardly wait to meet Pierpoint, one, she says, who "I think would kiss his feet!"

Mary Silverman and her late husband Frank spent time as Pierpoint's neighbors near the Montana home which became the family's retreat from White House rigors during his correspondent days and a regular destination during retirement. Not far from Yellowstone, it has become something of a Pierpoint family compound, surrounded by long-time friends. Following the controversy over the "double-standard" commentary in 1973, the

Silvermans witnessed first-hand how Pierpoint was not only a great speaker but an especially gifted listener—even in the face of belligerent opposing views.

"He always stuck to what he believed," says Mary Silverman. "We had a friend who really wanted to meet Bob, so we invited him to dinner," she remembered, but the guest "just kept talking and talking and talking so he didn't have to hear any of Bob's answers." After the man left, an apologetic Silverman told Pierpoint she was sorry to have invited the domineering guest. Pierpoint's reaction was "Mary, I've met a lot of people like that and I don't want you to worry about it." Argument came naturally to him and he never shied away from it. If he had not gone into journalism, he would have become a lawyer, Pierpoint once told his youngest daughter, Kim.[5]

"He had such a strong ethical sense as a journalist. It was a pretty high standard that he held himself to and he felt journalists should all be," said Nathan Gonzales, the University of Redlands archivist who sorted through Pierpoint's papers when they were given to his alma matter in 2002. "People getting their news from personalities instead of journalists ... one of the things he singled out was people getting news from Rush Limbaugh, instead of journalists."

Soon after the 2008 election, Pierpoint was quoted in an article in the local Santa Barbara newspaper. According to Gonzales, just before his death Pierpoint told him he was upset with the way the article was written. His objection? "It would lead the reader to believe Bob was not happy with the outcome of the 2008 election. Nothing could be further from the truth. Bob was a big supporter of Obama. The one criticism he was really hopeful he would come in and be a fighter like LBJ, but by 2010, he was concerned that he was not going to be a fighter, but a healer." Pierpoint disliked intensely being misquoted, since he had spent a lifetime being certain of the quotations in his own stories were absolutely accurate and fair—something at which he excelled.

Pierpoint also excelled, by all accounts, at synthesizing what he did for a living with how he lived. "His life was like his profession," says son Alan. "He chose the values he lived by." In the process, he adds, Robert Pierpoint "inspired a new generation of journalists with the ideals he lived and worked by." He was tremendously interested in people and their stories, living by the mantra "everybody's got a story," and the ones that were most important to him were those closest to home.

Kim Pierpoint knew who to call when she just needed to talk. "It took me time and difference to really reconcile my place with him," she says. "The last fifteen years, in particular, I've come to understand and admire him." It's telling of a man who treated his family as friends and his friends like family. If you were friend or family, you couldn't escape knowing where he stood and where you stood in relation to him. No sugarcoating. No embellishment. Like he once said about Gerald Ford, what you saw was what you got.

Much has been written, including here, about how Dan Rather was perhaps the major figure preventing Pierpoint from getting his full due as the great White House correspondent of his generation. Son Alan says the Pierpoint children were never brought up to dislike Rather. "Other than a word here and there, Dad kept whatever bitterness he may have had to himself. (Or maybe to Mom.) Those reporters all knew they were competing in a tough business; if you had a thin skin, you never got that far to begin with." "Thin skin" were not words anyone would apply to Pierpoint.

In the final analysis, those with whom he had the most professional differences—Rather certainly chief among them—might be in the best position to see more clearly Robert Pierpoint's legacy. "The longer I knew him, the more I respected him," Rather says. "Bob loved what he did. It was very satisfying to him; he felt he was a part of something bigger than himself. The lesson is that there are a lot of places in journalism where you can do good work, have a great life, whether or not you're a big star or make a lot of money." In the end, the Pierpoint legacy may be the inspirational story of a young kid who had no logical reason to believe he could go where he went or to do what he did—but still reached the highest peaks of journalism. The same kind of kid may be sitting in a college classroom somewhere today. Pierpoint's story "has the potential to inspire young people who are even thinking about getting into journalism," says Rather. Over forty years later, now that the cameras are off, two colleagues and competitors can finally agree.

Notes

Chapter 1

1. From R. Pierpoint, "Asthma and Education," unpublished writing, Robert C. Pierpoint Collection, University of Redlands, California.

2. This account is contained in two places: the first is in a eulogy written by his oldest son, Alan, in 2011; it also exists in J.M. Dobbs, "Robert Pierpoint: 1925–2011," *Och Tamale* (University of Redlands alumni magazine), Winter 2012, p. 21.

3. Personal interview with Eric Pierpoint, Redlands, California, November 2012.

4. Personal interview with Ruth Hogg, Redlands, California, November 2012. Subsequent references are to this interview.

5. http://monrovia.patch.com/groups/around-town/p/the-pottenger-sanatorium. The same kind of climate that helped those with tuberculosis—dry, with year-round mild temperatures—was also found to be comforting to those with asthma. The sanatorium closed in 1955, after Pottenger, then 88, retired.

6. R. Pierpoint, "From Hardshell Baptist to Secular Liberal," unpublished writing, Robert C. Pierpoint Collection, University of Redlands, California.

7. http://homepages.rootsweb.ancestry.com/~uscnrotc/V-12/v12-his.htm. The program was in full operation until 1983, almost forty years after the end of World War II.

8. The U.S. Navy's V-12 program also introduced him to his first friend at Redlands, Bryns Fagerburg. The meeting occurred when Pierpoint visited the university before his attendance there. "We were both in the Navy V-12 training program, and he stayed in my room during his visit," said Fagerburg, who would go on to work at the university as director of admissions from 1951 to 1968. "He was a close friend. We spent many summers together fly fishing for trout near west Yellowstone, and he loved to play tennis. Friendships were very important to Bob." Quoted from J. Dobbs, "Robert Pierpoint: 1925–2011," *Och Tamale* (University of Redlands alumni magazine), Winter 2012, p. 21.

9. From R. Pierpoint, "Marriage and the Family," unpublished writing, Robert C. Pierpoint Collection, University of Redlands, California.

10. From notes made by Pierpoint on his days living in Sweden. Robert Pierpoint Papers, 1943–1982, Wisconsin Historical Society, Madison, Wisconsin. Unless otherwise noted, information regarding this period in his life is taken from the WHS archives.

11. Pierpoint kept many of his original radio scripts from this period. Most are in

the Wisconsin Historical Society colleton; others are in the CBS archives.

12. The original film is housed in the Wisconsin Historical Society Pierpoint Collection.

13. Mary and Jack Silverman became lifelong friends, especially as neighbors in Montana, a spot where he would one day have a home. From personal interview with Mary Silverman, July 2012. Subsequent references to comments by her are from the same interview.

Chapter 2

1. From a typed letter in the Pierpoint Collection, Wisconsin Historical Society, Madison, Wisconsin.

2. M. McMahon. "Eyewitness to History; Veteran Journalist Recalls Years as White House Correspondent for Six Presidents," *Santa Barbara News-Press*, October 2, 2011.

3. McMahon, "Eyewitness to History."

4. From an interview with Pierpoint in the *Bodega Bay Navigator*, September 9, 1993.

5. George Herman was not only Pierpoint's boss but a legendary CBS News correspondent. The story about Pierpoint's fear of losing the jeep assigned to him by Herman has been variously retold, most recently by Pierpoint himself in 2005, the year Herman passed away. In a letter to Herman's wife, expressing his sadness, Pierpoint writes that on May 16, 1951, his 26th birthday, Pierpoint asked permission to take the CBS jeep to cover nighttime firefights taking place some distance away. According to Pierpoint, George worried that while Pierpoint was untested for such danger, he needed experience. Here are Bob's words: "So George told me to take the jeep, and if something bad happened to me, that was my mistake. But if I lost the jeep, something even worse would happen to me. I got the message, took the jeep, guarded it with my life and returned both it and me safely." The quote found its way into Herman's eulogy by their mutual colleague, Sid Davis, who provided it by e-mail, July 2012.

6. Pierpoint's account of the scenario is outlined in various places. He referred to it often in interviews and in his book, *At the White House: Assignment to Six Presidents* (New York: Putnam, 1981), pp. 154–155. It is also in his personal notes in the Robert Pierpoint Papers at the Wisconsin Historical Society, from which this quote is taken.

7. M. MacPherson, "Remembering Bob Pierpoint," Nieman Watchdog Blog, http://www.niemanwatchdog.org.

8. J.F. McDonald, "TV News and the Red Menace: The Video Road to Vietnam," http://www.jfredmacdonald.com/trm/11tvkorea.htm.

9. Pierpoint's reporter notebooks are a large part of the Robert Pierpoint Papers, 1943–1982, housed at the Wisconsin Historical Society. In all, there are four boxes of these books, beginning with Scandinavia (1949–1951), the Far East (1951–1957), the Middle East (1956–1958), the Eisenhower administration (1957–1960), the Johnson administration (1963–1969), several boxes related to the Nixon administration, and others from Ford's and Carter's time in the White House. The material in this and other chapters that records his personal observations, unless otherwise noted, is from the handwritten notes in this collection. When once asked why Wisconsin (in terms of donating so many of his papers and personal notes), Pierpoint, who had no personal connection to the state, replied, simply, "Because they asked."

10. A good account of the "Christmas in Korea" segment of *See It Now* is found in R. Engleman, *Friendly Vision: Fred Friendly and the Rise and Fall of Television Journalism* (New York: Columbia University Press, 2011), pp. 96–97.

11. R. Pierpoint, "The Forgotten War Recalled," *San Francisco Chronicle*, August 16, 1993.

12. J. Greenfield, "Not an Anchorman in Sight," *New York Times*, July 29, 1993.

13. The episode was titled "Goodbye, Farewell, and Amen." Audio of Pierpoint's

"cameo" can be heard at http://www.mash4077tv.com/2011/10/25/robert-pierpoint-1925-2011.

Chapter 3

1. From pay stubs Pierpoint retained and which are now in his papers at the Wisconsin Historical Society.
2. R. Pierpoint, *At the White House*, p. 14.
3. All of the scripts from this period in Pierpoint's career are in the archives of the Wisconsin Historical Society.
4. Interview with Mary Silverman, July 2012.
5. R. Pierpoint, "A Great Institution," unpublished writing. This was among a number of pieces Pierpoint wrote in retirement, reflecting back on his years in journalism. They were mainly intended for his immediate family, one of whom, his daughter Marta, made them available for this book. Subsequent references to this period are from this document, unless otherwise noted.
6. Unpublished letter to his daughter Marta. Now included in the Robert Pierpoint Papers, Wisconsin Historical Society.
7. The actual broadcast's impact was intensified by the fact it was repeated several more times on the CBS radio network and led to divisions over both Pierpoint's opinions and the attitudes of concerned advertisers. See http://www.jta.org/1973/03/30/archive/wcbs-editorial-differs-sharply-with-pierpoints-double-standard-charge.
8. All the letters transcribed in this portion of the text are taken from the archives of the Robert C. Pierpoint Collection, University of Redlands, California.
9. Interview with Nathan Gonzales, archivist, Robert C. Pierpoint Collection, University of Redlands, September 2013.

Chapter 4

1. Interview with Patricia Pierpoint, Redlands, California, October 2012.
2. The timeline here is established from Pierpoint's own unpublished account, "Marriage and the Family," previously referred to and now in the archives of the Robert C. Pierpoint Collection, University of Redlands, California.
3. Interview with Kim Pierpoint, July 2012.
4. Interview with Marta Pierpoint, July 2012.
5. From personal notes made by Pierpoint and contained in the Robert Pierpoint Papers at the Wisconsin Historical Society.
6. Pierpoint brought up this point several times in different forums. One is contained during a question-and-answer period following the speech "A View from the White House Steps," given in Wichita, Kansas, December 9, 1973. He also referred to being "shocked" by the Little Rock incident in a 1998 interview with California PBS television station KRCB.
7. R. Pierpoint, *At the White House*, p. 27. Pierpoint's own accounts from his book were used to establish his first days on the job, especially Chapter 1, "The White House Press."
8. Much of the material for Pierpoint's coverage of the Eisenhower years, unless otherwise noted, is from *At the White House,* Chapter 3, "The Press Conference," pp. 62–68.
9. "A Conversation with Robert Pierpoint: An American Reporter," Part I, KRCB-TV, Sonoma, California, April 21, 1998.
10. Pierpoint recorded this anecdote in one of his reporter notebooks, now included in the Robert Pierpoint Papers at the Wisconsin Historical Society.
11. Interview with Ed Fouhy from his home in Barnstable, Massachusetts, July 2012.
12. His writing about Kennedy, both during his working days and in retirement, comprises a large portion of his recollections about the six presidents he covered for CBS News. Many of them are contained in *At the White House,* others in his personal papers at both the Wisconsin

Historical Society and the University of Redlands. The early part of this section relies on *At the White House* as its source.

13. Pierre Salinger, quoted in *At the White House*. Salinger may have been, for this reason and others, Pierpoint's favorite among the press secretaries with whom he dealt. He writes that shortly after Kennedy's election, Salinger approached him "with the idea of a televised press conference." Pierpoint "endorsed it immediately and almost as quickly referred Salinger to my bureau chief for further exploration of policy and technical considerations."

14. *At the White House*, pp. 69–70.

15. "A Conversation with Robert Pierpoint," Part I, 1998.

16. "A Conversation with Robert Pierpoint," Part I, 1998.

17. "A View from the White House Steps," December 9, 1973. There's some reason to believe this was a repurposed speech, as Pierpoint had been brought in at fairly late notice to fill in for author Gore Vidal, who had cancelled that night. The audiotape is in the archives of the Wisconsin Historical Society (Tape UCD 1120A/2).

18. *At the White House*, pp. 49–50. Kennedy's "womanizing" was well known to those who covered the White House at the time. As demonstrated since, the propriety of reporting a president's sexual infidelity is an ongoing ethical dilemma for journalists. It was one that arose more than once for Pierpoint. See Chapter 6 for another incidence.

19. Interview conducted with Pierpoint by Sheldon Stern of the JFK Library, Boston, Massachusetts, November 18, 1982. A full transcript of the interview is available in the Robert Pierpoint Collection at the University of Redlands, California.

20. *At the White House*, pp. 100–101.

21. "A Conversation with Robert Pierpoint," Part I, 1998.

22. Pierpoint recounts the incident in the PBS interview of 1998, as well as in his memoir, *At the White House*, years earlier, in 1981. Clearly, the perceived snub was something that bothered him at the time and contributed to his overall impression of Jackie Kennedy as a peculiar woman, hard to predict or fathom.

23. Pierpoint spent much of his life reflecting on the events of November 22, 1963, at one point putting his recollections into a typed manuscript (unpublished), which is in the Robert Pierpoint Collection at the University of Redlands, California. The account related here has that manuscript as its basis.

24. The networks often use a "pool" system, by which one reporter files a story for multiple news organizations that are members of the "pool" but don't have their own reporter on the scene. The duty rotates among those reporters from organizations who join the pool, so that no one reporter has the responsibility all the time.

25. Interview with Sid Davis, July 23, 2012.

26. Pierpoint talked and wrote about what he saw as his biggest lapse as a journalist in many places and during numerous interviews. This quote is from "A Conversation with Robert Pierpoint," Part I, 1998.

27. Rachel Tillman, "Old News," previously appeared in *Aerie Big Sky*, Volume 32 (2012). Reprinted with permission from the author and *Aerie Big Sky*.

28. Handwritten note by Robert Pierpoint, in the archives of the Robert Pierpoint Papers at the Wisconsin Historical Society.

29. This is thought to be the last formal interview Robert Pierpoint gave. The interviewer was Marilyn McMahon, in "Eyewitness to History: Veteran Journalist Recalls Years as White House Correspondent for Six Presidents," *Santa Barbara News-Press*, October 2, 2011.

30. From a typed, unpublished manuscript by Robert Pierpoint, in the archives of the Robert Pierpoint Collection, University of Redlands, California.

31. Letter written April 11, 1997, now in the archives of the Robert Pierpoint Collection, University of Redlands, California.

32. The accounts of Pierpoint's White

House experience during the Johnson years comes from his memoir, *At the White House*, except where otherwise noted.

33. From a reporter notebook in the archives of the Robert Pierpoint Papers at the Wisconsin Historical Society. The excerpts that follow throughout this section are all derived from the same source.

34. McMahon, "Eyewitness to History," 2011.

35. LBJ's years as a teacher are detailed in "Students: Lyndon Johnson's School Days," *Time*, May 21, 1965, http://www.time.com/time/magazine/article/0,9171, 901708,00.html.

36. "Conversation with a Reporter," Part I.

37. This and the excerpt that follows regarding Johnson's Latin American trip are taken from CBS News coverage of LBJ's trip to El Salvador, July 1968. They are from an audio tape (1120A/3) in the Robert Pierpoint Papers at the Wisconsin Historical Society.

38. From "A View from the White House Steps," 1973.

39. Interview with Dan Rather, July 10, 2012. All subsequent quotations are from this interview, unless otherwise noted.

40. Interview with Eric Engberg, June 2012. All subsequent quotations are from this interview, unless otherwise noted.

41. "Black Rock" is the nickname given to CBS corporate headquarters on West 57th Street in New York City. It derives from the black granite of which the building is constructed.

42. Interview with Roger Mudd, July 9, 2012. All subsequent quotations are from this interview, unless otherwise noted.

43. Quoted from T. Fish, "All the President's Newsmen," *Santa Rosa Press-Democrat*, undated article in the archives of the University of Redlands, California.

44. All of this is detailed in *At the White House*, but also comes out during interviews with those who knew Pierpoint well and recall the incident firsthand. The Rebozo investigation receives a full account in the chapter titled "Anatomy of an Award" in Pierpoint's memoir, pp. 216–227.

45. A. Clymer, "Vicious Stories Attacked," *Baltimore Sun*, October 27, 1973.

46. B. Bagdikian, "Mr. Nixon and the Press: A 27-Year Conflict," *New York Times*, November 1, 1973, pp. 42–43.

47. R. Kuttner, "Television Turns on Nixon," *Rosebud* 4, no. 1 (1974), p. 2.

48. E-mail interview with James McManus, August 11, 2013. McManus says that, in general, radio reporters were treated especially harshly by the Nixon administration. In 1969, he points out that "old divisions, as between print and TV broadcast, were gone in the recent past. But the radio-only types, only a handful, were new arrivals and in their isolation on the basement floor of the press wing found comradeship among themselves."

49. Roger Mudd interviewed Pierpoint by phone on June 16, 2006, for his book *The Place to Be: Washington, CBS, and the Glory Days of Television* (New York: Public Affairs, 2008). Mudd shared the transcript of his interview for use in this book.

50. From a handwritten note in the archives of the Robert Pierpoint Papers, Wisconsin Historical Society.

51. The excerpts regarding Nixon and Pierpoint's father are from McMahon, "Eyewitness to History," 2011.

52. S. Schwieder, "Pierpoint: Straightforward Man," *Tampa Times*, December 3, 1974, p. 2-E.

53. Of all the presidents Pierpoint covered, Ford is the one about whom he wrote the least in his private papers and there are few significant notations in his reporter notebooks. Most of his insights on the Ford years come from *At the White House*, especially pp. 113–118.

54. "A Conversation with Robert Pierpoint," Part II, 1998.

55. He discusses this in detail in *At the White House*, especially pp. 119–121. Pierpoint, in the last years of his life, felt similarly about Barack Obama, telling an interviewer, "He's not a fighter. He surrenders to Congress before necessary. Lyndon Johnson was a fighter. He fought for what he believed in." McMahon, "Eyewitness to History."

56. From transcript of Roger Mudd's phone interview with Robert Pierpoint, 2006.
57. From transcript of Roger Mudd's phone interview with Robert Pierpoint, 2006.
58. Taken from transcript of an audiotape in the archives of the Robert Pierpoint letters at the Wisconsin Historical Society. Tape 2: 1120A/5, dated November 16, 1976.
59. Pierpoint discusses this in detail in *At the White House*, pp. 118–119.
60. Pierpoint tells the story with great aplomb in *At the White House*, p. 120.
61. Interview with Lesley Stahl, June 27, 2013. Stahl, who joined *60 Minutes* as a correspondent in 1991, also wrote about this and other interactions with Pierpoint in her own book, *Reporting Live*, in 1999. Future references to Stahl's comments are from this interview, unless otherwise noted.
62. He elaborated on this account in the chapter "The Press and the Presidents" in *At the White House*: "More than anything substantive said about domestic or world problems, the difference in personalities shown by such exchanges cost Jimmy Carter the debate" (p. 121).

Chapter 5

1. From the introduction to *At the White House*, p. 21.
2. G. Ostrom, "Why We Hid Robert Pierpoint," *Montana Weekly News*, September 3, 1975. Not unlike most reporters at any level, Pierpoint was constantly aware of the need to be in touch with his news desk, a complicated task in the pre-cellphone era. A correspondent's job at that time often involved identifying the location of all nearby pay phone booths.
3. C. Roberts, "How Important Is Tennis?" *Tennis*, April 16, 1976, pp. 29–32. Coincidentally, the author is the same Charles Roberts who was a constant tennis opponent for Pierpoint. He was a *Newsweek* correspondent from 1951 to 1972.

4. The original photo is in the archives of the Robert Pierpoint Collection, University of Redlands, California. It is also the cover photo of his 1981 book. When he passed away in 2011, it was the single photo most often used in articles about his life and career. At his request, he was buried in the same tennis attire he wore in the photograph.
5. Pierpoint tells the story in detail and with great wit in the introduction to *At the White House*, pp. 22–23.
6. F. Graham, *Happy Talk: Confessions of a TV Newsman* (New York: Norton, 1990). Graham, who worked at CBS News from 1972 to 1987, outlines the inner turmoil within the network during this period on pp. 220–225.
7. Interview with Phil Jones, July 16, 2013. Subsequent quotations are from this interview, unless otherwise noted.
8. Interview with Bill Plant, September 20, 2012.
9. From transcript of Roger Mudd's phone interview with Robert Pierpoint.
10. Quoted from F. Graham, *Happy Talk*, p. 223.
11. This conversation is outlined by Graham in *Happy Talk*. There is no other confirmation from other sources, but it appears reasonable, given the context of events at the time.

Chapter 6

1. A version of the speech was published in the University of Redlands alumni magazine, then named *Alumnus*. The speech had been delivered at the university's Alumni Day Dinner on June 8, 1964. *Alumnus* (1964): pp. 9–11. All quotations from the speech are attributable to this source.
2. J. Persico, *Edward R. Murrow: An American Original* (New York: McGraw-Hill, 1988), pp. 320–321. This was one of many instances where Murrow annoyed the CBS hierarchy, to the point where even his patron saint, CBS founder William Paley, began to distance himself from his

top newsman. The most famous *See It Now* program attacking Senator Joseph McCarthy's "witch hunt" against alleged communists in many fields, government and entertainment included, alienated sponsors. The program found itself without advertisers and, at one point, CBS wouldn't promote it, leading to Murrow himself buying space in the *New York Times* to spotlight the programs' airing.

3. Taken from a letter to the editor by M. Boden, *Santa Rosa Press-Democrat*, June 7, 1977.

4. Taken from a letter to the editor by R. McCormack, *Santa Rosa Press-Democrat*, June 7, 1977.

5. Taken from a letter to the editor, no name given, *Santa Rosa Press-Democrat*, June 7, 1977.

6. S. Swartz, "Rental Dispute Divides Bodega Bay Neighbors," *Santa Rosa Press-Democrat,* January 20, 1999. Pierpoint's quote on the issue is from the same source.

7. Older son Alan Pierpoint gave this perspective on the club's place in the Pierpoint family: "We moved to Pollard Rd. in the summer of '59 and dad bought a full family membership (or maybe he was already a member, I don't know). Anyway, the club was right around the corner from us. I could (and very often did) carry my clubs over in the hot afternoons when kids were let on the course. Eric and Dad, and for a while Mom, used it for tennis. Sometimes mixed doubles with the Charles Robertses. No black faces anywhere, except, as I recall, for the wait staff, etc. Kenwood was a big part of our lives. Dad and his friends (Chuck Roberts, Harold Sinrod, Milt Eisenberg, Lyman Wynn) would play there at least once a week, weather permitting. Eric became one of the top junior players in the area there. Kim was on a swim team."

8. The source for this account is an unpublished manuscript Pierpoint wrote, titled "Saga of the Kenwood C.C." His daughter Marta, who provided the manuscript for use in this book, called it "one of my absolute favorites."

9. J. Marshall, "TV News Incomplete, Says Broadcaster." *Oregon Gazette-Times,* October 15, 1974.

10. "A View from the White House Steps," lecture, December 9, 1973, Wichita, Kansas.

11. Personal letter dated June 29, 1977, now in the archives of the Robert Pierpoint Papers, Wisconsin Historical Society.

12. Personal letter dated July 8, 1977, now in the archives of the Wisconsin Historical Society.

13. The quotations used are from the College of William and Mary alumni magazine, not the address itself. The account was published in the Summer 1979 issue.

14. Pierpoint devoted an entire chapter to "Press Ethics" in *At the White House.* The account here is taken from it, pp. 193–194.

15. Interview with Robert Pierpoint conducted by Sheldon Stern of the JFK Library, November 18, 1982.

16. From the draft of the speech given to the annual banquet of the Society for College Journalists, 1979, in the archives of the Wisconsin Historical Society.

17. Persico, *Edward R. Murrow: An American Original*, pp. 318–319. This incident was similar to the omission of reporting on the spattered blood on Jacqueline Kennedy's clothes. Both disturbed Pierpoint throughout his working life and into retirement. Friends and colleagues still see Pierpoint's adulation of Murrow as sustaining throughout his life, but Persico suggests otherwise.

18. Persico, p. 318. The idea that Pierpoint saw a "cause-effect" relationship between the presence of cameras and altered behavior in the subjects of news stories was new for its day. Since then, researchers have documented this effect on participants in news stories.

19. Sperber, pp. 137–140.

20. P. Boyer, *Who Killed CBS? The Undoing of America's Number One News Network* (New York: Random House, 1988). This portion of the narrative surrounding the changes at CBS News from the Salant to the Sauter era relies heavily upon the

research of Boyer, in his exhaustive study of the news division during this period. Many CBS insiders cooperated with Boyer in the writing of his book, some of whom also assisted in the preparation of this book and confirmed the portions that have been cited.

21. Fred Graham, in his book *Happy Talk,* corroborates the idea that there existed at CBS News during this time a "quest for moments," which transformed the culture by capturing the attention of those correspondents who wanted to retain their jobs.

22. This is all according to Sperber, considered by many to be Murrow's major biographer. He details the situation leading to Murrow's departure from CBS on pp. 616–619.

23. Sperber, pp. 650–651. Given the high esteem in which Pierpoint held Murrow, it's understandable that he would put the story aside on Murrow's say-so. On the other hand, so is his later regret, based on principle alone.

24. His comments are from an address Pierpoint gave at the Montana School of Journalism in 1971, the Dean A.L. Stone Address. It was titled "We Must Be Doing Something Right." It is published in the *Montana Journalism Review* 14 (1971).

25. As evidence of how far he believed women had come, Pierpoint kept this clipping from the *New York Times* of September 3, 1975. It read: "The White House Correspondents Association broke two precedents as old as its 60-year history yesterday. It elected a woman, Helen Thomas of United Press International, as president, and Robert Pierpoint to its executive committee." In the White House press corps, women and broadcast reporters were equal in that the perception was that both were not as important as the male print reporters of the day—the main keepers of the tradition. A woman and a TV correspondent being elected at the same time, in the same year, did indeed break that tradition.

Chapter 7

1. Interview with Susan Zirinsky, September 17, 2012. Subsequent quotations are from this interview. Before *48 Hours,* Zirinsky was a senior producer for the *CBS Evening News with Dan Rather* from 1989 to 1992, and she has occupied other high-ranking positions within the CBS News division throughout her career.

2. From e-mail correspondence with James McManus, August 2013.

3. For broadcast correspondents, this is a very small, soundproofed room where they record what's called their "track," the audio portion of their report. Not exactly a "studio," it fulfills the function of a quiet spot that filters outside noise. Once the track is recorded, it is synched up with the video portion of the story to provide narration for what the viewer sees. Radio correspondents use the same setup to record their audio-only stories.

4. Christopher and Pierpoint first met while both were students at the University of Redlands. Christopher, however, transferred to the University of Southern California. The relationship with Michener was probably based around the fact that the Pulitzer Prize–winning author was widely traveled and also, like Pierpoint, served in the U.S. Navy during World War II. According to Alan Pierpoint, Michener established a scholarship for the children of Korean War correspondents, a move that would have endeared him to Pierpoint.

5. In fact, according to his sister, Ruth Hogg, "Bob intended to go to Stanford Law, but he had the G.I. Bill to study abroad and so he thought he would give it a try." Quoted from J. Dobbs, "Robert Pierpoint: 1925–2011," *Och Tamale* (University of Redlands alumni magazine), Winter 2012, p. 21. In various interviews throughout the years, Pierpoint would also mention his original plan to attend law school.

Bibliography

Bagdikian, Benjamin. "Mr. Nixon and the Press: A 27-Year Conflict." *New York Times*, Nov. 1, 1973, 42–43.

Bliss, Edward. *Now the News: The Story of Broadcast Journalism*. New York: Columbia University Press, 1991.

Boyer, Peter J. *Who Killed CBS? The Undoing of America's Number One News Network*. New York: Random House, 1988.

Clymer, Adam. "Vicious Stories Attacked." *Baltimore Sun*, Oct. 27, 1973.

Dobbs, James. "Robert Pierpoint: 1925–2011." *Och Tamale* (University of Redlands Alumni Magazine), Winter 2012, 21

Edwards, Bob. *Edward R. Murrow and the Birth of Broadcast Journalism*. Hoboken, NJ: John Wiley and Sons, 2004.

Engleman, Ralph. *Friendly Vision: Fred Friendly and the Rise and Fall of Television Journalism*. New York: Columbia University Press, 2011.

Graham, Fred. *Happy Talk: Confessions of a TV Newsman*. New York: W.W. Norton, 1990.

Greenfield, James. "Not an Anchorman in Sight." *New York Times*, July 29, 1993.

Kuttner, Robert. "Television Turns on Nixon." *Rosebud* 4, no. 1 (1974): 2.

Marshall, James. "TV News Incomplete, Says Broadcaster." *Oregon Gazette-Times*, Oct. 15, 1974.

McMahon, Marilyn. "Eyewitness to History; Veteran Journalist Recalls Years as White House Correspondent for Six Presidents." *Santa Barbara News-Press*, Oct. 2, 2011.

MacPherson, Myra. "Remembering Bob Pierpoint." *Nieman Watchdog Blog*. http://www.niemanwatchdog.org/.

Mudd, Roger. *The Place to Be: Washington, CBS, and the Glory Days of Television News*. Philadelphia: Perseus Books, 2008.

Ostrom, George. "Why We Hid Robert Pierpoint." *Montana Weekly News*, Sept. 3, 1975.

Persico, Joseph. *Edward R. Murrow: An American Original*. New York: Doubleday, 1988.

Pierpoint, Robert. *At the White House: Assignment to Six Presidents*. New York: Putnam, 1981.

———. "The Forgotten War Recalled." *San Francisco Chronicle*, Aug. 16, 1993.

———. "We Must Be Doing Something Right." *Montana Journalism Review* 14 (1971).

Rather, Dan. *The Camera Never Blinks*. New York: W. Morrow, 1977.

Roberts. Charles. "How Important Is Tennis?" *Tennis*, April 16, 1976, 29–32.

Schwieder, Sara. "Pierpoint: Straightforward Man." *Tampa Times*, Dec. 3, 1974, 2-E.

Sperber, A.M. *Murrow: His Life and Times*. New York: Freundlich, 1986.

Stahl, Lesley. *Reporting Live*. New York: Touchstone, 1999.

Index

At the White House 39, 74, 88, 139, 142, 149, 151

Bernstein, Carl 136–137
Bradley, Ed 106, 114

Carter, Jimmy 41, 70, 105–110, 114, 134, 138
CBS News 19, 23, 40, 48, 75, 113, 115, 119, 132, 136, 142–143, 145, 151
"Christmas in Korea" 33–34
Christopher, Warren 16, 138, 155
CNN 131, 133
Cronkite, Walter 1, 54, 75, 78, 93, 104, 106, 115, 120, 143–144, 147, 154

Davis, Sid 75–77, 112, 118–119
"Double Standard in the Middle East" 47, 50, 91, 156

Eisenhower, Dwight 55, 58–65, 143
Engberg, Eric 6, 90–91, 96–97, 104–105, 152–153

Far East Bureau 39–40, 45, 55, 119, 124
Field and Stream 135–136
Ford, Gerald 101–105, 109, 112–113, 158
Foreign Correspondents Club (Tokyo) 44–45
Fouhy, Ed 62–64, 69, 93–95, 112, 122, 131
Friendly, Fred 29, 32–33, 116, 119, 140–141

Gonzalez, Nathan 50, 157
Graham, Fred 115–117

Haggery, James 59–61
Hear It Now (CBS radio program) 24, 29, 35, 37, 140
Herman, George 29, 30, 114, 116, 144
Hoag, Ruth 16–17, 28, 38, 51
Hogsett, Dick 11, 15
Huntley-Brinkley 115–117

John Birch Society 127–128
Johnson, Lyndon 72, 76, 79–88
Jones, Phil 103, 106, 117–118, 121, 125, 135, 153, 156

Kennedy, Jacqueline 72–74, 76, 137, 143
Kennedy, John F. 64–74, 137–138, 143, 146; assassination coverage 74–78, 101
Kennedy, Robert 73
Kenwood Country Club 130–131
Korean War 25–27, 30, 32, 35, 37, 39, 44, 75, 103, 127, 141
KRCB-TV 132
Kuralt, Charles 123–124

Lebanon, coverage of by Pierpoint 46–47, 62–64

MacPherson, Myra 30, 67–69, 124, 131, 138, 154–156
*M*A*S*H*, Pierpoint's role in 35–36
McManus, James 97, 116, 124–125, 154

Middle East 38–39, 42, 45–50, 130
Moore, Peggy 43, 156
Mudd, Roger 91, 99, 106–107, 120, 122–123, 134, 142–143
Murrow, Edward R. 5–6, 24–27, 30, 33, 35, 37–39, 42, 118–119, 127–128, 131, 134, 140–142, 145–147
"Murrow's Boys" 24, 26, 114, 145

Nixon, Patricia 99–100, 137
Nixon, Richard 67, 71, 88–101, 110, 112, 139

Ostrom, George 111–112

Paley, William 96, 132, 146
PBS 59–60, 133–134
Pierpoint, Alan (Stan) 52, 66, 72, 133, 138, 140, 155, 157
Pierpoint, Charles 11, 13, 24, 28, 43, 53, 100
Pierpoint, Emma 10, 12–13, 53
Pierpoint, Eric 12, 14, 32, 52–53, 55, 61, 72, 77, 98, 129–130, 133, 153
Pierpoint, Kim 53–54, 72, 77–78, 134, 150, 157
Pierpoint, Marta 7, 54, 56, 66, 72, 76, 80, 150, 155
Pierpoint, Patricia Adams 51–54, 66, 71–72, 77, 80, 93, 98, 124, 134, 150, 152, 154
Plant, Bill 117–118, 123, 134–135
Pottenger Sanatorium 12–13
Powell, Jody 109–110

Rather, Dan 2–3, 75, 78, 89, 92, 94, 96–98, 101, 104, 106, 114–122, 147, 158
Reagan, Ronald 110, 122, 134

Rebozo, Charles "Bebe" 93–95, 120
Roberts, Charles 76, 82, 112

Salant, Richard 47, 96–97, 116, 143–145, 149
Salinger, Pierre 65, 71, 74, 143
Sauter, Van Gordon 115, 145, 147
Schieffer, Bob 103, 106, 117, 119
See It Now (CBS television program) 24, 33–37, 39, 55, 127, 141–142, 146
Silverman, Mary 21, 43–44, 66, 123, 156–157
Small, William 49, 97, 99, 113, 120–121
Smith, Merriman 58
Socolov, Sandy 120, 122
Stanton, Frank 91, 143
Stahl, Lesley 109–110, 114, 118–120, 123, 153–154
Stockholm, Sweden 18, 20, 23, 28, 31, 50, 124, 127

Tisch, Lawrence 132

University of Redlands 15, 17, 50, 86, 126, 128, 157

V-12 (college training program) 15–16
Vietnam, and LBJ 81–82

Watergate 92, 94, 96, 98, 100–101, 106, 112, 135, 137, 143–144, 155
William and Mary College 136
Woodward, Bob 136–137

Yellowstone National Park 124, 157

Ziegler, Ron 89, 97–98, 112–113
Zirinsky, Susan 151–152

www.ingramcontent.com/pod-product-compliance
Ingram Content Group UK Ltd.
Pitfield, Milton Keynes, MK11 3LW, UK
UKHW042016140426
5217IPUK00015B/1197